WOMAN'S COUNSEL

WOMAN'S COUNSEL

A Legal Guide for Women

Gayle L. Niles
and
Douglas H. Snider

ARDEN PRESS, INC.
Denver, Colorado
1984

Library of Congress Cataloging in Publication Data

Niles, Gayle L., 1944-
Woman's counsel.

Bibliography: p. 221
Includes index.
1. Law--United States--Popular works. 2. Women--Legal status, laws, etc--United States--Popular works.
I. Snider, Douglas H., 1946- . II. Title.
KF390.W6N54 1984 349.73'024042 84-11161
ISBN 0-912869-04-6 (pbk.) 347.30024042

Published in the United States of America
Arden Press, Inc.
1127 Pennsylvania Street
Denver, Colorado 80203

Table of Contents

THE COURTS

DEALING WITH THE POLICE

THE FAMILY

WOMEN AS VICTIMS

PURELY FINANCIAL

Introduction

Until recently, most women had no reason to familiarize themselves with the law. Only on rare occasions were they faced with legal decisions, and when such situations arose, they were generally handled by husbands, fathers, or male executors. But all that has changed. Today the great majority of women are taking on increased responsibilities—they are better educated than their female ancestors, more involved in community and political affairs, and are entering the labor market and the professions in large numbers. At the same time that the number of women earning wages, running businesses, and owning property has increased, more and more of them are remaining single or have become divorced and are now single parents. And as women's roles have changed and expanded, so have the laws. Many of the laws protecting the rights of women did not exist ten or twenty years ago, such as those related to sex discrimination and sexual harassment.

The average woman will face a continual series of legal problems throughout her lifetime. Unfortunately, few are prepared to face such situations, and their lack of knowledge of legal concepts and procedures results in uncertainty and fear. The outcome of a legal issue can have devastating consequences for the woman who is uninformed and unprepared. To protect herself, her family, and her property, she must be familiar with the basic principles of the legal system.

This book was written to demystify the law as it relates to those legal problems most often encountered by women. The law is complex and constantly changing, but with knowledge of basic rights, obligations, and legal procedures, women need no longer be intimidated by the legal system. They will know what their options are, when they need to seek legal counsel, and how to prepare themselves to enter the courtroom—whether for jury duty or as a plaintiff or defendant in a lawsuit. And the more knowledgeable they are, the better chance that the legal matter will be resolved to their satisfaction.

The law is rarely absolute. It is subject to interpretation and change, and decisions of the courts often vary widely from state to state as well as from courtroom to courtroom. For this reason, we cannot provide detailed information on every state's laws and statutes. Instead we have provided an overview of the legal system, outlining important legal considerations and procedures, guidelines on how to prepare your case, and in some instances examples of how the laws are interpreted by the various states.

Because the law is complicated and variable, we recommend in many cases that readers seek the advice of an attorney before proceeding, since every legal matter is in some way unique and often requires the personal attention of a professional. This book is not intended to take the place of competent legal representation. Because women are often intimidated by attorneys and uncertain as to how to select one for their particular legal problem, we have devoted Part I to this topic, including discussions on sources to use in selecting an attorney, what to expect from the attorney-client relationship, and the types of fee arrangements that are available.

Our research is based to a great extent upon current case law, federal and state statutes, and administrative guidelines. We have used the same tools that an attorney would use in preparing a case in a particular area of law. In some instances, case citations have been provided so that readers can locate additional information on a case that is of particular interest. References and footnotes appear at the back of the book for those who wish to investigate further. In many chapters, we have provided names and addresses of organizations and agencies that can supply further information on a subject, offer legal advice, or assist you with a complaint or lawsuit. Legal terms that appear throughout the book are defined in the glossary.

We are grateful to the many law librarians who assisted us during our long months of research, particularly those at the San Diego County Law Library, the University of Washington Law Library, Seattle, and the Colorado Supreme Court Law Library in Denver. Thanks also to the staff of the Women's History Research Center, Berkeley, California, who provided us with information on marital rape, and to the Honorable Walter L. Gorelick and Ms. Margie Cook for their helpful comments and suggestions. Finally, we would like to express our appreciation to John Dahl, who generously offered his time to assist us in our research.

DEALING WITH ATTORNEYS

1
Do You Really Need an Attorney?

Most women go to an attorney only as a last resort, when all else has failed, when in fact hiring or consulting with a competent attorney should be viewed as a business investment that could save time and money later on. Look upon it as preventive medicine for the good health of your business and personal ventures.

Not every legal problem will require an attorney's assistance, but in most instances you will need at least to consult with one before proceeding on your own. Every woman should have an attorney friend or acquaintance she can call for general legal advice, someone who can provide her with basic information and, if necessary, recommend another attorney who specializes in that particular area of the law. This will save her the trauma of trying to find an attorney to rely upon in times of stress, when it will be more difficult to make a wise decision. Once the landlord has thrown you out on the street or the bank has repossessed your car, it may be too late.

Many women express great apprehension at the thought of having to deal with an attorney. They immediately envision someone in a black cape leading them down the primrose path to their bank account. Unfortunately, few women have an attorney friend they can turn to for advice. This is partly due to the fact that only a small percentage of attorneys are women; in 1981 women accounted for only 14% of the total legal profession.[1] Beyond this, consider the fact that a great deal of legal information is freely and informally transferred over business lunches, on the racketball court, or over an after-work drink. A large percentage of women do not have access to this type of information, although the situation seems to be improving as more and more women enter the work force and the number of women practicing law increases.

To illustrate the types of problems that can result from not having taken the time to find a suitable attorney, consider the situation Beth found herself in after she co-signed for her roommate's car loan. Beth was held accountable by the bank when her roommate left the state for parts unknown. In a panic she went to an attorney recommended by a friend. She had convinced herself that the only solution was to declare bankruptcy, which her attorney agreed to without discussing her other options. After paying the attorney $500, Beth was unclear as to his plan of action, and she could never reach him by phone or find him in his office. She finally went to a second attorney, who fortunately was able to resolve the situation. Beth's first mistake was in not having consulted an attorney before co-signing the loan, but she compounded the problem by hiring the first attorney recommended. If Beth had taken the time to find a competent attorney, she could have saved herself $500 and much grief.

Another woman purchased a second home through a creative financing plan with a broker. It was not until several years later, right before foreclosure on her original house, that she began to realize the total ramifications of the broker's plan—*then* she consulted with an attorney. This type of predicament is common among women who seek legal advice only after they are entangled in such a quagmire that it takes a miracle worker, not an attorney, to straighten it out.

Many concepts of law turn on timeliness. For example, you have only so long in which to file a lawsuit after an injury or to appeal an adverse ruling by a court or governmental agency. Consequently, many of your options may be eliminated if you wait too long to seek legal advice. Many legal problems can be resolved to your satisfaction, without loss of possessions or great financial cost, if action is taken at the right time and with the aid of an attorney.

Let's take a look at some of the legal situations we will be discussing in later chapters and consider when you should seek legal advice. (Further references to attorneys appear in the individual chapters.)

IN SMALL CLAIMS COURT

If you are about to sue your neighbor for hitting your parked car (or vice versa), you do not need an attorney in many states, nor in some are you allowed one. You may consult one if you feel unsure as to how to gather evidence or how you should present your case before the judge, but he may not be allowed to make an appearance as your representative in the courts of many states. This is to your advantage financially, as you will not have to pay substantial legal fees to recover small dollar amounts. Everyone in the court is in the same boat, and the court is generally more relaxed to account for the fact that the individuals are representing themselves and are not knowledgeable in legal procedure. If you as the defendant decide to appeal your case to a higher court, you will probably be allowed to be represented by counsel if you wish. However, you will be paying higher court costs as well as attorney fees to contend over a relatively small amount in damages. Of course should the court rule in your favor, your costs, and in some instances your attorney's fees, may be added to your judgment (paid for by the other party). If your state is one of those that allows attorneys in small claims court, you can choose either to represent yourself or to seek legal counsel.

IN TRAFFIC COURT

Generally, unless your license is in jeopardy or you've been involved in an accident resulting in injury to any of the parties or damage to property, you do not need an attorney, although under the rules of the court in most states an attorney may represent you if you so choose. The thing to consider is the seriousness of the incident: will it reflect upon your driving record and thus increase your insurance rates or imperil your license? Last but not least to consider is the principle of justice: you may decide to hire an attorney, even though the charge is a minor one, simply because you believe you did not violate any law and that the chance of having the charge dismissed would be greater with legal representation.

AS AN ARRESTED PERSON

This depends upon the circumstances. If you are stopped for a traffic violation and taken to the local police station, you may or may not want an attorney present, depending on the seriousness of the charge. At certain stages of a criminal investigation you have a constitutional right to be represented by counsel, but if you do not ask for counsel it will be considered a waiver of this right.

If you are being detained under custody by the police, have been read your Miranda Rights, and are about to be questioned, it would be wise to contact your attorney at that point. Information given to the police can be used against you later in court. Thus, you should have someone there "on your side" to ensure that your constitutional rights are upheld and to provide some emotional support.

IN A DIVORCE CASE

You may not need an attorney if your marriage was of short duration, no real property was purchased during the marriage, and there are no children, no outstanding bills, and, most importantly, total agreement exists between you and your husband on how the assets, belongings, and debts are to be divided. Several states now have a simple dissolution procedure which can be followed by spouses in agreement to obtain a divorce without going to court. The clerk of the family law court in your jurisdiction can direct you to the necessary information if this procedure applies in your state.

On the other hand, you should consult an attorney if you and your husband cannot agree, or if property, accumulated debts, or children are involved. The majority of divorces involve conflict, which leads to decisions based on emotional issues rather than sound logic. It is not uncommon for husbands and wives to have vicious arguments over who gets the microwave, and in order to avoid such nasty scenes it is best to have a third party represent you. Do not allow yourself to be represented by your spouse's attorney. This can lead to a violation of your rights, and many courts will disallow the representation. The situation occurs most often when both spouses wish to have the family attorney represent them.

Your state may require that you file, along with the divorce petition, a financial declaration. On this form you will be required to list the assets and liabilities of the marital community as well as provide an estimated household budget, including maintenance care of the children if you are seeking custody. It is often beneficial, because of the emotional nature of the proceedings, to have an attorney's input in preparing the final version of the financial declaration, as this will lessen the chances of your missing important items or estimating an unrealistic budget.

IN JUVENILE COURT

Juvenile proceedings are civil, rather than criminal, and an attorney's representation is not required. Nevertheless, every juvenile going into court should be represented by an attorney, either court-appointed or self-obtained. Without an attorney present, a juvenile runs the risk of not being afforded nis constitutional rights, which can have devastating results.

IN A SEXUAL HARASSMENT OR DISCRIMINATION CASE

If you are being harassed or discriminated against at work, you should first determine what safeguards your employer or union may have set up. If these grievance procedures prove unsatisfactory, consider seeking legal assistance. Even if you decide to handle the matter yourself, an attorney can help you determine at the outset whether your case is valid and supply you with information regarding the regulations and procedures involved in filing a claim. Most states, as well as the Equal Employment Opportunity Commission (EEOC, the organization that oversees the federal law in this area), require that you notify your employer and attempt to resolve the problem before they will take action. If you decide not to seek the assistance of an attorney, you must follow the required filing procedures with the EEOC on your own. The difficulty is in keeping up with the strict time limitations set for the various steps and in negotiating a settlement with your employer. Some individuals are so emotionally involved with the situation that they find it difficult to remain objective and handle the employer negotiations effectively.

IN A RAPE CASE

If you have been raped, call the police or a rape hotline *immediately*. This crime is so difficult to deal with legally as well as emotionally that you must be apprised of your rights and choices before they are eliminated by the passage of time or the evidence is mishandled. Many local rape hotlines and organizations have been set up to aid the rape victim in obtaining legal and medical assistance and to help her with the emotional aspects of this crime. You may want to consult with an attorney as well, even though the district attorney or prosecutor will be representing you should the case go to court. If the state decides not to prosecute, you may want to file a civil suit, in which case you will need an attorney to represent you.

IN A BATTERY CASE

Unfortunately, neither the police nor the legal system offers much assistance to the battered woman. If you can afford an attorney, at the very least confer with him about your legal options and, if you wish, request that he obtain a restraining order or a vacate order against your husband. It is also advised that you hire an attorney if you've decided to file criminal charges or to sue your husband in civil court. If you do not wish to or cannot afford to hire an attorney, you may want to contact any number of organizations for assistance, such as the National Organization for Women.

WHEN WRITING A WILL

It is in your own best interest as well as your heirs' to ensure that your will is legally recognized in your state. Some states still recognize a holographic (handwritten) will, while others require a formally written will which has been signed by witnesses. Wherever you reside, seek legal advice before writing your will. Many people treat the writing of their wills casually and either do not seek legal assistance or do not write a will at all, leaving their families to deal with the court process of probating the will and settling the estate. It is equally important that a will be current. A will should be rewritten or amended any time there is a change in your family or financial circumstances, such as a divorce, remarriage, or a substantial increase of assets, or when you move to another state.

FOR SOCIAL SECURITY PROBLEMS

The main problem here seems to be in dealing with the bureaucracy and all the red tape that goes with it, especially now that so many changes are being made in the social security laws (this also applies to workman's compensation, unemployment compensation, and veterans administration problems). If you can sustain a lengthy and patient following of the regulations and time limitations involved in filing a claim, then you have no need for an attorney. However, if things become confusing or you are in a desperate financial situation, it is time to seek legal assistance. One thing to consider is that due to the nature of the bureaucracy, attorneys usually receive more attention and quicker results than the average citizen. On the other hand, the amount of the controversy may not warrant the cost of hiring an attorney. Many state and local agencies offer assistance with social security problems and are good sources of information.

FOR VIOLATIONS OF CONSUMER RIGHTS

It is impossible to make a blanket statement here because so many different agencies are involved and each one has its own procedures and requirements. Most federal agencies have specific administrative procedures for investigating, mediating, and filing complaints. When the matter involves a federal, state, or local law, you must exhaust all the administrative remedies of the agency that enforces the particular consumer act before you can file a civil suit on your own. If the problem is complex or the dollar amount substantial, you may want to consult with an attorney before proceeding. If the administrative remedies prove unsuccessful, you can bring a civil action, in which case you will probably need an attorney, unless the dollar amount is within the limit set by the small claims court. Many of the statutes provide for the recovery of attorneys' fees in addition to penalties such as treble damages (automatic tripling of the amount awarded).

WHEN DECLARING BANKRUPTCY

Well before you declare bankruptcy, in fact while considering it as a possible avenue of financial escape, consult with an attorney. Declaring bankruptcy involves making some choices between state and federal law, and you need to be fully informed of the long-term effects of these decisions. You can do this only with sound legal advice. There are many types of bankruptcy, and in each instance you will need to be informed of your liability. Find an attorney who is willing to discuss the other options that may be available, one who is willing to take the time to present you with all the facts and who does not view your case as just another $400 fee for the month. Your attorney should discuss the actual costs in terms of filing fees, attorney's fees, etc., as well as any financial repercussions resulting from bankruptcy that may occur three months or three years down the road.

2
Selecting an Attorney

The one question we hear over and over again is "How do I go about finding a competent, reliable attorney, one who will take a real interest in my problem?" This question is usually followed by a horror story about a friend who chose an unethical or incompetent attorney. Unfortunately, many women use all kinds of means short of the Ouija Board to determine which attorney will represent them; they may simply retain an attorney who was recommended by a friend or relative without investigating her area of expertise or past experience. It is important to remember that hiring an attorney is actually a business decision that can have far-reaching effects upon your life.

SOURCES TO USE

Several sources are available that provide information on attorneys in your area. The problem is in using those sources to find an attorney who has the ability to deal with your particular problem effectively. Reliable traditional sources are the local bar association and legal directories found in most county libraries (such as the *Martindale and Hubbel Law Directory*). Local bar associations will recommend attorneys in good standing (those who have never been disciplined for unethical practices) and can tell you what their specialty areas are. Legal directories (some local bar associations, as well as the American Bar Association, have them) will provide you with such information as date of birth, law school attended, bar membership, and specialty areas of practice.

Taking the advice of friends when selecting an attorney can be risky business. Perhaps your friend's attorney represented her in traffic court and you are considering filing for divorce. The attorney may never have taken a divorce case to court. Or perhaps your friend is recommending her father's corporate attorney, who has no interest or experience in cases such as yours. Most members of the legal profession, like those of the medical profession, are specialists and cannot be expected to be experts in all areas of law. If you do decide to take the recommendation of a friend, be sure to do some investigating on your own—consult your local bar association and several legal directories to determine the attorney's background and areas of specialty *before* calling her office for an appointment.

The yellow pages will usually give you only an alphabetical listing of attorneys in your area with their office addresses and phone numbers, but sometimes attorneys are listed by their area of specialty as well. Still, using the yellow pages to select an attorney is generally a hit-or-miss approach and should be considered only as a means of obtaining names that will be checked later against other sources of information. The most important thing to remember when consulting the sources mentioned here is that you will want to talk to several attorneys before you decide on the one who will represent you.

ADVERTISING

The canons of ethics now allow attorneys to advertise in a more direct manner. As a result, in some states you will see television ads as well as newspaper ads encouraging viewers and readers to call a particular legal clinic or law office for assistance in resolving legal problems. In California, legal clinics are advertising on television in droves. Ads are certainly a reasonable source for obtaining the name of an attorney and possibly the area of specialty, but you should consider the fact that the fees they advertise are often no real bargain, as a clinic or law office that runs a great deal of advertising most likely is passing on the costs to you as a client. If you decide to select an attorney from the comfort of your easy chair, you should still interview several attorneys before you decide to work with one.

Attorneys have mixed feelings about advertising, and individual state bar associations are closely watching the advertisements to ensure that they are done in good taste. For example, the Rhode Island Supreme

Court refused to allow attorneys to advertise on the front or back cover of the yellow pages but required instead that they be listed under the section designated for attorneys.[1] States are struggling to find a way to handle this issue with dignity and reasonable taste through their bar associations, which oversee this area by investigating complaints.

The traditional means of advertising allowed by most states is by a name on the attorney's office, special event pamphlets (such as the opening of a new law office), and business cards with the attorney's name and address. At least for now, skywriting is considered to be unprofessional, but this entire area is destined to grow and change in the future. The San Diego County Bar Association is currently investigating a legal clinic that has been sending out pamphlets to homeowners stating that their homes are in danger of foreclosure but that they as the Handy Dandy Legal Clinic will be able to help out. You can easily see the questionable ethics in this type of advertising.

A WORD ABOUT LEGAL CLINICS AND COST-FREE LEGAL SERVICES

The quality of service you will receive at legal clinics varies greatly. While you may in fact have a minor legal problem resolved to your satisfaction at a fraction of the cost of hiring your own attorney (such as the drawing up of contracts or deeds), you should consider the following drawbacks in dealing with legal clinics. They often use pretyped or computerized forms as well as word processor formats for similar cases. Obviously, under these circumstances, it is unlikely that you will receive the individual attention you would in a traditional law office. One memorable example from "60 Minutes" is the Dallas attorney who handled over 200 divorces in one day. You can see how this might affect the time spent with an individual client. The other consideration regarding legal clinics is the cost; not all clinics are inexpensive and many times you will be charged a fee just to walk in the front door.

Cost-free legal services also vary a great deal. Many of them are run by a single volunteer attorney and a large group of law students from the local law school. Group prepaid legal services are sometimes available through unions or employers. In addition, free legal advice is sometimes provided by the Department of Consumer Affairs, administrative agencies at local, state, and federal levels, and certain national women's organizations. When considering legal clinics or cost-free legal services, follow the same procedure you would if you were hiring your own attorney. Investigate their background and areas of specialization and interview several persons to determine which one you feel most comfortable with.

INTERVIEWING ATTORNEYS

Meet and interview several attorneys before selecting one. Remember, you are hiring this person to assert your rights and hopefully to simplify your life. This can turn out to be a long-term relationship, often longer than you had anticipated, so select someone you are comfortable with and someone you believe will be effective in dealing with the legal issues.

Most attorneys will not charge you until you decide to retain them. The reason is simple—they want to select the clients they will represent, weeding out those who may never pay them, those who may fail to show up in court, and those who may try to involve them in illegal activities. When calling an attorney's office for an appointment, ask about the policies of that particular office and at what point they start charging fees. If an attorney will not talk with you without charging a fee, you may want to consider looking elsewhere.

When you interview an attorney, attempt to determine her approach to problem-solving because that is what she will be doing for you if you become her client. Ask her questions about the various alternatives to a solution. An attorney who gives you only one choice or one who attempts to inflict her opinion upon you without allowing you to make the final decision is not one you want to retain. Make some common-sense judgments. Are you at ease with this individual? Do you trust her decision-making ability? Do you feel confident that she will work toward *your* best interests? Or do you have a feeling of being rushed when talking with her or find that many of your questions remain unanswered? Would you feel comfortable having this person argue your case should it end up in the courtroom? You will have to depend to some degree on your instincts when determining whether or not you wish to hire a particular attorney.

Communication is at the center of a good attorney-client relationship. An ongoing legal problem will require effective communication in both stressful situations (such as hostile courtroom environments) and more informal office settings. Without a good communication link between you, there will be problems on both sides. If you find it difficult to relate to your attorney, you will be reluctant to give her all the information she will need to represent you. Remember that the attorney-client relationship is a type of partnership—you both should be working toward the same end and feel comfortable in discussing all phases of your legal problem. Some decisions you will trust your attorney to make; some you will make alone; but most decisions will be made jointly. You will eliminate a potential disaster by finding an attorney you trust and one you can talk to easily. This also applies to the attorney's office staff, as you will be dealing with these people on an ongoing basis as well.

A typical interview involves the following steps:

1. Call the attorney's office and ask about areas of specialty, fees, etc. If you are satisfied with the response, make an appointment.

2. At the beginning of the interview, explain that you will be talking to several attorneys. Be open about this. Any good attorney will respect a potential client's desire to have the best possible legal representation. Remember that just as you do not want to hire just *any* attorney, most attorneys do not want to represent just *any* client. Generally, they shy away from prospective clients who are evasive, difficult to relate to, or distrustful, as such relationships make their job extremely difficult at best and lead the way to possible malpractice suits.

3. Explain your problem. Ask the attorney specific questions about her past experiences with similar cases. Listen to what she has to say. Does she have some definite ideas about how your case should be handled? Does she discuss ways of resolving the problem outside of court? Does she explain the actual costs to you, including witness fees, service of process fees, court costs, etc.? Be wary of the attorney who immediately wants to go to court because this is where your costs really begin to mount up.

4. Discuss fees on a dollar-and-cents basis, *not* in vague terms. If you decide to retain this attorney, be sure the fee arrangement is in writing and that you have a copy.

5. Unless you have a legal emergency, allow yourself time to make your decision. Thank the attorney for her time and explain that you want to think over all that has been discussed.

ATTORNEYS' FEES

The cost of hiring an attorney may vary greatly from city to rural areas as well as from state to state. It has been declared unconstitutional for state bar associations to set legal rates for attorneys within given areas of the law; therefore, fees *do* vary and are negotiable with most attorneys.

Selecting the attorney with the lowest fee is not necessarily the best decision, as attorneys who charge lower fees tend to have less experience. A more experienced attorney with higher rates may actually save you money by completing the work in much less time than a novice could. It is important that you select an attorney according to the complexity of your legal problem. If you decide that your case requires the expertise of an experienced attorney, ascertain who will be doing the actual work. It is common practice for law firms to assign less important cases to the less experienced attorneys, and even though the senior attorney you hired will be responsible for your case, much of the work may be done by paralegals and junior lawyers. You have a right to know who will be involved in your case and what their hourly rates will be.

Fee arrangements fall into several categories:

Hourly fees range from $15 to $300 and may be billed to the nearest one-tenth or one-fourth of the hour. This arrangement most often occurs in criminal cases and in business matters.

Contingent fees are most often used in personal injury cases. The attorney is paid a percentage of the amount you eventually recover, generally 30 to 40% (although this may increase if the case is appealed). It is generally considered unethical to use this type of fee arrangement in a criminal matter. Court costs and expenses (filing fees, service fees, etc.) will come out of your share of the settlement. Under this arrangement, your attorney's time is free unless or until you win.

Flat fees are often used in divorce cases, probate, and the writing of wills. The attorney is paid a fixed amount of money to complete a particular task.

A combination of two types of fees, possibly a flat fee for the attorney's time up to a certain number of hours, after which you are charged an hourly fee.

The type of fee arrangement you and your attorney decide upon can make a big difference in the amount of legal fees you will pay. Consider carefully the seriousness of your legal problem, the chances of your winning your case in or out of court, and the amount of time your attorney will need to spend preparing your case and possibly representing you in court.

An hourly fee arrangement may be preferable if your legal problem is a common, less serious one requiring little more than the completion of a few forms. In more complicated cases, the costs may be exorbitant, and a less-than-honest attorney may be encouraged to spend more hours than are necessary. On the other hand, in most cases you won't have to worry about paying a large amount in fees for a few hours' work. If you decide to pay your attorney on an hourly basis, insist on having in writing a reasonable estimate of the number of hours she expects to spend on the case.

In personal injury cases, the contingent fee is the most practical and cost-effective. You may have to pay your attorney a small fee at the outset, but in many cases her entire fee will come out of the amount awarded you by the court, should you receive a settlement. Hopefully, this fee arrangement will encourage your attorney to put many hours of hard work into your case, since the larger the settlement the higher the attorney's fee.

The flat fee method is appealing to many clients simply because they know from the beginning how much they will be paying in legal fees. On the negative side, you won't know how much effort and time your attorney will be willing to expend. Another thing to consider is that your case may unexpectedly be settled out of court, and your attorney may make an enormous profit for a relatively few hours of work.

Whatever type of fee arrangement you decide upon, be sure to ask about additional charges such as phone calls, paralegal fees, investigation charges, filing fees, service fees, etc. In other words, be sure you know what you are being charged for and always request an itemized bill from your attorney. If you have talked with several attorneys, you should have several sets of figures to compare.

The fee arrangement should be in writing, and both you and your attorney should have a copy so that you can refer to it at a later date, if necessary. If you pay a retainer, request a receipt. Many individuals have left their attorney's office without a written agreement and later have no recollection of what was agreed upon and no proof of their financial obligations. The results can be disastrous. One example is the Maryland attorney who attempted to extract an excessive fee from his client in a domestic relations case. The initial verbal agreement stipulated $2,000 as a retainer and $70 an hour thereafter. On the final day of the trial, the attorney requested that the client sign a different fee agreement, which the client agreed to for fear that a dispute might jeopardize his case. He was subsequently billed for $8,500, with no itemized hourly accounting. When the attorney filed suit for payment, the fee was increased to $23,000. Fortunately for the client, the court determined that renegotiation of fees during a trial constitutes unethical behavior, and it imposed a one-year suspension plus costs on the attorney.[7]

DISMISSING YOUR ATTORNEY

This seems to be one of the most difficult areas for women to deal with successfully. If you find yourself in the position of having retained an attorney and for whatever reason find that you are uncomfortable with the relationship, it is important to remember that you hired this person to represent your best interests and if you are not receiving the service you expected you have every right to terminate the relationship.

Obviously, you must consider how changing attorneys will affect your case. Bringing in a second attorney will slow down the process since he will need time to study your files and to devise a plan of action. It might be wise to consult with another attorney before you make the change. Then you can better determine if there is a possibility that the problem can be resolved or whether in fact you should begin the process of looking for another attorney.

If your problem is of a less serious nature (your phone calls are not returned, appointments are often cancelled), the best approach is to confront your attorney directly with your complaint. Give her the opportunity to improve her services. By all means, don't ignore the problem, hoping that things will improve later—you may be placing your case in jeopardy. If you decide to dismiss your attorney, offer to pay for the amount of work that has already been completed and pick up your file (lawyers are required to cooperate with whomever succeeds them on a case). If you feel that the bill presented to you is excessive for the services you received or you think money is due you for payments already made, discuss the matter with your attorney. If she is unwilling to resolve the problem, contact the local bar association, as most of them have a grievance or fee dispute procedure to review the charges made to you. The clerk of the local court or the clerk of the state supreme court also can give you information on your rights and your attorney's ethical duties.

Should you be approached sexually or suspect any illegal activity on the part of your attorney, contact the state bar ethics committee immediately. Local bar associations, in particular, are taking the problem of ethics within the profession quite seriously by following through on complaints by citizens and bringing charges against attorneys that can lead to disbarment. Since attorneys are licensed by the individual states, this process is handled by each state as it sees fit. An increasing number of cases based on ethical violations are reaching state supreme courts. For example, the court sent an Indiana attorney to the state prison because he had refused to acknowledge his prior disbarment and continued to accept clients.[3] In another case, two California attorneys were convicted of grand theft and disbarred for falsifying medical and damage reports sent to insurance companies.[4]

THE COURTS

3
Jury Duty

Before preparing an outline for this book, we asked many women, of various backgrounds and professions, what they would like to know about the legal system. To our surprise, many of their questions were related to the jury selection process. "Why am I never (or so often) called for jury duty?" "If I'm called for jury duty, what types of questions will the judge and the attorneys ask me?" "Why was I not chosen to be a juror once I got to court?" After reviewing all their questions on this subject, we decided to include a separate chapter on jury duty, starting with the summons to appear and moving through the final day of the trial. As is true of all other situations covered in this book, you will feel much more comfortable if you know what to expect and what will be expected of you.

THE SUMMONS

Initial reactions to a summons for jury duty range from mere curiosity to frustration at having to cancel planned activities or to miss work for an indefinite period of time. What should you do once you receive notice of jury duty? What will you observe in court? What will be required of you? And how was your name selected in the first place?

The summons for jury duty will be sent either by the clerk of the court or, in the larger jurisdictions, by the jury commissioner. In order to conform to the United States constitutional requirement of an impartial jury,[1] those summoned must represent a broad cross section of the community. Normally, names are taken from the voter registration list, although in some counties the clerk of the court may also use the list of names of those who have received driver's licenses or identification cards from the state motor vehicle licensing agency. Since the selection of names from these lists is totally random, you may be called for jury duty several times within a five-year period while someone else is never called.

Under common law, counties and states were able to exclude women from jury duty, thereby denying the participants in lawsuits jury panels that were representative of the community. In 1936, the United States Supreme Court ruled that women are qualified to serve as jurors.[2] Since the names of prospective jurors are generally taken from voter registration lists, it is important that all women register to vote so that a higher percentage will be eligible for jury duty.

WHO MAY SERVE AS A JUROR?

Certain laws have been enacted which specify who is qualified to be a juror. Though individual state laws may differ slightly, the following requirements are fairly standard:[3]

— A citizer of the United States, 18 years of age or over, who meets the residency requirements of the state electors. This requirement usually specifies that one must have lived within the jurisdiction (county) for a certain period of time, usually ranging from 90 days to one year.

— A person of sound mind and of ordinary intelligence, capable of seeing, hearing, and analyzing evidence presented during the trial. (Some states do not automatically exclude blind or deaf persons.)

— A person having sufficient knowledge of the English language.[4]

— A person who has not been convicted of a crime constituting a felony.

MUST YOU GO?

Upon receiving the summons for jury duty from the jury commissioner or clerk of the court, you are considered legally notified, and except in rare instances you will be expected to appear in court on the specified date.[5] Be sure to check the address on the envelope first. If the summons was sent to a previous address and then forwarded to your current residence in another county, you can simply call the number that appears on the summons and you will be excused from jury duty. Prospective jurors must reside in the county in which the court is located.

Should you have a previous appointment scheduled for that date, it would be to your advantage to reschedule it and arrive at the court at the time specified. However, if you feel that your appointment is important enough that it should have precedence over jury duty, contact the party whose name appears on the summons and attempt to reschedule the jury duty for a later date. It should be noted that certain jurisdictions will excuse a juror in advance only upon a finding that "the service would entail undue hardship on the person or public served by the person."[6] A recent example is a pharmacist who was excused from jury duty because her partner was ill and she was the only pharmacist available; it was determined that her absence could pose a threat to the health of certain members of the community.

Obviously, if you are employed full time, you will be concerned about your responsibility to your employer and your income during your absence. Your employer is required to allow you time off when you are called for jury duty, but unless a written agreement exists between you and your employer or your union stating otherwise, he is not required to pay your normal wages for those days you are in court, although many do. In most states, jurors receive a small fee for serving on a jury, ranging from $5 to $30 a day, and are reimbursed for mileage. And on the rare occasions when the jury must be sequestered (which means that they are not allowed to return to their homes until a verdict is reached), the jurors' meals and hotel accommodations are paid for by the court.

Should you fail to appear in court on the date designated, your absence will be noted and at the very least you will be promptly notified of a new date to appear. Or the court may call you and request that you appear immediately, where the judge may, if it is decided that you intentionally avoided jury duty, impose a penalty in the form of a fine and request that you appear at a later date.

SELECTION OF THE JURY

For some potential jurors, the first minutes spent in the court are not only confusing but frustrating and intimidating. You most likely will find yourself in a group of 50 to 100 strangers, most of whom will be experiencing similar emotions. Your group may be asked to meet for an introductory lecture on the judicial process or you may find yourself immediately being led into the courtroom where jury selection is about to begin. Once the clerk of the court has taken roll, the potential jurors will be sworn in, swearing or affirming that the answers they will give to the questions presented by the judge and the attorneys will be the truth. The clerk will then randomly select twelve of the prospective jurors, who will be asked to enter the jury box (in civil cases, juries may be comprised of only six persons).

The judge will normally introduce to all potential jurors the parties to the lawsuit, their attorneys, and the names of the witnesses. It is at this time that the judge will also briefly explain what the case involves—for example, that the defendant, Mr. Jones, is accused of the crime of burglary, or that Ms. Smith is bringing a civil action against Mr. Adams over a dispute involving property rights. All prospective jurors, those within the jury box as well as those who have yet to be called, should pay close attention during this process since the attorneys may later ask them questions regarding the witnesses or the charges in the case. A prospective juror must also be aware that she is going to be called upon to make two important determinations; that is, can she sit on this case and remain open-minded during the presentation of the evidence, and can she then deliberate with the other jurors and return with a verdict, if one is possible, which is based solely upon the law as presented by the judge and the evidence as presented by the exhibits and the witnesses? It is not easy to sit in judgment over another human being, and that is why the judge and the attorneys will ask specific questions of the prospective jurors to determine if they are impartial.

The Questions

The proceedings in which the jurors are questioned by the judge and by the attorneys are referred to as "Voir Dire," from the Latin for "to speak the truth." The following are examples of the types of questions that may be asked of potential jurors in an attempt to elicit any feelings of bias or prejudice:[7]

— Will you have any difficulty in following the law as given to you by the judge, even if you may disagree with it?
— Are you acquainted with the prosecutor, the defense attorney, the defendant, or any witness mentioned?
— Have you heard or read, from any source, anything about this case, or do you know anything about it other than what you have heard today?
— Do you have contact with any members of a law enforcement agency, the legal profession, or the court system through your employment?

— Are any of your relatives or close friends members of any law enforcement agency, or do any of them have contact with the legal profession or the court system?
— Would the fact that any witness may be a member of a law enforcement agency cause you to look with favor upon one side of this case and with disfavor upon the other?
— Will you have any difficulty applying the same standards to judge all of the witnesses' testimony?
— Do you have any feelings against the defendant solely because he/she is charged with this particular offense?
— Do you have any feelings about this particular offense that would make it difficult for you to be a fair and impartial juror?
— Do you belong to any group or organization which takes any definite position on law, crime, or offenses of this nature?
— Have you or any of your relatives or close friends ever been charged with any criminal offense?
— Have you or any of your relatives or close friends been the victims of crime?
— Does the mere fact that the defendant has been arrested and that a complaint has been filed against him/her cause you to conclude from those facts alone that the defendant is more likely to be guilty than not guilty?
— From time to time throughout the trial, the attorneys may make objections to questions asked of the witnesses. Would you look with disfavor upon such an attorney or the side of the case that the attorney represents for making such objections?
— If one of the attorneys in this case should exercise a peremptory challenge, would that fact cause you to be biased against that attorney or the side the attorney represents?
— Will you have any difficulty in refraining from discussing the case with anyone until it is submitted to you for decision, and then discuss the case only with the other jurors in the jury room?
— Will you have any difficulty keeping an open mind until you have heard all of the evidence and all the arguments of both sides and until the court has given you all of the instructions?
— Is there anything you did not understand in the statements made by the judge?
— Is there any reason why you would not want to sit as a juror in this case?

Should you answer any of the questions affirmatively, follow-up questions will be asked. For example, in a criminal trial should you state that you have a close friend in law enforcement, the attorneys may ask amplifying questions such as: "Where does your friend work?" "How close a friendship do you enjoy, and how often do you meet?" "Should you return a verdict of not guilty, would that in any way imperil the friendship?" If it is disclosed that the friendship could be affected by your verdict, it can then be argued by the attorney for the defense that you would find it difficult to be impartial in this matter and that to retain you as a juror would deny his client of the constitutional right to a fair trial.

If a question is asked that you do not understand, ask the attorney to rephrase it. Questions should be answered as directly as possible. You are not on trial—if you are sympathetic or unsympathetic towards either party, say so. If you should be asked a question which you consider too personal, you may ask the judge if he will allow you to respond to the question out of the presence of the other jurors. Since the judge is responsible for all the activities that take place in the courtroom, he will decide whether a question asked of a juror is proper, whether the conduct of an attorney or a juror is proper, and whether a particular matter should be discussed without the other jurors present. If you should be denied your request, you will be expected to answer the question in the presence of the other jurors.

Challenge for Cause

If either attorney has reason to believe that a prospective juror may be biased or prejudiced, he may ask that the court excuse that person, an action which is called "challenge for cause." A juror may be challenged for cause if it is discovered during questioning that she has a bias or prejudice that will interfere with her ability to arrive at a decision based solely on the evidence presented. A prospective juror who has recently been convicted of driving while under the influence of alcohol would likely be challenged for cause in a similar case. The same is true of a person who has already formed an opinion about the guilt or innocence of the defendant based on what she has read in the paper, or someone who is prejudiced against either party because of her or his race, sex, or religion.

Peremptory Challenge

The peremptory challenge allows an attorney to excuse a prospective juror for practically any reason whatsoever. Obviously, the attorney would like a jury composed of jurors who are sympathetic to his client's position, and when he wants to dismiss a prospective juror for reasons other than expressed bias or prejudice and thus cannot challenge for cause, he will utilize the peremptory challenge. A good trial attorney will observe the potential jurors from the time they enter the courtroom, looking for traits which he does or does not desire in a juror. As questions are asked of the individual jurors, he may observe their body language, their tone in answering, and their reaction to the specific questions. He may observe the dress of a potential juror to see if it conforms to the area's unwritten dress code or if it is a departure from the ordinary. An attorney may conclude that two persons who individually are the type of juror he desires may, during deliberation, stubbornly maintain different positions based solely upon their personality differences.

Unlike the challenge for cause, peremptory challenge allows the attorney to excuse a potential juror without asking a single question or stating the reason for her dismissal. And while an unlimited number of prospective jurors may be challenged for cause, the number of peremptory challenges is limited—for example, some states allow only ten in a misdemeanor criminal trial.[8]

May an attorney exclude prospective jurors solely because of their race, sex, or religion? Most jurisdictions allow peremptory challenges to be exercised without court control on the premise that the excusing of a certain group or class of people does not establish unlawful discrimination.[9] According to this rationale, an attorney may excuse as many women as he wants to until he has used all of his peremptory challenges. However, if it is proven that a peremptory challenge is used solely for the purpose of excluding a particular race, or ethnic or similar group, such a group exclusion will be held to be a denial of the right to trial by an impartial jury, and should the matter be appealed to a higher court, a new trial may be ordered.[10]

Should you be dismissed from the court, you are free to leave if there are no other courts in session seeking jurors. A person excused from one court because of perceived bias or prejudice may be considered an impartial juror in another since the circumstances may be entirely different.

SWEARING IN OF JURORS

Once the jury has been selected, the members will be sworn in by the clerk. (In lengthier trials, alternate jurors may be selected; the alternates are required to listen to all the evidence but will not be involved in deliberation unless one of the jury members becomes ill or for some other reason cannot be present.) You will be asked to affirm that you will hear the case and at its conclusion reach a verdict based only on the evidence presented and on the law as read by the judge. The judge will then give you instructions on how you should conduct yourself during the trial. For instance:

Don't speak with anyone, including the attorneys, until the trial is over.

Don't decide the case until you have heard all the evidence.

Avoid reading about the case in the newspapers.

You may (or may not) take notes during the trial.

Each time you leave the courtroom the judge will remind you of these instructions.

THE TRIAL

The trial will be divided into four segments—the opening statements, the prosecution's case, the defense's case, and closing arguments. Though the following makes reference to a criminal trial, civil trials are quite similar.

Opening Statements

The attorney for the prosecution (the plaintiff in a civil matter) will make an opening statement. What he says is not evidence but rather an introduction to what he expects to prove. He may decide to present an outline of his case, telling you who will testify and what that testimony will consist of. At the end of the prosecution's opening statement, the defense attorney may, if he wishes, make an opening statement, although in many instances it is presented after the prosecution has concluded its case.

The Prosecution

In the next segment of the trial, the prosecuting attorney will present evidence to show that an illegal activity has taken place and that the defendant illegally participated. For example, in a burglary case, the owner of the house may testify under oath that someone without her permission entered her home and took certain items; and then an officer may testify that immediately following the burglary he arrested the defendant after finding the stolen items in his car. The defense attorney has the right to cross-examine each witness presented by the prosecution. Although the prosecution may have presented a strong case against the defendant, it is too early to reach any conclusions regarding his guilt or innocence since you have heard only part of the evidence.

The Defense

Once the prosecution has presented its case, the defense will be allowed to present evidence. It may produce witnesses who will testify that the defendant was not in town on the night of the crime, or that this is a matter of mistaken identity. In the above burglary case, the defense may produce evidence that the defendant legally owned the items he was charged with stealing—such as receipts of purchase or testimony by the clerk who sold him the items or the friend who was with him at the time of the purchase. The prosecuting attorney has the right to cross-examine each witness for the defense.

Closing Arguments

After all the evidence has been presented and each attorney has rested his case, the judge will allow the attorneys to summarize the evidence that has been presented and to attempt to convince the jury that their client (or the state, in some cases) is in the right. The prosecutor, who presents his oral arguments first, may point out areas of conflicting evidence in the opponent's case. As each attorney points out the strengths of his case and the weaknesses in that of the opponent, it is important to remember that their arguments are not evidence. You must consider as evidence only the testimony you have heard by the witnesses under oath and those exhibits that have been accepted as evidence.

The Judge's Instructions to the Jury

After the attorneys have finished their final arguments, the judge will provide the jury with instructions. This is not a lot of legal mumbo jumbo but important information that will clarify how the jury should apply the law to that particular case. For example, the judge may instruct you that if you find one part of a witness's testimony false you may discount her entire testimony. The jury instructions may be lengthy and a bit dry, but with a little concentration you should find them to be understandable and informative.

Deliberation

Following the judge's instructions, the jury will move to the jury room for deliberation. Its first task will be to select a foreman, or chairman, who will be responsible for ensuring that the discussion is open to all of the jurors, that the issues are freely and openly reviewed, and that the balloting process is proper. During the discussions, differences in opinion will be expressed by the jurors. The fact that the attorneys have presented conflicting testimony illustrates that there are at least two points of view on the matter.

If you have a question during the deliberations, ask the foreman to write it out and give it to the bailiff. The bailiff will then present it to the judge. For example, if you and another juror are in disagreement as to what a witness said, you may request that the court reporter who has taken down the testimony read it back to the jury from the court record.

Once you have thoroughly discussed the case among yourselves, it is time to vote. It will be the foreman's responsibility to ensure that the vote is in accordance with the judge's instructions. Some states require a unanimous vote, while others require a majority. If a verdict is reached, the foreman will inform the bailiff; if a verdict cannot be reached, you will be asked to discuss the evidence once again and to go over the points of disagreement.

The Hung Jury

If after repeated discussions and votes a verdict cannot be reached, the jury is considered "deadlocked" and the foreman will report this to the judge. The judge may ask the jury to report to the courtroom, where he will inquire whether or not there is a good chance that a verdict could be reached if the court were to allow the jury to continue its deliberations. If the foreman answers "yes," the judge will ask the jury to return to the jury room. If the foreman answers "no," the judge will ask the foreman if there is anything he can do to assist the jury with its deliberations. If he feels that a verdict is not possible, he may declare a mistrial and dismiss the jury.

The Verdict

If a verdict has been reached, the foreman will sign the verdict forms and inform the bailiff. The jury will then return to the court, and, depending on the type of court, either the foreman or the court clerk will read the verdict. The judge will then thank the jurors for their service and dismiss them. He will also inform them that they are now free to discuss the trial with the attorneys and with their families and friends.

4
Small Claims Court

Almost all women, at one time or another, find themselves in need of a simple method of settling disputes over relatively minor matters. Perhaps you have received a bill for auto repairs which far exceeds the original estimate, or repairs have been made which you did not authorize, or the repairs were not done properly. Your landlord refuses to refund your $300 security deposit. The furniture or stereo you ordered is delivered in damaged condition and the proprietor refuses to refund your money or to replace the item. In these and similar instances, if you feel you've been wronged and the other party is unresponsive to your complaints, you may want to consider taking the matter to small claims court.

The purpose of this court is to give the citizen an opportunity to air her grievances and to collect small debts owed to her without having to become involved in costly and complex legal proceedings. The most beneficial aspects of the small claims process are these:

- You have the opportunity to represent yourself. In many states attorneys are not allowed to represent a client in this court, and the large majority of claimants represent themselves.
- Generally, once a claim is filed you have to wait only a matter of weeks for a hearing.
- The filing fees are minimal, usually ranging from $2 to $10.

— The atmosphere in small claims court is generally much more informal than in other courts.

DO YOU HAVE A VALID CLAIM?

You must first decide whether or not you have a valid claim and a good chance of receiving a favorable judgment in small claims court. Just because someone treated you unjustly or made your life miserable does not mean you have a valid claim. The following is a checklist of requirements that must be met before filing a claim in small claims court:

1) Your claim must be based on a sound legal concept. For example, if the contract you signed with Harry the Handyman stipulated that he would paint your house by Christmas for a fee of $300 and the work is still not completed on July 4, you may have a valid claim based on a sound legal concept involving contract law. But if your neighbor refuses to trim his tree which drops leaves into your yard, you may have a difficult time convincing a judge that you are entitled to some kind of compensation.

2) You must have evidence to support your claim.

3) Your claim must be within the dollar limitation of the jurisdiction of the court.

4) You must file your claim within a specified period of time.

5) You must file your claim with the court that has jurisdiction over your case.

6) Many courts require and common sense dictates that you contact the other party and attempt to resolve the dispute before going to court.

7) Be sure that your opponent is in a position to pay the amount you are claiming in damages. It is a waste of time to file a claim against someone who has no money or assets.

Taking the time to determine whether or not your case is based on a sound legal concept will save you the trouble of preparing a case that has no chance of winning in small claims court. The following is an example of a valid claim:

Six months after signing a three-year lease on a house, Joanne found that the stove wouldn't work. When she contacted the management company, she was told to arrange to have a local appliance store repair the stove and that she would be reimbursed for the cost of repairs. Three months and $75 later, Joanne had yet to be reimbursed. Receiving no response to her several written demands for payment, she brought a small claims action against her landlord (who was represented by the management company). While she had complied with her obligation (the stove had been repaired and she had a receipt for the work done and a cancelled check to prove that she had paid for the repairs), the landlord had failed to fulfill his obligation (to reimburse Joanne for the expenses).

Small claims court is a civil court, which means it handles only cases seeking a dollar amount of damages for an injury or loss or, in some jurisdictions, equitable relief such as the enforcement of the performance of a promise. This court does not deal with criminal matters, though you may feel your landlord is a criminal and should be thrown in jail. In other words, the court generally cannot require that a specific act be done, but it may order monetary damages. It all comes down to what you want the court to do. In the example of Harry the Handyman, whom you hired to paint your house, the small claims court may be unable to demand that he complete the job since it cannot oversee his work, but it does have the power to award you the amount you paid him. Some courts, however, by suspending judgment and asking the parties to report back after a specific period of time, have been able to ensure that a certain task be completed (such as the painting of the house). Once the defendant has fulfilled his obligations according to the terms of the contract, the case is dismissed. Other small claims courts are allowed to grant equitable remedies such as the return of your property, the changing of a contract, or the rescinding of a contract. These are remedies that do not involve dollar amounts.

Most small claims cases involve a contract, an injury to property, or a personal injury. Take the time to go to your local law library and do some reading about the type of claim you are considering. Most law libraries are county-supported, open to the public, and excellent sources of information.

Contracts

If you are dealing with a breach of contract, you must be able to prove that a contract actually existed. Learn the difference between a gift and a contract. If a friend promised to give you a car for your birthday and later changed her mind, there is no contract involved since the car was intended as a gift. But if the same friend promised to give you a car in exchange for your refinishing her furniture, a valid contract exists and can be enforced in a small claims court.

Injury to Property or Person

In injuries to property or person, you must be able to prove that intentional or negligent behavior was the cause of the injury. For example,

Fran's car was hit broadside by a Cadillac that was being backed out of a parking space at the Alpha Beta grocery store. The driver of the Cadillac was very apologetic and insisted that she would pay for the damage done to Fran's car, which consisted of a dent in the right front door. After obtaining an estimate of damages from a mechanic, Fran contacted the woman, who then refused to pay for the damages, claiming that Fran was the one who had been negligent by failing to stop when the woman started to back her car out of the parking space. The matter was brought before a small claims court. Although Fran had failed to obtain the names and phone numbers of any witnesses to the accident, she had taken pictures of the parking lot and the damage to her car, which were admitted as evidence. The judge concluded, after examining the photographs and hearing the testimony of both parties, that Fran had the right of way and that the driver of the Cadillac had been negligent by not checking in all directions before backing out.

HOW MUCH CAN YOU SEEK IN DAMAGES?

This is a court of limited jurisdiction, which means that it handles only those claims within a limited dollar amount. These limits vary from state to state, but generally range from $500 to $1500. The limits are often revised, so contact your local small claims clerk before processing your claim. (State laws regarding small claims can be found in any county law library.)

If when you sit down to figure out the dollar amount of your damage you find that it is greatly in excess of the amount allowed, you have two choices. You may settle for less and go through small claims court without incurring high litigation costs or you may bring the cause of action in a higher court with a higher dollar limit. Of course if you decide to sue for the full amount in a higher court, you will undoubtedly need an attorney to represent you—so you must decide which option will be more beneficial. If your small claims limit is $750 and you have determined that the defendant owes you $1000 in damages, would it be to your advantage to pay an attorney's fees to take it to a higher court?

If you decide halfway through the process to go to a higher court, some states will allow a transfer of the case but others will not. The thing to remember is that if you reduce your claim you forever waive recovery on the balance. Most courts will not allow you to "split" a cause of action, or divide a claim, so your case must be under the dollar limit unless you can creatively distinguish this claim as independent of the other (such as claiming that it is actually based on two contracts or two separate personal injuries). If you attempt this, you run the risk of having the second claim thrown out with no chance of refiling in a higher court.

When figuring dollar amounts of damages there are some basic things to consider. In a case involving a breach of contract, you are entitled to claim damages that would put you in as favorable a position as you would have been in had the defendant honored the contract. Generally, in property damage cases, you may claim the fair market value of the property before the damage or the cost to repair it, whichever is less. If the cost to repair your car is $800 while the actual value of the car is $300, you may claim only the $300 as damages. Since older property has less of a return, you may not be able to replace it for the current market value, especially in this time of inflation. In a personal injury case (you slipped on a banana peel at the grocery store), figure your actual dollar loss, such as medical expenses, loss of pay, etc., to determine the amount you can claim. In some instances, you can also claim damages for your physical suffering and mental anguish, but generally such cases involve a higher amount in damages than is allowed in small claims court.

At this point, you may want to consider consulting with an attorney just to be sure that you have considered all the options. You actually may be entitled to much more than could be recovered through small claims court. In addition, she may be able to direct you to a state or local regulatory agency that would be willing to handle your claim. If your local small claims court does allow attorneys to represent claimants and you have retained one, check with the small claims clerk to see if your attorney's fees can be recovered from the defendant should you win—some courts do allow this.

SHOULD YOU NEGOTIATE FIRST?

Yes, unequivocally yes. Try to resolve the problem outside of court. After all, going to court at the very least will cost you time off from work, not to mention the time to gather evidence and fill out and file forms with the court. Take your matter before the court only when you have no other avenue left to recover the debt. In addition, most states require that you attempt to resolve the problem yourself before you go to small claims court. Many times a dispute reaches small claims court which really could have been resolved beforehand with some compromise between the parties (such things as deciding which one of the parties is the actual owner of a cider press that has been borrowed back and forth over the years).

Your attempt to solve the problem should be in written form (called a "demand letter" or a "settlement letter," which is sent to the person you are considering suing). In the letter, summarize your grievance in a simple, logical manner, explain why you feel your opponent is at fault, express your willingness to reach a compromise, and state that should you not receive a satisfactory settlement you are prepared to take the matter before the small claims court.

In many cases, a settlement letter is all that is needed to get your opponent to negotiate, as most people dread the thought of having to go to court. Even if your letter brings no response, you will have made the attempt, and most courts require proof that you have contacted the other party in an attempt to resolve the dispute. When you write your letter, keep in mind that a judge may later read it in court (it will be considered evidence, so it should be clear and exact), and keep a copy for yourself. Send your letter by registered mail with a return receipt request, as this form will serve as evidence that your opponent was notified.

Should your opponent express interest in negotiating a settlement and yet put off discussing the matter with you, be aware that he may simply be stalling until the deadline to file your claim has passed (see "Statute of Limitations" on page 37). Even after a claim has been filed, the parties are encouraged to settle out of court. Some small claims courts offer the services of legally trained mediators (often attorneys) who will assist you in your negotiations in an attempt to resolve the dispute before the trial. Check to see if these services are available in your court system. If a settlement is reached after you have filed your claim, make sure the agreement is in writing and signed by your opponent and try to collect the full amount before the trial date. If you do not receive payment before that date, contact the court clerk to arrange for a postponement (or adjournment) of the trial until such payment is made. If you receive full payment before the date of the hearing, notify the court clerk immediately so that the case can be dismissed.

RULES OF THE COURT

Any court you enter will have specific regulations that must be observed. In California, claimants must meet the following requirements before they are allowed to enter the court. (Although most states have the same or similar requirements, be sure to verify this with the court clerk in your own city.)

1) You must be over 18 years of age or have filled out special forms. (In many courts, a parent or guardian is allowed to file a claim on behalf of a minor.)
2) You must have previously made an oral or written demand upon the defendant for the payment of the damages.
3) The injury or damage to person or property must have occurred within the judicial district of the small claims court. (Your judicial district may not be the same as your county. Some judicial districts encompass only part of a county.)

4) The obligation must be one that was to have been performed within the court's jurisdiction.

5) The defendant must have resided or the corporation to have done business in this jurisdiction at the time the contract was entered into (if your case involves a contract).

Apart from these requirements, in most states your right to bring a suit against another individual may not be transferred ("assigned") to someone else. For example, you are not allowed to have an insurance company sue someone on your behalf in small claims court.

STATUTE OF LIMITATIONS

You must file your claim within a specified period of time. These time limitations, called "statutes of limitations," vary from state to state and according to the type of claim being filed. They may range from six months up to three or four years, so be sure to check with the small claims clerk to see what limits apply to your case.

HOW MUCH WILL IT COST YOU TO FILE?

You will be required to pay a filing fee, which most states have kept very low since you are allowed to recover a limited amount in damages. The fees vary from state to state but generally range from $2 to $10. Many courts also charge a minimal fee for service of the claim (notifying the defendant) either by an officer of the court or by mail. All witnesses whom you subpoena must be served, and you may have to pay them witness fees and mileage costs. If you wish to subpoena a police officer, you may or may not have to pay a deposit ($75 in California). The officer's time will be charged against the deposit, so you may receive a refund depending upon the length of time he is in court. If the judge rules in your favor, you may be able to recover these costs.

FILING THE CLAIM

Once you have determined that you have a valid claim and the other party has failed to respond to your demands, you should contact the clerk of the small claims court. These are the steps you will need to take to file a claim:

1) Call the court clerk and provide him with the following information: the full legal name and address of the individual or company you are suing, the type of claim (breach of contract, etc.), the amount of damages you are claiming, and the pertinent dates. If the clerk verifies that the court has jurisdiction over your claim, ask him when you can file, the amounts of the filing and service fees, and what types of documents you should bring to his office. (If your opponent lives in another city, you may have to file your claim there.)

2) Prepare a folder to take with you to the court clerk containing a brief summary of the incident as well as any documents or items that may be used as evidence (contracts, leases, settlement letters, receipts, estimates of damage, cancelled checks, accident reports, etc.). Be sure to make copies of all documents.

3) Fill out and file your claim for damages with the clerk of the small claims court. Clerks are generally very willing to assist you.

4) A notice will be sent to the defendant informing him that he is being sued for a specific amount of damages and will be expected to appear in court on the date designated. The notice will be sent by certified or registered mail with a return receipt or delivered in person by a sheriff, a marshal, or some other authorized person. Before you go to court, check with the court clerk to be sure the defendant has been served.

5) Fill out subpoena forms for witnesses who may be reluctant to appear in court and have them served. Again, the clerk will assist you. Consider, though, that a witness who is ordered to court against her will may do your case more harm than good. There is no need to subpoena other witnesses who have already agreed to appear; simply notify them of the date and time of the trial. You may also subpoena documents if need be by filling out a form directed to the person in charge of the documents.

6) After you have filled out the plaintiff's statement and paid the filing fee, the clerk will give you a receipt which will include a case number and the court date. This date should be convenient for you and allow time for proper service of the defendant.

PREPARING FOR TRIAL

From the date you filed your claim, you have been collecting all your evidence to present in court—anything that will convince the judge that you have a valid claim. In an injury case, you will have taken photographs of the injury and the scene where the injury took place. If possible, you should plan to bring damaged goods to the courtroom (the jacket that started out as a size 14 and now is a size 6 due to the cleaning process). You will have collected all the necessary documents that are pertinent to your case, including the letter you sent to the defendant in an attempt to settle out of court. In addition, you will have notified all of your witnesses of the time and date of the trial.

During this period between filing and the trial, which may be from two weeks to several months, you may receive notice that the defendant has filed a counterclaim (a claim made by the defendant against the plaintiff). If this should occur, your claim and the counterclaim will be presented at the same time, unless of course the defendant's counterclaim exceeds the jurisdictional limit. In that instance, the court may transfer the case to a higher court. Although many counterclaims are filed simply to intimidate the plaintiff into settling the dispute out of court, be prepared to defend your case.

YOUR DAY IN COURT

Generally, the rules of evidence are very relaxed in small claims court, so you don't have to be a Philadelphia lawyer to survive the experience. When you have been seated in the courtroom and the judge has entered, the clerk will read the calendar or list of cases to be heard to determine that all the parties are present. When your case is called, you will be sworn in by the clerk. Some small claims cases are heard by arbitrators rather than judges; these persons are appointed by the court and have all the qualifications and authority of a judge.

Should the defendant in your case fail to appear at the trial, the judge or arbitrator will request that you present your case, and if you can prove that you are entitled to recover damages you will be awarded a default judgment (which will include court costs). If your opponent is present, the trial will begin with your testimony.

State your case simply and briefly. Present all of your evidence to the judge or arbitrator, including the settlement letter that was sent to the defendant, documents, and any physical evidence (such as photographs, diagrams, or the damaged item). Inform the judge of the costs you have incurred in bringing the case to trial, as you may be able to recover these if he rules in your favor. When you have completed your presentation, you may ask your witnesses to testify on your behalf. The defendant (or his attorney) is allowed to cross-examine you and your witnesses, and the judge may ask questions as well. Respond to all questions with a brief statement, and be courteous to the judge, the defendant, and anyone else involved with the trial.

Once you have presented your case and cross-examination has been completed, the defendant will have the opportunity to present his side of the dispute. Do not interrupt, no matter how outrageous you consider his statements to be. You will have a chance to cross-examine him and his witnesses once he has completed his presentation.

Most small claims hearings take no longer than fifteen or twenty minutes. When the judge or arbitrator has heard both sides of the case, he will either render a decision at that time or mail the decision to both parties a short time after the trial.

COLLECTING THE JUDGMENT

The next hurdle is getting your money. The court does not collect for you. The direct and courteous approach works best so request (preferably in writing) that the defendant pay you the amount of the judgment. The next step, if you are unable to collect within a reasonable period of time (several weeks), is to consider levying or garnishing wages and bank accounts or seizing real property or other assets. Not all of your opponent's assets are automatically subject to levying or seizure. Property owned by both the defendant and his wife is not always exempt but may be more difficult and complicated to reach. If your claim is against a corporation, you cannot touch the personal property or bank accounts of any of the individuals who own or run the business. In some states, a portion of the equity in a motor vehicle may be exempt from levy. For example, if the defendant's truck is worth $4000 but he owes $3000 on it, his equity is $1000 and $500 of the equity may be exempt from levy. If the truck is used for business purposes, the exemption may be even higher.

The following steps should be taken to collect a judgment that the defendant refuses to pay:

1) Ascertain the defendant's assets as best you can. If necessary, you can arrange to have the defendant appear in court to answer questions regarding his assets—bank accounts, real property, etc.

2) Contact the small claims clerk and fill out a Writ of Execution or Writ of Garnishment (there is a minimal charge).

3) The clerk will direct you to the county sheriff or marshal, who will notify the defendant that he must pay the judgment.

4) If payment still has not been made, the sheriff or marshal may seize your opponent's assets or levy against his wages or bank accounts. A levy against real property (such as a home, a building, or land) requires that you record an Abstract of Judgment, a form supplied by the court at the records office, with the county clerk where the property is located. This gives you a lien on the property, which means that the judgment must be satisfied before the property title can be transferred to a new owner.

5) To recover service and filing fees not awarded in the original judgment, you must file a Memorandum of Credit with the court and obtain

court approval. One copy is filed with the small claims court clerk and another is sent to the judgment debtor (your opponent).

6) Once you are paid in full you should file a Satisfaction of Judgment with the clerk of the small claims court. Failure to file the Satisfaction of Judgment may in some states subject you to liability should the judgment debtor suffer any damage. For example, if you recorded an Abstract of Judgment against the defendant's residence but failed to file a Satisfaction of Judgment after being paid in full, the Abstract of Judgment is still in effect. If the defendant loses a buyer for his home because the judgment is still filed, you may be personally liable for any damage.

WHAT IF YOU ARE THE DEFENDANT?

If you receive notice that you are being sued in small claims court, study the notice carefully to determine what the suit involves and what your rights and obligations are and then contact the claimant and attempt to settle the matter out of court. If a settlement is reached, it should be in writing and include a statement that the claimant will drop the suit. Retain one copy and send another to the clerk so that the claimant cannot accept payment from you and still go ahead and sue.

If you are unable to reach a settlement and must defend your case in court, in some jurisdictions you will need to complete and file a Defendant's Response (attached to the claim form); you will be charged a small fee, usually around $4. In other jurisdictions you need merely collect your evidence and appear in court on the specified date. Or perhaps you will decide to bring a counterclaim against the plaintiff and file a Claim of Defendant. If the counterclaim involves the same dispute and the amount of the damages is within the small claims limit, you must file with the small claims clerk prior to the court date (the fee will be around $8). The court will hear both cases at the same time. If you wish to bring a claim for an amount greater than that allowed in small claims court you will have to file in a higher court, where you most likely will want to be represented by an attorney. You must decide in which court you wish your case to be heard before the date of the small claims court hearing so that the judge can decide whether or not to transfer the remaining portions of the case. If you file a counterclaim, you will have to arrange for the plaintiff to be served, subpoena or notify witnesses, assemble pertinent documents, and present your case to the judge.

THE APPEAL

If the plaintiff loses her case in small claims court, she generally cannot appeal it to a higher court. In most states, this is not true of the defendant. However, before you appeal, consider the following:

- You must file a Notice of Appeal with the clerk of the court within a set time period (usually soon after the judgment of the small claims court) and pay a filing fee that is greater than the one for small claims.
- Since the entire case will have to be presented again, you will have to prepare your evidence, subpoena or notify witnesses, etc.
- In a higher court, the environment will be much more formal and the legal procedures more complicated, so you may want to hire an attorney, which will increase your costs.
- There will be a longer waiting period before the case is heard.

Few small claims cases are appealed since the odds of winning are slim and even the most favorable outcome is rarely worth the time and cost involved. Should you appeal and lose, you will not be allowed to pursue the matter further.

5
Traffic Court

Traffic court can be a frightening experience for women simply because, for many, this is the first contact they have with the judicial system. It is generally one of the busiest and liveliest of the courts, having been compared upon occasion to a three-ring circus. Most traffic courts operate daily, and many communities have at least one night session of court for those who work during the day.

Knowledge of the law could save you a traffic violation or at least be useful when determining whether you should "fight" a ticket. You are expected to be familiar with the traffic regulations in your state. Any questions you have can be easily answered by looking up the state vehicle code at the local law library or by the clerk of the traffic court or the Department of Motor Vehicles.

Unfortunately, states have not unified their traffic codes, which causes motorists great confusion when driving from one state to another. Some states have been known to use this to their advantage by increasing state traffic revenues at the expense of unsuspecting out-of-state motorists. Although Congress adopted the Uniform Vehicle Code in 1926, it is merely a suggested code and is not legally binding upon the states, serving instead as a model and reference for state legislatures in drafting motor vehicle and traffic laws for their jurisdictions.

TYPES OF TRAFFIC TICKETS

The first thing you need to be aware of is that traffic tickets vary in their degree of seriousness, depending upon how your individual state vehicle code defines the offenses. Your traffic violation will be either an infraction (less serious), a misdemeanor (increasingly serious), or a felony (very serious, such as vehicular manslaughter in some states).

An infraction is an offense for which you cannot be punished with a jail sentence. The sentence is usually a fine, although occasionally the court will suspend or revoke an individual's driver's license. The fines generally run from $50 to $200, depending upon whether this is your first, second, or third offense within the same year. In some states, the fourth offense within the same year automatically becomes a misdemeanor. Exceeding the speed limit and running a red light are examples of this type of violation.

A misdemeanor is an offense for which you can be fined and/or given a jail sentence. If you are found guilty of a misdemeanor in Montana, the fine would range from $100 to $5,000 and the jail sentence from 30 days to one year, for a first offense, while in Alaska you would receive a fine in the neighborhood of $200 and/or a 90-day maximum sentence in jail. Misdemeanors often include such violations as failure to report a traffic accident, reckless driving, and non-injury hit and run.

A felony is defined as a driving offense which results in death or serious injury to another party. Again, sentences vary from state to state. In Washington, a felony traffic violation is punishable by a maximum fine of $5,000 and/or 10 years in prison; Ohio calls aggravated vehicular homicide a felony of the fourth degree and penalties range from 18 months to 5 years in prison and/or $2,500, but if there have been prior convictions the sentence would be a maximum of 5 to 10 years in prison and/or $5,000. California's fines for such offenses range from $1,000 to $5,000 and/or 1 to 5 years in prison. Offenses such as vehicular or negligent homicide often fall into this category of violation.

If you receive a citation, technically your ticket represents an arrest for which the officer is releasing you from his custody on your own recognizance based on your promise to appear in court on the specified date to answer the charges or mail in the fine (if allowed). The officer will ask you to sign the citation—don't refuse, even if you consider yourself innocent. Your signature does not represent an admission of guilt. Should you receive a citation for not having your driver's license or registration card with you when you were stopped, the case will usually be dismissed if you appear in court with the valid documents.

Whether you receive a warning or a citation is often a judgment call of the officer. A warning does not represent an arrest or require a court appearance and in most states is not reported to the Department of Motor

Vehicles. Warnings are often given for parking violations and for defective equipment (a turn signal that doesn't work or a headlight that has burned out). In the latter instance, the warning will usually stipulate that the defect must be corrected within a certain number of days and that proof of the repair be mailed in.

WHAT HAPPENS IF YOU IGNORE THE TICKET?

If you decide to ignore the ticket and do not appear in court or pay the fine, a "bench" warrant may be issued for your arrest. This means that a judge, after noting your absence, will rule from the bench that you have violated your promise to appear and will order you arrested and brought before the court. In many cases, however, you will not be arrested on the bench warrant until you are stopped for some other violation and the police officer calls your license number in to see if there are any outstanding violations.

The thing to consider here is that your traffic offense may be only an infraction but by the time you have failed to appear you have committed a more serious offense—in many states failure to appear is considered a misdemeanor. An individual brought in on a bench warrant will be required to answer both the original charges and the charge of failure to appear. A fine is often imposed to cover the additional court costs.

THE OPTIONS

The following options are available to you when you receive a traffic ticket:

1) Send in your fine, which is considered the same as a conviction.

2) Plead guilty at the arraignment, in which case a penalty will be imposed.

3) Plead not guilty at the arraignment, in which case a trial date will be set and you will be required to post bail (usually the amount of your fine).

4) Plead guilty with an explanation (allowed in some jurisdictions). This will appear on your record as a guilty plea, but you will be allowed to offer an explanation of any extenuating circumstances (poor weather conditions, your excellent previous driving record, etc.) which you would like the court to take into consideration when assessing a penalty (hopefully resulting in a reduced or suspended fine).

5) Plead *nolo contendere* (no contest). You are not admitting guilt but are not contesting the charge either. This is considered the same as a guilty plea in terms of your driving record. The only advantage is that this plea cannot be used in a later civil suit against you as an admission of your guilt in the incident.

Before deciding which option to take, you should ask yourself several questions. Is the matter serious enough to warrant the time and cost involved in going to court? What effect will a guilty plea have on your driving record and insurance rates? Is your license in jeopardy? (Some states operate on a point system, in which a certain number of points are assigned to each violation and if that number exceeds the maximum allowed within a set period of time, the driver may lose her license.) Will you need to hire an attorney?

If you are guilty of the violation and a small fine is all that is involved, simply mail in your check. Should you consider yourself innocent of the violation and wish to spend the time to fight it, you will have to appear in court. If the incident is minor, there should be no need to hire an attorney to represent you. As in small claims court, traffic court hearings generally don't last long and are quite informal.

In more complicated or serious matters, such as offenses punishable by large fines, a jail sentence, or loss or suspension of your driver's license, as well as those involving an accident in which there was damage to property or injuries to any of the parties, you should seriously consider hiring an attorney. If you should find yourself accused of such an offense, start immediately to collect any evidence that could be used in court to substantiate your innocence—take down the names, addresses, and phone numbers of any witnesses to the incident, make notes on everything you can recall about the weather and traffic conditions and the speed and direction in which all the parties were traveling, take photographs or draw diagrams, etc. You will want to be well prepared should you find yourself standing trial and challenging a police officer's testimony.

ARRAIGNMENT

Your first appearance in court is called the arraignment. When you arrive, locate the court dockets (a listing of the cases and the courtrooms in which they will be heard), and inform the clerk or bailiff that you are present. Be prepared to wait for a while for your case to be called. Once the judge reads off your name and the charge that has been made against you, you will be asked how you wish to plead. If you plead not guilty, the court may require that you post bond (usually the amount of the fine), which will be returned to you if you are acquitted (found not guilty). In some states, the trial is scheduled for the same day, in which case you will move to another courtroom. In others, the trial is set for a later date.

In most states, you are guaranteed the right to a jury trial only in the case of a misdemeanor or a felony, not an infraction. You will be asked at the time the trial date is set if you wish to have your case heard by a judge or a jury (there may be a fee in the range of $25 for a jury trial). This is a constitutional right that should not be waived before giving it considerable thought.

You have the constitutional right to request that the police officer appear at the trial, so do not agree to a trial by deposition, in which the officer does not appear but only his sworn statement is admitted as evidence against you. In your attempt to convince the judge or jury that you are not guilty of the violation, or at least that there were extenuating circumstances beyond your control, you will need to cross-examine the police officer and any of the prosecution's witnesses.

CONTINUANCE

If you find you are unable to appear on the date set for your trial, it is your responsibility to ask the court for a continuance (postponement). You must have a reason that the court deems acceptable, such as the need for more time to prepare your defense or the inability of a witness to appear. Some courts will accept phone requests made to the court clerk, but if you request a continuance by phone be sure to get the name and title of the person you talked to and send a follow-up letter that refers to the new trial date and reiterates your reasons for requesting a postponement.

If you do not seek a continuance and simply fail to show up in court, you will probably forfeit bail and the charge will be recorded as a conviction. If instead of paying bail you were released on your own recognizance, you may find that a bench warrant for your arrest has been issued.

A continuance may very well be to your advantage—the police officer may be unable to appear or after a longer period of time be unable to recall the incident except for what is contained in his notes. However, you should be aware of the fact that if you are granted a continuance you waive your right to a speedy trial (usually one to three months), which was guaranteed at the time you pleaded not guilty.

THE TRIAL

You will have started preparing your defense from the moment you received your traffic ticket. You've made notes, taken photographs, prepared diagrams—whatever will strengthen your case—and have, with the assistance of the court clerk, subpoenaed witnesses to testify on your behalf. In addition, you will have anticipated what will be said in court and how you will respond and what questions you will ask of the police officer and any witnesses.

The atmosphere in traffic court is usually quite informal, and most people choose to represent themselves, although you may be allowed to have an attorney represent you if you wish. (In some cases, attorneys are successful in plea bargaining for their clients, a form of negotiation between the judge and the attorney whereby the judge may agree to dismiss the charge if the attorney can show good cause, or perhaps reduce the charge to a lesser offense if the defendant agrees to plead guilty to that offense.) Again, once you are seated in the courtroom you may have a long wait until your case is called. The prosecution will present its evidence first, which in many cases will consist solely of the police officer's testimony. (If the officer fails to appear in court, the judge may dismiss the case.) Listen closely to the officer's testimony in order to detect any discrepancies or inaccuracies, as once the prosecution has presented its evidence you will have the opportunity to cross-examine.

Your purpose at this point is not necessarily to convince the judge or jury of your innocence but to establish a reasonable doubt about the accuracy of the officer's interpretation of the incident. If you produce evidence (such as photographs) which conflicts with the officer's testimony and the officer is found to have been mistaken, there is a good chance that the case will be dismissed. For example, you may present a photograph of the intersection which shows a double turn lane and you were given a ticket for an improper turn from the outside turn lane. All you're trying to prove here is that the officer was in error. Remember, the burden of proof is on the prosecution to prove that you are guilty beyond a reasonable doubt. If you can establish a reasonable doubt as to your guilt, you have a chance of having the case dismissed.

When cross-examination is completed, you will be allowed to present your argument. Explain exactly what occurred as simply and concisely as you can, present any evidence that will strengthen your case, and call any witnesses you may have to testify on your behalf. When the prosecution cross-examines you, answer as directly and courteously as possible.

TYPES OF SENTENCES

The verdict is usually announced immediately after the case has been heard. Although the judge is not allowed to look at your past record before or during the trial, she can, and undoubtedly will, refer to it before she sentences you, and the severity of your sentence most likely will depend on your prior driving record.

If you are found not guilty, any bond you posted will be refunded and the violation will not appear on your driving record. If you are found guilty, the judge will impose a sentence. In some cases, the court will penalize you to the maximum of the law but suspend all or part of the sentence, usually upon a certain condition—such as that there be no similar violation for one year or that you attend a traffic violators school. The violation will appear on your driving record, but in some cases if you produce evidence that you have completed the traffic school the citation will be taken off your record.

THE APPEAL

Appealing traffic convictions is usually a costly process with a limited number of successes. In many states, traffic courts are not courts of record so there are no transcripts of the trial, which means that if you appeal to a higher court the entire case must be presented again. (In some jurisdictions, a tape of the proceedings will be made upon request.) In addition, the court costs will be higher; there will be a longer waiting period before the appeal is heard; and you most likely will want to hire an attorney to represent you.

DEALING WITH THE POLICE

6
Your Rights as an Arrested Person

What is the extent of your knowledge regarding your constitutional rights should you be detained or arrested by the police? If you are in the majority of women (and men), you probably have not considered such an event; it may be that your only contact with the police occurred when your home was burglarized or when you were stopped for driving five miles per hour over the speed limit. You may feel the chances are very slim that you, a friend, or a member of your family will ever have an unfortunate encounter with the police and therefore that the following information will be of no use to you. However, if you have ever been abusive to a police officer when stopped for a traffic violation, driven home after an office or cocktail party where alcohol was served in abundance, or inadvertently placed a pen in your purse while shopping, you may want to read further. Remember that many innocent persons are confronted by the police solely because of their association with others who are suspected of illegal activities (perhaps you are at a party where illegal drugs are being used) or because of their own absentmindedness (you forget to pay your bill before leaving a restaurant or hotel).

Should you be arrested (this includes for driving under the influence of alcohol), you may find yourself with your hands on top of the police car as you are searched for contraband or weapons. After this is concluded, you may be handcuffed, placed in the back seat of the police car, and transported to the local jail. Once in the jail, the female jailer will conduct a search. Your belongings will be inventoried, your picture and fingerprints taken, and perhaps questions will be asked of you. After you have made your phone call, you will probably be placed in a concrete room (possibly the size of a walk-in closet) with other arrested women. And that may be only the beginning. Tomorrow when you consider your situation, you most likely will be full of self-doubt and concern, desiring to clear yourself and get the matter behind you as quickly and painlessly as possible.

The woman who has been arrested often becomes paranoid and gets caught up in the game of Monday morning quarterbacking the police's actions—"Should I have reacted differently?" "Did they have the right to arrest me?" "They didn't give me my Miranda Rights until several hours after the arrest; does that make the arrest illegal?" Today she is embarrassed, confused, and scared, and it suddenly dawns on her that her knowledge of criminal procedure is limited to what she has seen on "Hill Street Blues" and "The Rockford Files." If she'd been familiar with her rights as a citizen and known what a police officer can and cannot do, the experience might have been less traumatic.

The laws in the area of criminal procedure have been changing constantly during the past two decades, and police agencies and departments conduct frequent refresher courses in an attempt to keep the officers informed of recent Supreme Court cases and how the rulings will affect their jobs. The reason for this training is obvious: an officer's failure to conform to the proper procedures during even the most basic period of an investigation may result in the entire case being thrown out of court and the suspect set free.

The following is not intended as the last word on how to deal with the police in every situation but as an overview of criminal procedure. The information presented here hopefully will help you understand your own rights and obligations and the basic principles of criminal law. Except in the case of minor traffic violations, should you run afoul of the law it is recommended that you promptly seek legal counsel, since every situation is different and not every one can be covered in a book. We begin this discussion by reintroducing you to your constitutionally protected rights, the ones you were forced to learn in the eighth grade. After quickly reviewing them, we will examine when the police have the right to detain, question, and arrest you, what constitutes excessive force and false arrest (and what you can do if you suspect either applies to your situation), and finally what you can expect should you be arrested for driving while under the influence of alcohol.

CONSTITUTIONAL RIGHTS

All citizens are given certain rights through the United States Constitution. These rights are guaranteed irrespective of one's guilt or innocence. For example, the Fifth Amendment states that a person shall not "be compelled in any criminal case to be a witness against himself" (self-incrimination), and the Sixth Amendment states, "in all criminal prosecutions, the accused shall enjoy the right to a speedy and public trial, by an impartial jury ... and to have the assistance of counsel for his defense." These amendments represent the minimum standards with which the government must comply when dealing with individuals suspected of illegal activities. The more of your liberty the police agency desires to take away from you the greater the reason and necessity for intrusion it must show. If during an arrest or investigation the government or the police fail to adhere to these standards, they are guilty of violating your constitutionally guaranteed rights. This is not mere rhetoric. Evidence gathered during a constitutionally invalid search may not be admissible in court. More than one jury has returned a verdict of not guilty only to find out later that highly incriminatory evidence was withheld at the trial due to an officer's improper search, investigation, or arrest.

STATE LAWS

State laws differ, depending on the way the individual states interpret the United States Constitution. The Constitution and its amendments set forth the *minimum* rights guaranteed to individuals, and the individual states may, through judicial decisions or changes in their constitutions, increase their citizens' rights when dealing with state-related matters. Some states are considered to be more liberal, having interpreted the Constitution broadly and finding individual rights to be paramount; others are considered to be conservative, having adopted a strict interpretation of the Constitution and therefore being more willing to grant the police agencies broader powers. Irrespective of the way the individual states interpret the Constitution, the final interpretation is made by the United States Supreme Court.

Should an individual who has received an adverse ruling raise the issue that a certain state's law is not in keeping with the law as set forth by the U.S. Constitution, that is, that the state law and the manner in which it is enforced inhibit an individual's rights, the federal court and ultimately, if necessary, the U.S. Supreme Court will review the law and the manner in which the state's courts have interpreted it. Should a finding be made that the law is in fact contrary to the U.S. Constitution, it will be ruled unconstitutional and the state will be required to eliminate it or rewrite it to conform to the Constitution.

WHEN MAY AN OFFICER DETAIN YOU?

For an officer to be able to stop you on the street or in your car, that is to detain you, most states require that she be able to show that there are specific facts which cause her to believe that criminal activity has occurred (or is about to occur) in the area and that you were involved in that activity. Clearly this does not infer that an officer cannot request an individual to stop and provide certain information. However, should she not be a suspect in the illegal activity and refuse to assist the officer, she is free to continue on her way.

Consider the following hypothetical:

While working the evening shift in a residential area, an officer was notified by the police dispatcher that a residential burglary, a felony, had just been committed in the area by three Caucasian males who fled in a blue 1981 Camaro. Immediately after the call, she noticed a vehicle matching the description and noted that there were three individuals in the car. She promptly turned on her flashing light, and the vehicle pulled off to the side of the road. When she approached the car, she found not the male suspects but three ladies on their way to dinner.

The officer had the right, based upon the information she had received from the dispatcher, to conclude that there was illegal activity occurring in the area, and based upon the similarity of the vehicles, it may be fair to assume that she had a reasonable belief that the occupants of the automobile were involved in the activity. Therefore, she had the right to stop and detain the occupants of the vehicle for the purpose of investigation. However, once she observed seated inside the Camaro not the suspected male burglars but three women, she was then required to allow them to proceed to their destination. Had the dispatcher's broadcast merely stated that the suspected burglars had fled in a light-colored car, the officer's detention of the women may have been improper since the description was too vague.

WHEN MAY AN OFFICER ARREST YOU?

An officer can arrest you only under one of the following circumstances: 1) she has seen you commit a crime, 2) she has in her possession an arrest warrant (an official document issued by a judge approving such an arrest), or 3) she has probable cause to believe you have committed a crime. The officer is required to have more information to arrest you than is necessary for her simply to detain you. To arrest you, she must reasonably believe that an offense (a crime) has been committed and that you did in fact commit the offense.

WHEN MAY AN OFFICER QUESTION YOU?

Every woman who has ever watched television is aware that the police are required to read a group of rights known as Miranda Rights to an arrested person before they can begin questioning. These are designed to protect that person's Fifth Amendment right against self-incrimination during the period known as "custodial interrogation." Custodial interrogation occurs when a person is in the custody of the police for allegedly committing a crime and the police desire to question her regarding her involvement. This is an area of the law that most people find confusing. Many individuals have observed such a situation only as portrayed in 1940s detective movies—a small dark room in the basement of the police station furnished only with a table and a chair, a single light bulb suspended by a long cord hanging directly over the table. The suspect is seated at the table, and two officers in their rolled-up Arrow shirts stand over him demanding that he confess to the crime. Many hours later, after having been continually badgered and threatened by the officers, the suspect admits his guilt (unless he is the hero, in which case he just grins and bears it).

The name for these Fifth Amendment rights against self-incrimination arose from the famous case of Miranda v. Arizona.[1] In 1963, Mr. Miranda was arrested at his home and taken by the police to the local police station, where he was identified by the complaining witness. He was then taken to "Interrogation Room No. 2" and questioned by two police officers. After two hours in the interrogation room, the officers emerged with a written confession signed by Mr. Miranda. The trial court allowed the confession into evidence, even though the officers admitted during the trial that Mr. Miranda had not been advised that he had a right to have an attorney present. Mr. Miranda was found guilty, and the case was appealed to the Supreme Court of Arizona, which held that his Fifth Amendment right against self-incrimination had not been violated by the police, and affirmed his conviction. In 1966 the case was heard by the U.S. Supreme Court, which stated:

> We reverse [the ruling of the lower court].... From the testimony of the officers ... it is clear that Miranda was not in any way apprised

> of his right to consult with an attorney and to have one present during the interrogation, nor was his right not to be compelled to incriminate himself effectively protected in any other manner. Without these warnings the statements were inadmissible.[2]

From this case came the Miranda Rights and the requirement that individuals arrested for an offense must knowingly and intelligently waive their constitutional rights before they may be questioned by the police.

Miranda Rights can be broken down into four categories:

YOU HAVE THE RIGHT TO REMAIN SILENT. You are not required to discuss the matter with anyone after you have been arrested, and the police cannot entice you to speak about the offense by resorting to bribery, promises of leniency, or threats of physical or emotional harm. The courts have ruled that the only information you are required to give to the police is such things as your name, address, and next of kin (when you are admitted, or "booked," in jail).

Consider the following situation:

An officer stopped Mary outside a department store for suspicion of shoplifting after having been informed that a woman matching her description had just left the store with a light-weight winter jacket in her shopping bag. She has the right to ask Mary for her name and address (Mary may choose not to reply), but should she place her under arrest for shoplifting, the officer is required by law to inform her of her right to remain silent before questioning her about the incident.

It is important to understand that a person who desires to invoke this right will be considered no more or no less guilty than one who desires to waive it, that is, agrees to talk with the police about the matter. This right is absolute, meaning that should you remain silent the police will be required to act as if you did not give up this right and will not be allowed to question you.

ANYTHING YOU SAY CAN AND WILL BE USED AGAINST YOU IN A COURT OF LAW. Should you waive your right to remain silent and discuss the matter with the police, be aware that an officer may be called to testify as to any statements that you made should your case end up in trial. This includes the so-called "off the record" statement. For example, at the time of her booking, a woman charged with driving under the influence of alcohol stated to the officer, after waiving her rights, that she had consumed three alcoholic drinks during the hour before her arrest. During the trial, she testified under oath that she had had only one alcoholic drink during the three hours before her arrest. The prosecutor called the officer to testify as to her prior statement. In this situation, the jury had to decide who was telling the truth and who had the most to gain by misstating the facts.

Even though you initially waive your right to remain silent, you can reinstate the right at any time by merely informing the officer of your decision. Returning to Mary's situation, after being advised of her rights, she decided to waive them and informed the officer that she had not been in the department store that day. However, when the officer questioned her about the contents of her shopping bag Mary requested that all questions cease until she could speak with her attorney. At that time, the officer terminated the questioning and, based upon the observations and positive identification by a store employee, placed Mary under arrest for theft.

YOU HAVE THE RIGHT TO TALK WITH AN ATTORNEY AND HAVE HIM PRESENT WHILE YOU ARE BEING QUESTIONED. IF YOU ARE UNABLE TO AFFORD AN ATTORNEY, ONE WILL BE APPOINTED TO REPRESENT YOU BEFORE YOU ARE QUESTIONED IF YOU WISH. Should you invoke your right to remain silent in order to speak with your attorney, the questioning will cease until you have had an opportunity to discuss the matter with him. After your conference, you can decide whether you wish to answer the questions or remain silent. If you cannot afford an attorney, one will be appointed to represent you, as the United States Supreme Court has interpreted the Sixth Amendment clause regarding right to counsel to include *all* persons accused of criminal violations regardless of their financial situation.

DO YOU UNDERSTAND EACH RIGHT WHICH I [the officer] HAVE EXPLAINED AND WITH THEM IN MIND DO YOU WISH TO TALK WITH US NOW? An individual must knowingly and intelligently waive each right before any questions can be asked. The officer's responsibility is two-fold: she must inform the arrested person of her rights, ensuring that there is no ambiguity or confusion; and she must ensure that once the suspect has reached a decision it is respected. Should the individual be unable to understand any of the rights or be willing to waive all but one, the officer must explain that they must all be understood and all waived before questioning can begin.

These rights must be given any time you are arrested for an offense *and* the police desire to question you about that offense. Should they decide not to question you, they are not required to inform you of these rights. Many an individual after an arrest has immediately run to her attorney exclaiming that since she was not informed of her rights the arrest must be invalid, when in fact no questioning had taken place.

What is your recourse should the police fail to inform you of your rights before questioning you? It does not make the arrest invalid, since the arrest came before the questioning, but it may make not only your statement but any evidence discovered because of your statement inadmissible as evidence against you in a trial. Any information the police derive through procedures that violate your Fifth Amendment right against self-incrimination is not admissible in court when considering your guilt or innocence, and if it is presented the court may order a mistrial.

EXCESSIVE FORCE/FALSE ARREST

Excessive force, or police brutality, involves many types of behavior, and determining when an action would be considered excessive is not always cut and dried. If you were handcuffed and offered no resistance, it is a clear case of excessive force if the officer hit you in the stomach with her club. However, the matter may not be so clear cut if the officer grabbed your arm as you reached into your purse for your wallet, as she could have reacted out of her fear that your purse contained a gun.

Perhaps you feel that you were wrongfully denied your freedom of movement and that your arrest or detention was not legally justified. For example, say an officer stops and detains you as you are walking down the street at 10 p.m. If there has been no known criminal activity in the area and yet the officer arbitrarily decides to detain you in the back seat of her car for no other reason than that she thought you looked suspicious, she may have violated your right to freedom of movement and you may have a bona fide case.

If you feel that a police officer has acted improperly in any way (resulting in what you consider to be excessive force, false arrest or detainment, or a violation of any of your constitutional rights), don't hesitate to take action. You can bring the officer's behavior to the attention of her superiors by sending a written complaint to the police department. In many jurisdictions, such complaints are followed up by an in-house investigation. If the investigation reveals that the officer did violate your rights, the complaint will be noted in her personnel file and in many cases disciplinary action will be taken.

You or your attorney may also bring a legal motion requesting a judge to rule your arrest illegal if you feel the officer violated one or more of your constitutional rights. All participants will be required to appear in court for a formal hearing, and after all the testimony has been presented and the laws on the subject have been reviewed, the judge will be required to exercise judicial hindsight and rule whether the arrest or detainment was reasonable. If the judge finds that the officer was justified in her actions, the arrest will be upheld, and if you deny your guilt a trial date will be set. Should the judge rule that the arrest was improper, the case will probably be dismissed and the charges dropped.

Lastly, you may want to hire an attorney and bring a civil suit against the officer and the police department for false arrest or assault, though this litigation will have no effect on the criminal matter should you prevail. The police agency may be ordered to pay you money damages equal to the harm that was proven.

DRIVING UNDER THE INFLUENCE OF ALCOHOL: A CASE STUDY

It used to be that individuals cited for this violation could often simply hire an attorney, who would plea bargain for a lesser offense, say reckless driving, and never appear in court. In recent years, however, families of victims involved in alcohol-related accidents have begun speaking out against the legal system's slap-on-the-wrist punishment, and insurance companies have been quick to terminate insurance coverage of those convicted. In response to the public's outrage and the increasing number of fatalities due to drunk drivers, many states have toughened their laws in this area. What this all means is if you are drinking, don't drive, and should you disregard common sense and drive anyway, be prepared to accept the consequences.

Many women asked us what would happen to them if they were stopped for driving a vehicle while under the influence of alcohol. We were surprised at the lack of understanding of the possible consequences and of the process they would go through after they were stopped. It is with that in mind that the following case study is offered.

The office party concluded after four hours of good humor and free drinks. Getting in her car after the final round, Janice rolled up the windows and locked the doors, a task which took a little more time than usual. She entered the freeway she travelled daily to work, concentrating on her driving but at times abruptly changing speed as she maneuvered around the other cars. Nearing home she turned onto a multilane street, swerving between lanes in what the officer later testified to as an "inattentive manner." Observing a flashing light in her rearview mirror, Janice promptly pulled over to the side of the road. The traffic officer approached her car and identified himself by placing his badge up against the closed window for her view. She then rolled down the window and after some fumbling presented the officer with her driver's license and vehicle registration. The officer later testified that he noticed an odor of alcohol when she rolled down the window and that it took her a long time to get her license out of her wallet.

Based upon his observations (her driving pattern, the odor of alcohol, and her difficulty in locating and removing her license), the officer requested that she step out of her car in order to perform what are known as Field Sobriety Tests. These tests, sometimes referred to as "roadside ballet," are designed to measure coordination and the ability to follow instructions. Janice was first instructed on how to perform the "finger to nose touch." "Stand erect, place your arms out to the side, and extend your index finger. Then place your head back, close your eyes, and touch your index finger to the tip of your nose." The officer demonstrated the test and then asked Janice to perform it. In her first attempt, her index finger ended up between the top of her nose and the middle of her forehead. Two further attempts produced similar results. After recording the results, the officer introduced another test, "walking heel to toe." It consisted of walking heel to toe in a straight line for six steps, then turning around and returning to the original position. For Janice, finding the tip of one foot with the heel of the other was easier than keeping the movement in a straight line, and upon turning she lost her balance and had to begin again. Four tests were given, and in the officer's opinion she failed them all, leading him to believe that she was under the influence of alcohol.

Janice was placed under arrest for driving under the influence, patted down for weapons, and requested to lock up her car (a tow company would be called so that it could be impounded). She was then handcuffed and placed in the back of the police car for the trip to the local jail. Prior to leaving the scene, she was informed of her constitutional rights, which she elected to invoke, stating to the officers that she wanted to speak with her family attorney before making any statements.

Once at the jail, Janice was informed that her state had adopted an Implied Consent Law, which states that all motorists who are licensed by the state to drive a motor vehicle have, by the act of accepting their license, consented to take a chemical test to determine the alcoholic content of their blood. If she refused to take the test, she could lose her driving privilege for a period of six months to a year, as her refusal would be considered an admission of guilt. She was further informed that she had the right to a blood, breath, or urine test and that she did not have the right to consult with an attorney before making her decision, the courts having concluded that the chemical test requirement is not in violation of the Fifth Amendment right against self-incrimination.

Janice was informed that the results of the breath test would be determined immediately, while the blood and urine tests would require laboratory analysis. She chose the breath test, which required that she blow into a plastic mouthpiece for a short period of time. The other end of the mouthpiece was connected to a Breathalizer machine, which through a chemical process analyzes the oxygen in the lungs to determine the amount of alcohol. The machine produced a printed form showing her alcohol level to be 0.l6. In her state, any person with an alcohol level of 0.10 or above is assumed to be under the influence of alcohol. Janice was then booked into the jail.

After the administrative procedures were completed, including fingerprints, photograph, and an inventory of clothing and other belongings, she was allowed to make a telephone call to her husband informing him why she was not home and when he could come and get her (her state required that she remain in the jail for six hours before she could be released). After the call, she was taken to a cell established for females arrested on similar charges and later released on her own recognizance.

For Janice, the problems had just begun. She was later arraigned by the court, that is, the charge was read to her by the judge and she was informed of the maximum sentence the court could impose should she desire to plead guilty and of her right to speak with an attorney before entering a plea. Ultimately the matter went to trial, where a jury heard the testimony of the officer, the official who administered the breath test, and the chemist who was responsible for the accuracy of the Breathalizer machine. Janice testified in her own defense. The outcome? The jury found Janice guilty, she paid a fine of $400, was required to attend special night classes for those convicted of DUI, and the offense went on her driving record, which caused her insurance company to cancel her automobile insurance (the premium for her new assigned-risk insurance was three times the amount she'd previously paid). And Janice got off easy. She could have lost her license, received a jail term, or suffered the agony and guilt of knowing she'd injured or killed another person simply because she'd "had a few too many."

7
Searches

Let's suppose that tonight when you arrive home from work you prepare dinner and sit down to relax and enjoy the latest escapades of J. R. Ewing. Your new roommate will be out of town for a whole week, and you are finally able to spend a quiet evening at home. Totally absorbed with what is taking place on television, you hardly notice the slight commotion outside your door, but before you know it three police officers have barged in and are ransacking your apartment in search of contraband. They tell you only that they have reason to believe your roommate is involved in buying and selling cocaine. How do you respond? Are you required by law to answer their questions? Do they have a right to search your apartment without your consent? Must they have a search warrant?

Although the situation described above is not a common occurrence, it *does* happen—and sometimes to innocent persons. The point to be made here is that although you most likely will not find yourself in this situation, what if you should be stopped for a traffic violation (a more common occurrence) and the officer asks to inspect your trunk or your glove compartment? What if you are arrested and the police attempt to search you and your car? What are your rights regarding searches by the police and under what circumstances do the officers in fact have the right to search?

Searches generally can be conducted only under the following circumstances: 1) as part of a lawful arrest, 2) the police officer has a valid search warrant, 3) he has received your consent to search, or 4) the officer has reason to believe that his life or safety is in jeopardy. The reason for these limitations is that the Fourth Amendment of the Constitution guarantees you certain rights and prohibits unreasonable intrusion into your private life:

> The right of the people to be secure in their persons, houses, papers, and effects, against unreasonable searches and seizures, shall not be violated, and no warrants shall issue, but upon probable cause, supported by Oath or Affirmation, and particularly describing the place to be searched, and the persons or things to be seized.

Should you feel that a search has taken place without sufficient cause or that correct procedure was not followed, you have the same courses of action open to you as you would as a victim of excessive force or false arrest (see page 60).

WITH OR WITHOUT A WARRANT

A search can be conducted with or without a warrant. If a search warrant is issued, it is to be used for a specific, limited purpose, for example to recover stolen or embezzled property, property used in the committing of a felony, or evidence that suggests that a felony has been committed. A search warrant is "an order in writing ... signed by a magistrate, directed to a peace officer, commanding him to search for personal property, and bring it before the magistrate."[1] Before the judge will issue a warrant, the officer must present the information that leads him to believe a search should be conducted as well as the source of that information, and describe what the search is expected to uncover.

Most searches are made without a warrant and occur at the time of an arrest. For example, in a recent California case, one which broadened the police's authority to search an automobile, the California Supreme Court upheld an officer's search of a closed glove compartment. The episode began as a routine speeding violation, but before the police were able to stop the car they were notified that the vehicle matched the description of the getaway car in a robbery that had occurred minutes before. When the officers approached the car, they observed that the occupants fit the description of those involved in the robbery and placed them under arrest. On the dash and the front seat, within plain view, were items similar to the ones reported to have been stolen. Based on the initial observation, the officers then proceeded beyond what was within plain view and began searching the car. Upon opening the glove compartment, one officer found a closed shaving kit containing what appeared to be, from the outline, a pistol. He opened the kit and discovered that it was indeed a pistol—a loaded one. The court, which had previously ruled that searches of closed glove compartments were illegal without the owner's permission, ruled that this search was proper due to the exigent circumstances (the robbery). It stated further that an immediate, warrantless search of a vehicle is justified when an officer has information which causes him to conclude that those whom he has stopped are involved in a serious crime and that the vehicle contains contraband. This is not to say that the law allows the police unrestrained authority to search every vehicle. They are authorized only to search for that which they believe is concealed. Knowledge that a television set has recently been stolen would not justify a search of a glove compartment.[2]

OBSERVATION

Where most individuals get into trouble is by not understanding what is considered proper police observation and what is considered unreasonable government intrusion. The court will allow evidence that has been acquired by way of police observation as long as the area that was observed is one in which the owner has no reasonable expectation to privacy, the items are in plain view, or the owner has consented to a police search. Let's look at these one at a time.

REASONABLE EXPECTATION TO PRIVACY. Although citizens have no reasonable expectation to privacy regarding items that are in plain view, they are protected against police observations of those items that are not exposed to the public. Such observations are considered a form of government intrusion. For example, consider the use of binoculars by the police to view a particular item within a home. The question is not did the police use a magnifying device to observe an item in the home from two blocks away, but could an individual standing on the sidewalk in front of the house have seen the same item with the naked eye.[3] If the item was observable from the sidewalk, the owner could not argue that she had a reasonable expectation to privacy; the observation is not considered a search and therefore the item could be used as evidence in court.

PLAIN VIEW. If items are observed in an area where the police have a right to be, no search has taken place. For instance, if Chris is stopped for a vehicle violation and the traffic officer observes in the passenger seat a clear baggie containing a substance that resembles marijuana, she may be arrested for possession of a controlled substance since the item was in plain view. Another example of this occurs when an officer makes a traffic stop for driving under the influence of alcohol and observes empty beer or liquor containers in the car. Even if it is dark and he must use his flashlight to observe them on the passenger floor, the observation is considered proper and may be used as evidence in a trial.

CONSENT TO SEARCH. You can refuse to give your consent to a search in any situation, preferably with a witness present. Should the police proceed anyway and the matter end up in court, they will have to justify searching your property without your approval. If you give the police permission to search either yourself or your property and they discover contraband, relying on the consent to justify the lawfulness of the search, the burden is on them to show by clear and positive evidence that the consent was freely, voluntarily, and knowledgeably given.[4] As with other constitutionally protected rights, an individual may consent to waive this right and unless there is evidence that the police used coercion or threats, the search is valid. Should you give the police the right to search a specific item, they are limited by the extent of your consent. For example, when Lisa was stopped for a faulty taillight the officer asked if she would like him to check the bulb. By consenting to the officer's request, Lisa authorized him to open the trunk, and if in the trunk there were any items of contraband which the officer could readily observe, they would be allowed as evidence in court. However, as long as the officer had no reason to believe that she was involved in illegal activity, he would not have the right to open and search a closed suitcase lying in the trunk.

SEARCHES OF YOUR HOME

The examples above apply equally to one's residence. In the absence of exigent circumstances, that is a situation requiring immediate action by an officer to prevent the loss of life or damage to property, the police may not enter your residence without a search warrant.[5] Should you consent to their entry into a portion of your home, they may not wander into other areas and later claim that what they observed was in plain view; to do so would exceed the scope of your consent. For example, the police asked Laura's permission to walk through her home in order to investigate a report that her neighbor was growing marijuana plants, which were visible from Laura's back yard. Laura immediately showed them the direct route through her home to her back yard. Any contraband which the officers observed as they walked through the home or any they observed in the back yard would be admissible in court since Laura had consented to their entry. However, had the officers strayed into another room and searched a closet or drawer, any observation would be the result of an illegal search and therefore would not be admissible in court.

SEARCHES DURING AN ARREST

As a general rule, should an officer fear for his safety, he has the right to order you out of your car. He may also have the right, depending on the circumstances, to search you and your property during an arrest. For the person stopped for driving under the influence of alcohol or other traffic violations, there may be a cursory "frisk" or "pat down" search for weapons. Once arrested, the officer can proceed to search you fully to remove any weapons. In addition, he may also seize any evidence on your person such as drugs which you might attempt to conceal or destroy en route to the jail.[6] The United States Supreme Court, in the landmark case of Chimel v. California, stated that " ... it is reasonable for the arresting officer to search the person arrested in order to remove any weapons that the latter might seek to use in order to resist arrest or effect escape."[7] The Court went further in explaining when an officer may search an arrested individual should there be the possibility that evidence could be destroyed after she is in police custody: "It is entirely reasonable for the arresting officer to search for and seize any evidence on the arrestee's person in order to prevent its concealment or destruction."[8] The Court also determined that a police officer has the right to search that "area within his immediate control," defining that to mean the area from which the arrestee may gain possession of a weapon or evidence.[9] In other words, the police may be exceeding their authority if they search any room other than that in which the arrest occurred, but should they have information that leads them to believe the home contains contraband, they can, after they book the suspect at the jail, seek a search warrant from the local magistrate.[10] As in all judgment calls that an officer is required to make, he must be able to substantiate his actions should the matter end up in court.

BOOKING SEARCHES

Once an arrestee enters the jail and the admission procedure has begun, her personal belongings will be searched for the purpose of establishing an inventory. Since in most jails the prisoner receives a jail uniform, all items within pockets will be inventoried, but jailers are not authorized to open a closed container and examine its contents. In most cases, a female jailer will also conduct a full body search.

THE FAMILY

8
Divorce

It used to be that the majority of people stuck it out when the marital relationship became difficult, and the divorced woman was generally considered to be somewhat of an outcast, a shady lady. Today the scene has changed. Divorce is so common that a first marriage that survives up to the death of one of the spouses is considered unique. Increasing numbers of women for individual though categorical reasons are choosing to terminate their marital relationships. At some point in the relationship, the marriage ceased being enjoyable. Perhaps you simply decided that you wanted your independence or that you and your husband no longer had anything in common. Or maybe you had good reason to believe that your husband was involved with another woman. Regardless of the reasons, you began questioning the "state of the union" and decided to feel out the options.

Most women's initial reaction is panic. No matter how disastrous the marriage, the alternative looks even more hopeless. "Can I survive financially and emotionally without my husband?" "How will a divorce affect the children?" These questions are not easy to answer, but if you will take the time to prepare yourself for what lies ahead you will be able to deal with the legal issues and procedures as well as the emotional pain as an intelligent adult rather than as a helpless victim. It is *because* divorce is such an emotional issue that you need, more than ever, to be in control and capable of making sound decisions that will ensure your future well-being and financial security.

This chapter does not attempt to discuss every legal issue relating to divorce (also termed dissolution in some states), nor do we recommend that you use it as a step-by-step guide on how to obtain a divorce. Instead we have provided an overview of the divorce process, including legal, financial, and emotional factors, in order that you will have a better understanding of what to expect and will be better able to protect your interests and come out of the divorce in the best possible position. Whether you are the petitioner/plaintiff (the party seeking the divorce) or the respondent/defendant (the spouse being sued for divorce), the following information will point out your options, help you assess your current and future financial situation, and give you an idea of what you can expect to encounter during the legal process.

In preparing this book we reviewed the laws in as many states as possible in order to provide a broad overview. However, it would be impractical to cite each state's laws and unique exceptions. This information is intended to help you prepare for a divorce, not to provide you with laws to quote to the judge. Before you proceed with any legal action, it will be necessary to seek competent professional assistance, or at the very least review your state's divorce laws. (These will be found under the titles Marriage, Husband and Wife, Divorce, Custody, and Annulment.)

THE ALTERNATIVES

If you are considering setting aside your marriage, be sure to consider the options that may be available to you. Besides divorce, these include annulment and legal and informal separation.

Annulment

There is a big difference between a divorce and an annulment. When a divorce is granted, the court rules that the marriage is over, terminated; when an annulment is granted, the court rules that the marriage never existed. Should you be granted an annulment, you may legally state that you were never married. Although in recent years, with the advent in many states of no-fault divorce and simplified filing procedures, the courts are less willing to grant annulments, some women prefer to seek an annulment in order to avoid the stigma of divorce. Possibly they have heard that their neighbor Sally, the wife of Bob the Bigamist, was awarded an annulment because Bob "forgot" to divorce his first wife before marrying her, or that Rachel's marriage was annulled because she was only 15 at the time she married Ken.

Your right to petition the court for an annulment is set forth in your state's statutes. Annulment laws vary from state to state, and it is recommended that you contact an attorney to help you determine how to proceed. In order for an annulment to be granted, you must show that some circumstance at or before the time of the marriage ceremony invalidated the marriage, something which you were not aware of or were incapable of correcting. For example, Sally was not aware that Bob was still legally married to another woman, and Rachel, being only 15 at the time of her marriage, was legally incapable of consenting to marry. An annulment will be granted only when you can show that your marriage was either void or voidable.

Void Marriage. In a void marriage the imperfection is such that the marriage is not and never will be legal and therefore may be terminated at any time by either spouse. Sally's marriage was not legal since Bob could not legally enter into a marriage with her when he was still married to another woman; therefore, most states would consider this a void marriage.

A void marriage is invalid from the day of the ceremony. Irrespective of either spouse's desires, the court will treat a void marriage as never having existed. Most states consider incestuous marriages as well as bigamous marriages to be void from their inception. Incestuous marriages are those in which the spouses are closely related. This includes marriages between parents and their natural children, brothers and sisters, half-brothers and half-sisters, uncles and their nieces, and aunts and their nephews. Marriages between first cousins may also be considered void.

Voidable Marriage. A voidable marriage is one which the court will consider to be legal unless one of the parties within a certain time period seeks court approval to annul the marriage. Rachel's marriage was not valid since at the time of the ceremony she was under the age of consent. However, if she continues to live with Ken after having reached the legal age to marry, most states will assume that she has ratified the marriage. Her marriage was voidable only until she reached the age of consent. Should she decide to terminate the relationship after she reaches the age of consent, she will be required to proceed with a divorce.

Fraud. Annulments are often granted for marriages that were entered into through fraud. Fraud is defined as a false representation or concealment of a fact by one of the spouses which goes to the essence of the marital relationship. A woman seeking an annulment on these grounds must be able to prove 1) that the fraud was perpetrated, that is acted out, at or before the time of the marriage ceremony, 2) that she, the innocent party, was unaware of this misrepresentation or concealment, and 3) that upon discovering the fraud she no longer voluntarily lived with her husband. Should she be unable to prove these facts, it is unlikely that an annulment will be granted and she will be required to file for divorce if she desires to end the marriage. Besides bigamy, which was discussed earlier, the types of fraud which the courts have stated go to the essence of a marriage include:

—A spouse who claimed that he desired to have children, yet at the time of the statement was aware of his sterility. For example, should your husband fail to inform you that he had a vasectomy three years before the marriage and lead you to believe that he wants to have two children, you may have little difficulty having the marriage annulled if you act as soon as you become aware of the fraud. However, if you both are in your fifties and have been married for 20 years, the courts will view the situation differently.

—A husband who promises before the marriage to engage in normal sexual intercourse while having no intention of doing so. If after the marriage ceremony your husband carries you over the threshold, walks promptly to the bedroom, drops you on the bed, and then walks away and takes up residence in the den, you are a likely candidate for an annulment.

—A husband who refuses to reside with you after marriage. This is similar to the preceding situation except that instead of retreating to the den he goes back to Mother.

—Concealment at the time of marriage of your pregnancy by one other than your husband. It is not grounds for an annulment, however, if you falsely led your husband to believe that you were pregnant by him. The courts have ruled that this act, though fraudulent, does not go to the essence of the marriage.

Other misrepresentations that have been ruled do *not* generally go to the essence of the marriage include:

—Misrepresentations of wealth or promises to furnish you with items which would elevate your social status. For example, your husband promised you a yacht and a limo and you end up with a rowboat and a station wagon.

—Misrepresentations of proper moral character or false statements regarding his chastity. Your husband, who acted like a saint before the marriage, turns out to be a member of the American Nazi Party or you discover that he previously had girlfriends at every truck stop.

Effect of an Annulment. Unless the couple was married for more than a short time or had children during the marriage, an annulment will usually return the parties to the same legal and financial status they enjoyed before the marriage ceremony. However, if it appears that the petitioning spouse believed in good faith that the marriage was valid, the court will generally allow her the same rights as a woman who is seeking a divorce. This means that if you, as the person seeking the annulment, had no reason to believe that your husband was married to another at the time of your marriage, you may be eligible for spousal support and a share of the property (as well as child support) according to your state's laws. A religious annulment has no legal effect, and the marriage will be considered legally valid unless a civil annulment or divorce has also taken place.

Separation Agreements

After 16 years of marriage, Judy realized that the relationship she had once enjoyed with her husband was falling apart. The more effort she put into maintaining the marriage, the worse things got, and before long neither of them was able to voice a civil word. Because of her religious beliefs, divorce was not an acceptable solution. After a year of wrestling with the problem, Judy sought the advice of a local attorney specializing in family law. After discussing her dilemma with the attorney—she wanted to live apart from her husband but for moral reasons would not file for divorce—Judy decided that a legal separation would be the best solution. The court ruled that the assets of the community be divided according to the state property laws, that joint custody of the children be established, and that Judy receive alimony for one year in the amount of $600 a month to assist her as she made the transition from homemaker to wage earner.

There are two common types of separation, legal separation, in which the court decides the terms of the separation, and informal separation, in which the spouses simply agree to live apart.

Legal Separation. A legal separation is designed not to terminate the marriage but to allow the spouses to live separately and to settle their financial responsibilities to each other and to their minor children. It is not for the couple who have decided to live apart only temporarily, but for those who know that they will never reconcile yet choose, for moral, religious, or other reasons, not to seek a divorce. The spouse seeking a legal separation must conform to the local laws, which usually require that a Petition for Legal Separation be filed stating the grounds for the separation, and that a property declaration be submitted. In some states, the spouse may also be required to file a Property Settlement Agreement with the court. Should the husband and wife fail to reach an agreement, the court will divide the property according to state laws and the judge's discretion. As you can see, a legal separation is closely related to a divorce.

Because of its complexity, it is recommended that you confer with an attorney, especially when property division, spousal support, and child custody must be decided.

Some women file for legal separation when they have no grounds for divorce, while others view the separation as the first step towards an eventual divorce. Occasionally a woman who desires to dissolve her marriage has not resided within the state long enough to satisfy the residency requirements for divorce so she files for a legal separation. For example, your state may require that you reside within its boundaries for six months before you may petition the court to dissolve your marriage but may allow you to file immediately for a legal separation. Rebecca left her husband of eight years, taking their only child with her to California, where they would reside temporarily with her parents. Being unable to support herself, she immediately filed for a legal separation and further petitioned the court for an order granting her temporary spousal support and child support. The court, after confirming that her husband had been served with the proper papers and had been notified of the date of the hearing, heard her request. Her husband not only failed to appear in court but to submit a response to her request; she was granted temporary support of $400 a month and child support of $200 a month. After residing within the state for the six-month statutory period, Rebecca was then eligible to petition the court for a divorce.

In deciding whether a legal separation is the best solution to your predicament, the following should be considered:

1) A legal separation does not affect your status as a married person, even though you are living apart.

2) Usually, the same court action is required in a legal separation as in a divorce, including the division of community assets and the establishment of spousal support and child support and custody.

3) In petitioning the court for a legal separation, you may be required to state the grounds for the separation.

4) After you are legally separated, you and your spouse must file your federal income tax returns as single taxpayers.

5) In most states, any income received by either spouse after they have begun living separate and apart will remain the property of that spouse. Unless the two of you have signed an agreement specifying otherwise, you will not be responsible for your husband's debts, nor he for your debts.

6) It will be necessary for you to review your estate planning, your will, and your insurance policies once you are legally separated. You may

not want to leave your estate to your husband should you die before him. (Should you fail to rewrite your will and die after your husband, leaving no children or relatives on your side, that sister-in-law you always despised may receive the entire estate.)

7) You will be unable to remarry since the marriage is still valid. This may cause you problems later should you meet Mr. Right, as you will be required to file for divorce and wait the statutory time before you can remarry.

Informal Separation. A couple may decide to separate yet wish to avoid both the expense and the hassle of obtaining court approval. Whereas a legal separation settles the questions of property rights, spousal support, and child support and custody, an informal separation postpones these decisions, at least in the legal sense. We are dealing here with the informal separation that is planned to last indefinitely, not the sudden separation that occurs after a fight when you spend a few days at the home of a friend. The informal separation may be well thought out in advance or be based on nothing more than a note stating: "I've had it—am quitting my job and moving to Bakersfield."

The informal separation raises the same questions as a legal separation or divorce. How is the property to be divided? How will you support yourself if you've never worked outside the home? Who will be financially responsible for the children and with which parent will they live? Can the house continue to be held jointly? Will you be legally responsible for your husband's bills, or he for yours? Although you may feel secure knowing that you and your spouse parted amicably and agreed upon your financial obligations, be aware of the fact that many such oral agreements, made with good intentions at the time, cause serious problems later on. Many states have adopted the position that spouses who live together are responsible for supporting each other in the manner in which they're accustomed, subject to the earning potential of the spouses, but that once they live apart the duty is eliminated. If the courts do not recognize your husband's financial responsibilities to you, how can you enforce the agreement if he later refuses to carry through with his promises?

The court's power is limited in enforcing informal separation agreements. For example, Sue and Jeff agreed that during the separation she would care for the children and reside in the family home while he would contribute $200 a month for the care of the children plus $420 a month for a year to assist Sue while she completed her master's degree. Although the child support checks arrived on time the first of every month, Sue's checks stopped after two months. When Jeff explained to her that he could not afford to continue her payments, Sue could only respond with, "But you promised!" She was shocked to learn, after speaking to an attorney, that she could not petition the family court to enforce the agreement, since that option is available only to women who have received a legal separation, an annulment, or a divorce. Sue was informed that her only recourse was to file a civil complaint, that is, to sue Jeff for breach of contract. The problem was, how could she prove that he had promised to assist her financially? Since their agreement was oral, it would be her word against his.

As you can see from the preceding illustration, informal separations are not as informal as they sound. If you do decide to go this route, the very least you should do is get everything in writing. In those states that do not grant legal separations, the courts usually recognize a written separation agreement if it is properly drawn up and covers all of the financial issues that need to be resolved. It will be to your advantage to consult with an attorney before deciding what you are willing to settle for, and once you and your husband have come to an agreement have your attorney prepare the contract.

THE DIVORCE PROCESS

As contrasted to an annulment, divorce is the dissolution of a valid marriage, concerning itself with acts occurring after the ceremony which were not of sufficient grounds to justify an annulment. As compared to a legal separation, a divorce is a final judgment, enabling the parties to remarry.

Pre-Divorce Considerations

After considering your options and deciding that you do in fact want a divorce (or if your husband has informed you that he has reached this decision), you may feel overwhelmed, unsure of how to proceed and whom to contact for assistance. If you have already moved your husband's personal belongings out into the street and have called the Salvation Army to come and pick up your old wedding presents, perhaps you are moving too quickly. Don't do anything in haste. Now is the time to consider your situation carefully, to review the events that have brought you to this point, and to get an idea of the whole picture. Unless there is a compelling reason to act immediately (your husband has become violent or threatens to harm you or has refused to support you financially), take the time to consider whether you are absolutely sure that divorce is the only solution. If there is any chance that in a day or two you may change your mind or decide to seek counseling in an attempt to make the relationship work, put off taking any action. Many an attorney has interviewed a prospective divorce client who swore that she would never return to her spouse and wanted the divorce papers prepared that very day so that she could get out of the marriage as soon as possible only to inform the attorney several weeks later (after the petition has been filed and the papers served) that she and her husband are going to give it another try.

Unless the relationship has deteriorated to the point where there is no hope of rational communication, you may want to attempt to talk your husband into visiting a marriage counselor. The courts in some states take the position that the spouses should consider counseling before filing for divorce in an attempt to reconcile or if that is impossible at least to make the divorce a little more amicable.

Fault vs. No-Fault

Traditionally, most states required that one spouse, in seeking a divorce, allege and prove that the other spouse was at fault, that he or she somehow violated the marriage contract and that the violation destroyed the marriage. Although the majority of states have changed over to no-fault divorce, some still require a spouse to prove fault (see the chart beginning on page 82). Grounds for fault vary from state to state but generally include any number of the following:

1) Adultery. You have information that causes you to believe that your husband has voluntarily had sexual intercourse with someone other than yourself during your marriage.

2) Bigamy. Your husband married someone else while your marriage still legally existed.

3) Physical and/or Mental Cruelty. Repeated physically violent behavior by your husband which would make it unsafe for you to continue living with him, or conduct by your husband which seriously endangers your mental well-being (such as continued threats of physical violence).

4) Desertion. Your husband voluntarily abandoned you without justification for a certain length of time (determined by state law, generally a minimum of one or two years).

5) Insanity/Mental Illness. In most states, your husband must have been declared legally insane or be confined to a mental institution for a certain period of time.

6) Non-Support Which Imposes Hardship or Privation. You must be able to prove that your husband is financially able to support you but is unwilling to do so (he owns three rental properties with all the creature comforts but refuses to either update or move from the family home that has no indoor plumbing).

State Divorce Laws*

	Residence Requirement	Waiting Period before Remarriage	No-Fault Divorce: Living Separate	Incompatibility	Irretrievable Breakdown	Irretrievable Breakdown and Traditional Grounds	Judicial Separation and Maintenance
Alabama	6 months	60 days		x		x	2 years
Alaska	none	none		x		x	
Arizona	90 days	none			x		
Arkansas	60 days	none	3 years				
California	6 months	none			x		
Colorado	90 days	none			x		
Connecticut	1 year	none	1½ years	x		x	no set period
Delaware	6 months	none		x			x
Florida	6 months	none			x		
Georgia	6 months	judge determines	2 years			x	
Hawaii	6 months	none	2 years		x		2 years
Idaho	6 weeks	none	5 years			x	
Illinois	90 days	none				x	
Indiana	6 months	after proof of child support				x	
Iowa	1 year	none			x		
Kansas	60 days	none		x			
Kentucky	180 days	none			x		
Louisiana	none	none	1 year				1 year
Maine	6 months	none				x	
Maryland	1-2 years	none	1-2 years				
Massachusetts	1 year	none				x	x
Michigan	180 days	none			x		
Minnesota	180 days	none			x		½ year
Mississippi	6 months	1 year if adultery				x	
Missouri	90 days	none			x		
Montana	90 days	none			x		
Nebraska	1 year	none			x		
Nevada	6 weeks	none	1 year	x			
New Hampshire	1 year	none	2 years			x	
New Jersey	1 year	none	1½ years				
New Mexico	6 months	none		x			
New York	1 year	none					1 year
North Carolina	6 months	none					1 year
North Dakota	1 year	court decides				x	4 years
Ohio	6 months	none	2 years			x	x
Oklahoma	6 months	6 months		x			
Oregon	6 months	court decides			x		
Pennsylvania	6 months	none	1 year			x	
Rhode Island	1 year	none	3 years			x	
South Carolina	1 year	none	1 year				
South Dakota	60 days	none					
Tennessee	6 months	none				x	2 years
Texas	6 months	30 days	3 years			x	
Utah	3 months	appeal period					3 years
Vermont	½-2 years	none	½ year				
Virginia	6 months	appeal period					1 year
Washington	none	appeal period			x		
West Virginia	1 year	none	1 year			x	
Wisconsin	6 months	6 months			x		1 year
Wyoming	60 days	none			x		
District of Columbia	6 months	none	1 year	x			½ year

*As of January 1984. A few of the grounds listed, such as insanity/mental illness, may be limited to a certain time period (e.g., in some states the condition must have existed or the spouse to have been institutionalized for a certain number of years). Grounds that are unique to a particular state do not appear on the chart (such as "abuse and neglect of a

State Divorce Laws*

Traditional Grounds

	Adultery	Mental/ Physical Cruelty	Desertion/ Abandon-ment	Impotency	Alcoholism/ Drug Addiction	Insanity/ Mental Illness	Bigamy	Non-Support	Pregnancy at Marriage	Felony Conviction/ Imprison-ment
Alabama	x	x	1 year	x	x	x			x	x
Alaska	x	x	1 year		x	x		x		x
Arizona										
Arkansas	x		1 year	x	x	x	x	x		x
California						x				
Colorado										
Connecticut	x	x	1 year		x	x				x
Delaware										
Florida						x				
Georgia	x	x	1 year	x	x	x			x	x
Hawaii										
Idaho	x	x	x		x	x				x
Illinois	x	x	1 year	x	x		x			x
Indiana				x		x				x
Iowa										
Kansas	x	x	1 year			x				x
Kentucky										
Louisiana	x									x
Maine	x	x	3 years	x	x	x		x		
Maryland	x		1 year	x		x				x
Massachusetts	x	x	1 year	x	x			x		
Michigan										
Minnesota										
Mississippi	x	x		x	x	x	x		x	x
Missouri										
Montana										
Nebraska										
Nevada						x				
New Hampshire	x	x	2 years	x	x					x
New Jersey	x	3 months	1 year		x	x				x
New Mexico	x	x	x							
New York	x	x	1 year							x
North Carolina	x		x	x		x			x	
North Dakota	x	x	1 year		x	x				x
Ohio	x	x	1 year	x	x		x			x
Oklahoma	x	x	1 year	x	x	x			x	x
Oregon										
Pennsylvania	x	x	1 year			x	x			x
Rhode Island	x	x	5 years	x	x			x		
South Carolina	x	x	1 year		x					
South Dakota	x	x	x		x	x				x
Tennessee	x		1 year	x	x		x		x	x
Texas		x	1 year			x				x
Utah	x	x	1 year	x	x	x		x		x
Vermont	x		7 years			x		x		x
Virginia	x	x	1 year							x
Washington						x	x			
West Virginia	x	x	6 months		x	x				x
Wisconsin										
Wyoming						x				
District of Columbia										

child" in West Virginia). Pennsylvania is the only state that has the condition that an adulterous spouse may not marry the other party to adultery during the lifetime of the ex-spouse.

7) Alcoholism and/or Drug Addiction. Your husband has a habitual addiction to drugs or alcohol.

8) Impotency. Generally, your husband's impotency must be incurable and he must have been impotent at the time of the marriage ceremony.

9) Imprisonment or Felony Conviction. Your husband has been convicted of a serious crime and/or is confined to prison for a certain period of time (according to state law).

If you reside in a state that requires that fault be proven, research your state's laws and procedures before filing. It is one thing to be aware through rumors that your husband is having an affair with a co-worker and quite another to prove it. And remember, some grounds are easier to prove than others; the reason you want a divorce may be quite different from the grounds you are trying to establish.

Most states no longer require that one spouse prove specific acts of wrongdoing or fault before granting a divorce. With the adoption of no-fault proceedings, the courts are not interested in determining which spouse is at fault, but whether in fact the marriage has disintegrated to the point where there is no hope of its ever being workable. The grounds for divorce in no-fault states may be termed irreconcilable differences, incompatibility, or irretrievable breakdown of the marriage—all meaning the same thing. In a state that adheres to this principle, you may need merely to state that there were "irreconcilable differences which led to the irremediable breakdown of the marriage and that there is no chance for a reconciliation," or something similar.

Emotional Factors

Even in the most "friendly" divorces, most spouses experience some pain, some anger, and some regrets. During what may be the most difficult transition of your life, you will need not only to familiarize yourself with your state's laws and procedures but to deal with all the strong emotions you will be experiencing throughout the divorce process. Many hasty and disastrous decisions have been made by divorcing women who were unable to gain control over their emotions.

The majority of women go through three distinct emotional stages during this time, and each one can adversely affect their judgment and their ability to be objective. As you experience each stage, your perception will change along with your ability to deal with the problems in a logical manner. Neither the time at which you experience these emotional states nor their order of appearance is set, but you will undoubtedly experience each of them at least once during the divorce. Hopefully, if you know what to expect, you will be prepared to face them head on, knowing that eventually they will pass—and that other women have gone through them and survived.

The first phase generally occurs in the earlier stages of the divorce. Rather than taking a good look at the events that led to the disintegration of the relationship, you start remembering the good times you once shared and the qualities that first attracted you to your husband (this is easy to do when you're feeling lonely and scared, especially when you're no longer dealing with him on a daily basis). So you go back over your own actions, blaming yourself for the breakup—"If only I had done this or not done that." You may find some temporary satisfaction in accepting responsibility and persecuting yourself for the failure of the relationship, but if these feelings continue, you'll need to use all your will power to snap yourself back into reality.

In the second phase, you feel completely drained, having spent hours and hours talking with your attorney, trying to reach some kind of settlement, and debating with yourself whether or not you're doing the right thing. You're tired of the whole thing and want the situation resolved immediately so that you can get on with your life. You've adopted a fatalistic attitude—"Whatever happens, happens; all I want is to get this over with as quickly as possible no matter what it costs monetarily or emotionally." It's easy to see that such an attitude can have disastrous consequences.

The third and last phase is one of vindication and hatred. Suddenly all of your energies are geared toward getting back at him for subjecting you to so much pain. "How can he be so cruel and selfish after all the years we spent together?" "How does he expect me to support myself when I have to take care of two children?" Life is unfair, and your rage is nearly uncontrollable. You may find your anger and frustration directed not only toward your husband but toward friends and relatives as well. It is during this phase that some women make the mistake of seeking revenge "at any cost."

It may be necessary to remind yourself constantly that all of these emotions and reactions are normal and that they will pass, but that you cannot afford to let them impede your ability to make wise decisions. The terms of the divorce will have long-range effects on your future—and if you want to have peace of mind and be financially secure, you'll have to control your emotions and be ready to defend your rights and interests.

Because of the emotional nature of divorce and the vulnerability of both spouses, it may be wise to arrange to have all communication and negotiation between you pass through the attorneys' offices. Such an arrangement may cause the divorce to proceed more smoothly and will lessen the chances of you and your spouse becoming entangled in bitter and destructive arguments.

Finances

How much do you know about your family's financial situation? Do you know how much money you would need a month to live on? Do you earn this much yourself or will you need at least temporary support from your husband? Do you know where the financial records are kept? Have all major bills been paid? What about the car? the mortgage? school loans? Do you understand your tax situation? These are just a few of the questions you should be able to answer *before* you begin divorce proceedings.

Most family law courts require that you submit a financial statement along with a prospective budget at the time you file for divorce. You will need to provide a list of all assets and liabilities as well as a monthly breakdown of projected income and expenses. Unfortunately, many women are not that knowledgeable of their family's financial situation. You may have always turned over your earnings to your husband, who then paid the bills and balanced the checkbook. When income tax time rolled around, he met with the accountant and asked you to sign on the X at the bottom of the tax form. Your involvement in family finances should have begun on the first day of your marriage. If it didn't, it's time to do your homework.

Jane found out about her family's financial status the hard way. After 11 years of marriage to a successful salesman, she decided to file for divorce. At her attorney's insistence she reviewed the joint checking account for the previous year so she could see where the money had gone. She also reviewed the previous year's joint tax return in order to determine the family's assets and liabilities. When she had concluded her research, she felt that she had a good understanding of the situation. Only after her attorney decided to gather all previous tax forms, forms which she had signed without reviewing, was it uncovered that during the marriage her husband had purchased out-of-state property with community funds, which he later sold for a sizable profit. The unique part of the deal was that the profit was deposited not in a joint savings account but in an out-of-town investment company in his name only. Had Jane's attorney not discovered this transaction, her share of the final settlement would have been significantly decreased.

This is not to say that in every divorce one of the spouses will attempt to hide assets from the other. However, if you were never involved in managing the family money, it is imperative that you do some investigating and familiarize yourself with the facts. Better safe than sorry.

This process may be extremely distasteful to you, especially if you've never been involved in the day-to-day management of the family funds and have no desire to start now. Nevertheless, once you're divorced you will be responsible for handling your own finances anyway, so you might as well learn now. More importantly, though, if you dig in and learn all you can about your financial situation at this point, it is much more likely that you will receive a fair settlement and that the rest of the process will go smoothly. You'll be prepared and organized when you meet with your attorney, and your knowledge will cause you to have more confidence when you're involved in later negotiations.

How do you begin? First of all, familiarize yourself with the divorce laws and procedures in your state regarding filing and residency requirements, division of property, support and custody of children, and spousal support (alimony). Next you'll need to research your financial situation to determine how much it costs to support the family. Using all of your cancelled checks for the past year, figure out your monthly expenses—house payments, mortgages, or rent, utilities, groceries, car payments, medical expenses, credit card payments, etc.—as well as annual, biannual, or quarterly expenses—loan payments, taxes, insurance, tuition, etc. Then list all the assets, everything that you and your husband own that has a cash value—houses, rental properties, businesses, cars, checking and savings accounts, stocks and bonds, life insurance policies with cash value, pension or profit-sharing plans, etc. (You'll need to list purchase prices and actual market values for such items as real property and vehicles). Inheritances and gifts should be listed as well, although whether they will be considered community property will depend on your state's laws. Make a separate list for liabilities, those amounts you still owe—such as mortgages, loans, charge account balances, unpaid taxes, etc. Then you'll need to make a list of all personal property (and their values), such as furniture, appliances, china, stereos, and televisions, as well as any assets or debts that you or your husband had before your marriage. Finally, make copies of your federal and state tax returns for the past three years. If these are unavailable, the Internal Revenue Service will send you copies for a small fee.

Obviously, this is a tedious process. Because of its importance, however, allow yourself three or more weeks to compile and organize the information so that you are familiar with every aspect. Although you will need to do most of the work yourself, you may want to contact an accountant or financial advisor if you run into problems. The information you've compiled must be accurate, as the financial statement and budget you submit to the court will be based on these figures and reference will be made to them during negotiation of the property settlement.

One more step before you proceed. Using the financial statement you've compiled, prepare a detailed personal budget, listing all your projected expenses on a month-by-month basis. This budget should present a realistic picture of the minimum amount of money you will need to live on. You'll have to face the reality that few divorced spouses are able to sustain their previous standard of living. While you'll be required to weed out a lot of the luxuries you've become accustomed to (unless you or your husband's income is substantial), don't sell yourself short. You'll want to include the cost of reeducating yourself if you've been out of the work force for a number of years, and perhaps the cost of day care or babysitters. In most cases, the court will order the husband to make at least temporary support payments to his wife. Remember when preparing your budget that although the court will want to ensure that your monthly support check covers your basic expenses, it recognizes that your husband may lose his incentive to work if most of his income goes toward your support.

Attorneys

You may feel you don't need an attorney, and you may be right, but only under the following circumstances—you have been married only a few years, you have no children, your husband will not contest the divorce, you don't own a house or have other substantial assets or debts, you are in total agreement as to how the property and personal belongings are to be divided, and both you and your husband are self-supporting. Some states have adopted simplified divorce proceedings for those who have no minor children and no real property interest, and then there are numerous books and materials available for the individual who wants to handle her own divorce.

While these methods will generally produce the desired result, a divorce, you should still give serious thought to hiring an attorney, even if your marriage meets all the above requirements. No book or forms can anticipate all the situations that may arise throughout the divorce process. An attorney can offer you professional advice regarding your particular situation, and since she has handled previous divorce cases she knows what the problem areas are and can recommend how they should be handled. In addition, you may decide to seek an injunction against your husband (a court order to freeze money or property so that he cannot dispose of your share) or to arrange for depositions (more on this later). If you decide on a "do it yourself" divorce, you may still want to consult with an attorney before proceeding.

Lynn's situation illustrates what can happen in even the most amicable of partings. When she and her husband agreed to divorce after four years of marriage they felt confident that they could handle the matter themselves without assistance from attorneys. They sat down one afternoon and calmly discussed how the property should be divided. Lynn would take the station wagon and he would take the 280Z. She would get the home and give him a second trust deed. Everything seemed to be going so smoothly. However, soon after Lynn filed for divorce, things began to change. They began to fight over small items that had been overlooked in the initial division, such as the wok and the photograph albums. Before long they found it difficult even to be civil to each other and ended up hiring attorneys to represent them. What had begun as a friendly parting of the ways ended up as a 14-month legal battle complete with investigators and appraisers.

Chapter 2 provides general information on how to interview and select an attorney, what you should expect from the attorney-client relationship, the types of fee arrangements available, and when to consider changing attorneys. Because divorce is such an emotional issue and the final settlement will have such far-reaching consequences, it is crucial that you hire an attorney who will represent your best interests and who is experienced in divorce law. If you are having difficulty finding an attorney you feel comfortable with, you may want to visit a few sessions of divorce court in order to observe several attorneys in action. Are they well prepared and professional? How do the judge, the opposing attorneys, and their clients respond to them? You may have found yourself an attorney and at the same time have gained some insight into divorce proceedings.

A word of caution. Do not allow yourself to be represented by your husband's attorney. Some couples rationalize that since they both agree to the divorce why not save some money and be represented by the same lawyer? You and your spouse may not have any conflicting views or interests at the time you file for divorce, but it's unlikely that you'll get through the entire process without conflicts. An attorney cannot possibly work toward the best interests of both the husband and wife and preserve each spouse's confidence; consequently, most attorneys refuse to represent both parties.

Once you have retained an attorney, you will want to supply her with as much information about the marriage as possible. Present her with the financial statement and budget you prepared earlier as well as copies of your tax returns. You will be very relieved (and so will your attorney) that you completed your financial investigation beforehand and that, unlike many other women who immediately run to an attorney completely unprepared and with Kleenex in hand, you've gotten your emotions under control and are ready to proceed. After your attorney has reviewed your financial statement and budget, she will ask you further questions about your financial situation, your marriage, your education, and your employment history. When were you married? Did you work before the marriage? Are you presently employed? Did you own any property at the time of your marriage? Did you support your husband at any time during the marriage? Was money banked together or separately? How many children do you have? Do either you or your husband have children from a previous marriage? What are your children's ages and health, and what future education was planned for them? Additional questions will relate to your husband—his employment history, present employer, his attitude regarding the divorce, and any history of violence or hostility.

At this time you will begin a series of discussions on how you would like to see the major issues resolved—who should remain in the family home or whether it should be sold, who should have custody of the children, how the property should be divided, how much spousal support you'll need, and whether or not your husband should pay for your attorney's fees (this will depend on the circumstances of the divorce). Of course if you and your husband signed a prenuptial agreement, these matters may already have been decided, and you can move on to the next step as long as you are both willing to honor the agreement. Agreements prepared before marriage are considered contracts in most states. Courts will generally uphold such contracts, or at least give them serious consideration, if they are in writing and signed by both spouses and do not impose undue hardship on either party.

After several meetings with your attorney, you will begin putting together what you feel to be a reasonable property settlement, and as further information is revealed or discovered, you may want to revise your financial statement and budget accordingly. Your goal here, of course, is to come to an agreement with your husband and his attorney so that the matter will not end up in a lengthy and expensive court battle.

Division of Property

In almost all divorces, the battle lines seem to be drawn over who owns what. Will he be able to prove that the business is entirely his? Will she be able to prove that she has a right to the home and the vacation retreat? The biggest property interest is normally real estate. This may include your home, the empty lot you purchased in the mountains, or the apartment building across town. Personal property is everything else—your furniture, your car, your clothing, etc. Though the following discussion deals primarily with real estate, the division of personal property is generally subject to the same criteria.

Historically, under the old "common law" system that the English forefathers brought over with them, at the moment the marriage vows were recited the ownership of the wife's real property was transferred to her husband. Upon his death, a partial interest would be returned to her (usually one-third to one-half), and the remainder would be passed on to either the children of the marriage or the husband's heirs. Fortunately we've come a long way since then. In the middle of the nineteenth century, many states enacted the Married Women's Property Acts, which gave women the right to retain property owned before marriage, although in some cases the husband retained the right to manage it. These laws also specified that women be allowed to retain their own earnings and any income that resulted from ownership of their separate property. Three states have continued to follow the pure common law concepts as revised by the Married Women's Property Acts (Mississippi, South Carolina, and West Virginia). In these states, whichever spouse paid for and holds legal title to the property owns it. Property acquired during a marriage can be considered totally the separate property of one of the spouses and remains such after the marriage or it can be held as the property of both spouses. For example, if a husband and wife purchased a home in West Virginia but the title was in the husband's name only, it would be considered his separate property and the wife would be denied an interest in it should they later seek a divorce. However, if the title to the home was in both their names, the court would conclude that it was owned jointly and would probably order that the equity in the home be divided equally. The problem with this system, as far as women are concerned, is that if the wife does not work outside the home and all property is in the husband's name, the court will usually consider him the owner of all the property.

The second property ownership system was patterned after the Spanish property laws. The states that follow community property laws are primarily in the west (California, Arizona, Nevada, Texas, Washington, Idaho, New Mexico, and Louisiana, as well as Puerto Rico). Community property states divide the property that was acquired during the marriage on a 50-50 basis, the only exceptions being property that was owned separately before marriage, property acquired individually by gift or inheritance, or that acquired after separation. Even though only one spouse's name appears on a title or deed for property acquired during marriage, it is considered community property. Though the states may interpret their community property laws somewhat differently, a basic premise of community property law is that the court honors the *labors* of each spouse rather than their income. In other words, even if the wife has never worked outside the home she is entitled to one-half of the property since the law considers her contribution to be as valuable as the husband's income.

Property can be owned by only one of the spouses, of course, and the courts will not consider it community property as long as the property is not combined with community property. For example, if a woman inherits $25,000 from her grandmother, this money would be considered her separate property. But if she deposits the money in a joint savings account, it becomes community property unless she can prove otherwise.

The last group of states, all those we have not already mentioned, can be defined as "equitable distribution" jurisdictions. The laws in these states are based on concepts from both the common law and the community property systems of property division. While they allow property acquired during a marriage to be considered separate property of one of the spouses, they give the court broad discretion to divide property accumulated during a marriage in what it considers to be a fair manner. (In some states, the court can also determine how property that was acquired before the marriage is to be divided.) The courts in these states base their decisions on a number of different factors. They may look at such things as the length of the marriage, the occupations of the spouses, their ages, the amount of their income, and their employability.

Besides personal and real property, certain nontangible assets should be considered in the property settlement. Particularly if you are near retirement age, be sure to ask your attorney if you have a right to a share of your husband's retirement, social security, and pension benefits according to your state's laws.

In 1981 the Supreme Court held in McCarty v. McCarty that federal law does not allow a state to divide military retirement pay as an asset of the marital community in a divorce, just as prior cases had not allowed the division of railroad retirement benefits. This caused a great uproar, resulting in a 1982 federal law called the Military Spouse Protection Act, which now allows the states to treat military retirement pay just as they treat other pensions. This means that in a community property state a military retirement benefit, like a pension benefit, can be divided in a divorce. But in an equitable distribution state it may or may not be considered divisible depending upon how the state handles other pension benefits. Some that do consider it divisible are Alaska, Delaware, and Indiana, and some that don't are Kentucky, Missouri, and South Dakota.[1]

Although the new social security law has made it easier for widows and divorcees to collect their share of social security benefits (see pages 186-87), such benefits are still generally considered separate property in a property settlement. They may be considered by the courts, however, when deciding on the amount of alimony to be paid.

Spousal interest in degrees and licenses is a running battle in the divorce courts. Some states have allowed repayment to the community equal to that spent on education (California, Minnesota), while others have not allowed it at all (Colorado, Michigan). If you have put your husband through school, check to see if your state considers licenses and degrees marital assets.

As you can see, there are no magical formulas that can be used to determine what your share of the property settlement will be. The best you can do is to be aware of the laws of your state, anticipate problems that may arise, and attempt to reach a compromise with your spouse before going to court.

Spousal Support (Alimony)

It used to be that alimony, or spousal support, was automatically awarded to the wife in a broken marriage and that the payments would continue for the rest of her life unless she remarried. Recently, this concept has changed so that the duration of alimony payments is limited by one or more factors. While some states have a set limit, such as three years, that alimony must be paid, most states require that it continue only for the amount of time it takes the spouse to establish herself in a job (allowing for training or necessary education).

The most recent and dramatic change occurred in the 1979 U.S. Supreme Court case of Orr v. Orr.[2] The Orrs' divorce decree stipulated that the husband was to pay alimony to his wife on a monthly basis. Two years after the decree, Mr. Orr got behind in his payments and his wife brought contempt proceedings for failure to pay. At the hearing, Mr. Orr argued that the Alabama statute was unconstitutional because it specified that only women were eligible for alimony. Ultimately the case was heard by the Supreme Court, which ruled that there is no reason "to use sex as a proxy for need," that males as well as females may need financial assistance. The Court went on to say that states, by establishing "legislative classifications which distribute benefits and burdens on the basis of gender, carry the risk of reinforcing stereotypes about the proper place for women and their need for special protection. No longer is the female destined solely for the home and the rearing of the family and only the male for the market place and the world of ideas." Still, because very few women have incomes considerably greater than their husbands, we will limit our discussion to the average situation.

Generally, the court requires the husband to pay at least temporary support to his wife. Hopefully you, your husband, and your attorneys can agree on temporary and if necessary more permanent support payments rather than allowing the court to decide for you. In most cases, the court will accept the agreement that has been negotiated outside of court. Although most courts follow guidelines that have been established in their state for determining the amount of alimony, they are usually allowed wide discretion. Their primary concerns are need and the ability to pay, although the amount awarded will also be affected by the length of the marriage, the ages and health of the spouses, their employability, and the degree to which each will be responsible for the care of the children.

The court must balance all of these considerations to ensure that both spouses are able to maintain as closely as possible their previous standard of living. In the majority of divorces, however, this is a difficult task. While there may have been sufficient income to support the spouses comfortably in one household, the division of income and assets often results in a much lower standard of living for both.

There are a few other points that should be taken into consideration when negotiating the amount of alimony to be paid:

1) In some states requiring that guilt of one of the spouses be proven before a divorce is granted, the courts will not allow the guilty spouse to be paid alimony.

2) If you receive alimony, you must report it as income on your annual tax return; your spouse will claim it as a deduction.

3) Alimony is occasionally paid in one lump sum; this can drastically change your tax liability, so you will want to consult with an accountant.

4) The amount of alimony payments can be altered by the court if there is a substantial change in the financial situation of either spouse (for example, if the husband's income increases dramatically or the previously financially dependent wife obtains a high-paying job).

5) Depending on the court and the state, divorced women living with another man may or may not have their alimony payments reduced or terminated. The decision is often based on whether or not the woman is "holding herself out" as the other man's wife.

Filing for Divorce

Since the great majority of divorce actions are instigated by women, we assume here that you are the one who is filing for divorce. However, should you be the respondent rather than the petitioner, the only information that does not apply to you is that regarding the filing of the petition (you will be required to file a response, an answer; otherwise the procedures are the same).

The divorce action must be filed with the proper court, which, depending on the state, will be the family law, superior, domestic relations, or probate court. If you do not have an attorney, contact the clerk of the local court, who will inform you which court in your area hears divorce cases. Because you have already familiarized yourself with the divorce laws and proceedings in your state, you are aware that you must meet certain residency requirements before filing (usually one year or less; consult the chart on page 82 for the requirements in your state).

Your attorney will assist you in preparing the necessary documents—the Petition for Divorce or Divorce Complaint and the final financial statement and budget—that will be filed with the county clerk (you will be required to pay a filing fee). On the petition, you will be required to provide some basic information about the marriage—the length of your marriage, birth dates of you, your husband, and the children, your occupations, and the grounds for divorce. These documents will be of immediate use to the court if you are requesting temporary spousal or child support. In addition, it is at this time that you inform the court of any temporary orders you want the court to consider: these may include alimony, possession of the home, child custody or support (see chapter 9), and, if necessary, orders that your husband not annoy or harass you. These are temporary orders which you are requesting the court to enact at the preliminary hearing, orders that will remain in effect until the divorce is final.

Finally, you will need to fill out a summons, a notice to your husband that you have filed, which will be delivered to him personally by a court marshal or independent process server. Once the summons has been served, your husband is allowed a certain period of time (usually 30 days) in which to respond. If he does not, he is considered to be in default, which means that he has agreed that the divorce should proceed according to your wishes and your state's laws. If he does not respond, you should fill out a Request for Entry of Default (the county clerk will send you the form), on which you will state which papers were served, how your husband was served, and that you have waited the required time. If the court finds that the summons was served in the proper manner and that your husband failed to respond, you will be allowed to continue with an uncontested divorce. In this case, the court will divide the property of the marriage and grant spousal support according to state law and the judge's discretion. If your husband is bringing the divorce action, be sure to prepare a response, even if you both agree at the time how the property should be divided and who should get custody of the children. The chances of your receiving a fair settlement will be greater if the court has both sets of financial declarations.

Preparing for Negotiation

If you and your spouse have already reached an agreement as to how the property should be divided, it will be filed with the court. If not, you will be required to appear at a preliminary hearing, where you and your spouse will be asked questions relating to your marriage and your finances. It is at this time that the court will decide on temporary spousal and child support. When you leave the court, you will be considered legally separated from your husband.

Before negotiation with your spouse and the attorneys begins, you may become involved in the legal process called discovery, in which you and your attorney attempt to uncover additional financial information that was not included in your preliminary investigation. This is not always necessary, but if yours is a complicated or bitter divorce, be prepared. Even though you may have no desire to dig any deeper, your spouse may decide to make your life a little more difficult by refusing to supply certain information that is crucial to the property settlement. This is where the use of interrogatories and depositions becomes necessary. Interrogatories are lists of questions sent by attorneys to the opposing party that must be answered in writing under oath. These are usually sent for the purpose of uncovering additional financial information, although in some cases the primary purpose is to harass the other spouse. A deposition is an oral questioning that takes place in one of the attorney's offices, and serves the same purposes as the interrogatory. Your attorney will explain what your rights are and what to expect should you find yourself confronted with either of these situations.

It is important to remember that the act of divorce is one of those legal battles in which both armies are paid out of the same treasury. The more involved the divorce becomes, the more it will cost. The more money you spend on specialists and investigations, the more money your husband will spend trying to do you one better, which will leave less in the community treasury to divide once a settlement is reached.

During this time you and your attorney will be refining your version of the settlement agreement. You will want to consider once again whether you wish to continue to live in the house or if it would be better to sell it and divide the proceeds (many women have fought to keep the house but find out later that they cannot afford the payments and upkeep). If the house has not been appraised, you should have it done now. You will also want to review the settlement from another point of view, remembering that any property you receive may change your tax situation (you may want to consult with an accountant at this point). Once you and your attorney are satisfied that your proposal is complete and that it represents a fair division, you are ready to start negotiations.

The Property Settlement

Unless yours is one of those rare divorces in which both spouses are in complete agreement as to how the property should be divided, be prepared to spend a great deal of time negotiating. In some cases, it takes a year or longer to reach a final agreement. The time will be well spent if you can agree on what you both consider a fair settlement and avoid the expense of going to court where a judge will determine your fate. On the other hand, the longer the negotiation period, the higher the attorneys' fees. There comes a point when the possible benefits do not justify the time and trouble, and you will want to be as fair and as flexible as possible to avoid haggling over replaceable items.

Either you or your husband will make an initial offer in writing and send it to the opposing attorney. Although you may luck out and find your husband's proposal to be quite generous, in most cases some of the terms will be unacceptable and you will have to discuss these with your attorney and offer a counterproposal. If all goes well, a final agreement will be reached without too many more meetings.

Going to Court

Once the negotiations have concluded, the matter will be set for a hearing before the judge of the family court. If the spouses have agreed on the division of property, child custody and support, and spousal support, the judge will review the agreement. If she finds it to be proper, she will then, depending on the state, either grant the divorce at the time (a final decree) or set a date in the future when the divorce will be final (an interlocutory decree). Those granted an interlocutory decree are not allowed to remarry during the waiting period.

If the parties are unable to agree, the matter will be set for trial, where both spouses will be allowed to present their side of the case. The trial usually consists of the testimony of the spouses as well as of any witnesses who may be able to substantiate their cases, such as accountants or investigators. When all the evidence has been presented, the judge will make her ruling as to how the items in dispute will be settled.

Once the court has made a ruling, the parties are obligated to comply, unless they appeal the ruling. However, it is not uncommon for one or the other to disregard their responsibilities as outlined by the court. Should your ex-husband fail to honor any part of the settlement—the payment of spousal or child support, the signing over of a title, etc.—contact your attorney. She will request a court order, and your ex-husband will be required to attend a hearing. If the evidence shows that he purposely violated the court's ruling, the court has the power to hold him in contempt of court and order him incarcerated until he complies.

9
Child Custody and Support

CHILD CUSTODY

If you are considering separating from your spouse, a major concern will be how the divorce will affect your children. Will there be a custody dispute? Will the children be torn between you and your husband? What can you do to minimize the difficulties they will encounter during and after the divorce? As a judge in a New York dissolution case stated, "It is well recognized that the children of divorce are subjected to severe strain and that the children often experience loss of security and feelings of rejection [when their parents separate]."[1]

Although dissolution ends the marriage, it does not terminate the obligations of either spouse toward the children. In spite of any ill feelings that may exist between the spouses, it is expected that they have a shared commitment and responsibility toward the children of the marriage. The question is, can you and your husband put aside your differences and hostility in order to work out a custody agreement that will minimize your children's emotional trauma? The primary concern should be that the matter of custody and visitation rights be handled in a manner that is least disturbing to the children.

Negotiation of the Custody Agreement

Child custody battles can be particularly nasty, as well as costly and time-consuming. If at all possible, work out a custody agreement with your husband in advance, rather than allow the court to make the decision for you. This will save you the humiliation and aggravation of being subjected to extensive interrogation by the court to determine your fitness as a parent. The court will usually uphold a custody agreement prepared by the spouses except in the rare instances in which it has good reason to believe that the parent is unfit or unable to care for the child properly.

Discuss the options with your attorney. Having previous experience with custody matters, he will be able to offer you professional advice and point out potential problems. If there is any chance that you and your husband may come to an agreement, have your attorney arrange a meeting with your spouse and his attorney. If a satisfactory solution is reached, it will be put in writing, signed by both parties, and submitted to the court.

If either you or your husband is unwilling to compromise, consider visiting one of the many public and private counseling services available. You will want to do everything possible to settle the matter outside of court so as to minimize the children's involvement in the legal process. Some courts will appoint a mediator to interview the parents and children in an attempt to resolve the dispute outside of court. The mediator is usually a social worker, possibly an employee of the family court or the probation department, who will attempt to assess the needs and interests of the children. After she has reviewed the situation, she will make a recommendation to the court regarding custody and visitation.

The Best Interests of the Child

The final determination of where the children are to reside is made by the judge of the family court, who is allowed broad discretion in making his decision. He must decide who is more capable of caring for the children and who will be able to provide an environment that will be physically, mentally, and emotionally healthy. Even if the parents have already agreed on the matter of custody, the court is required to review the agreement to ensure that it is in the children's best interests. Absent an agreement, the court will require each parent to testify as to why he or she would be better able to care for the minor children.

During the inquiry into the parents' fitness, the court will admit evidence in the following areas:

Cooperation. Which parent is more likely to allow the children frequent contact with the non-custodial parent (the parent not given custody)?

The Child's Preference. If the children are of sufficient age and capacity to reason, the court will usually consider and give due weight to their preference. Some courts have held that a child is of sufficient age to reason at 15,[2] absent evidence to the contrary. Other courts have considered the preference of children who are as young as 8.[3] A judge will normally confer with the minor in his chambers in order to ascertain whether he is capable of making such a decision or if his stated request to live with one or the other of the parents is a result of coaching or intimidation.

The Parent's Mental and Physical Health. The court will take into consideration the mental stability of the parents as well as their physical health. Much has been written about the ability of disabled or handicapped parents to properly care for their children's needs. During the examination, the court may question the disabled parent on how he or she has adapted to the handicap, how the family has adjusted, and whether there are any special contributions that are made to the family unit despite or because of the disability. After all evidence is submitted, the court will determine whether the condition is likely to have a substantial and lasting adverse effect on the children. Absent a finding of an adverse effect, the disability of the parent will not be considered when granting custody.

Stability of the Parent. Will the parent be able to maintain a stable physical and emotional environment for the children? The court will consider each parent's willingness to assume "the continuous and full responsibility of the children." It is not "engaged in a disciplinary action to punish parents for their shortcomings as individuals nor to reward the unoffending parent for any wrong suffered by the sins of the other."[4] Rather, it attempts to serve the children's best interests by selecting the most fit parent.

Under the topic of stability, two other matters may be considered by the court: the parent's sexual conduct and sexual preference. These are highly inflammatory issues that are handled differently from state to state and from court to court. Society's increasing acceptance of cohabitation, homosexuality, and sexual activity between unmarried adults has affected the way the courts deal with the issues to a certain degree, but in general they still consider that such an environment may not be appropriate when raising a child. A statement made by a North Carolina judge in regard to cohabitation illustrates the general attitude of the courts: "Cohabitation by unmarried persons of the opposite sex is not condoned by the laws of this state, [however,] evidence of cohabitation alone is not always sufficient to support a finding that a party is not a fit and proper person to have custody of minor children."[5] While cases are decided on an individual basis, it seems that most courts regard cohabitation and homosexuality as significant considerations when deciding on custody matters, although they may not be reason enough to revoke custody. Again, the courts are concerned primarily with how such behavior affects the welfare of the child.

The Quality of Companionship and Ability to Supervise. The court will attempt to decide which parent will be better able to supervise and spend time with the child. This does not mean that a working parent will automatically be denied custody; the courts seem willing to allow part-time supervision through day care centers and pre-schools.

Temporary Custody

You may request temporary custody of your children when you file for divorce (see "Filing for Divorce," in chapter 8). Temporary custody will be granted to one of the spouses for the duration of the dissolution proceedings, while the non-custodial parent will be granted specific visitation rights. Should the parents disagree on who should have temporary custody, the court may request both spouses to supply evidence as to why they feel they would be better able to serve the children's best interests.

Though you may be willing to have your children stay with your spouse during the divorce, thinking that you'll need a little time to pull yourself together before they come to live with you on a permanent basis, you should be aware that the court may be inclined to grant final custody to the spouse who cared for them during the divorce, rather than disrupting the children by moving them to another residence. This is not always the case, but as we stated earlier, the court's primary consideration will be the children's welfare, and of course the amount of time the parents are willing to spend with them. Custody rulings can be altered at a later date, but generally the courts will require evidence that the custodial parent has neglected to care for the children properly and that the home environment has adversely affected them.

Joint Custody

Traditionally, the courts almost always awarded custody to the wife. She was considered solely responsible for the raising of the children, while the father was primarily responsible for their financial support. As the woman's role as mother expanded, the father's involvement diminished, his legal obligation to the children having been met when he deposited the monthly support check in the mail. The weekends spent with Dad were often a cross between Disneyland and the Inquisition. The father, in an attempt to make up for his absence from the home, would shower the children with gifts while simultaneously quizzing them about their mother's new boyfriend. And in spite of the parents' good intentions, the children became pawns.

In recent years, the more liberal states have enacted laws which prohibit the courts from granting or denying custody to a parent solely because of his or her sex. And as further evidence of dissatisfaction with the traditional approach to child custody matters, there has been a trend toward joint custody, in which both parents retain legal custody of the children, sharing the responsibility of raising them and providing for their financial needs. This new approach is designed to "assure minor children of frequent and continuing contact with both parents ... and to encourage parents to share the rights and responsibilities of child rearing.... "[6]

There are those who feel that joint custody is an untested concept that may cause serious adjustment problems for the child as he is transferred from one environment to the other. A Florida court, when considering the issue of joint custody, stated: "The question may be ... narrowed to the one whether the welfare of the child will be promoted if he is placed with first one parent and then the other, his home life interrupted every half year. It is thoroughly established that in such circumstances the primary concern of the court is the well being of the child, and we have grave doubt that an infant of three years old can develop normally and thrive if at the end of every six months he is removed from surroundings familiar to him and forced to become accustomed to new ones."[7]

Other states have responded favorably to joint custody, viewing it as a partial solution to the rising number of single-parent homes and the best alternative to the traditional authoritative mother and Disneyland father arrangement. The child is able to enjoy the companionship of both parents, the father is allowed continuous contact with the child, and the mother is relieved of the burden of single parenting. In 1979, the California Legislature enacted its Joint Custody Law, which states that "there shall be a presumption ... that joint custody is in the best interests of the minor child," and that should a parent's request for joint custody be denied the "court shall state in its decision the reasons for denial."[8]

When first contemplating the matter of custody, you will need to ask yourself a great many questions before deciding which type of arrangement would work best for you, your children, and your husband. If your preference is for both of you to retain custody, consider the following:

Will you and your husband be able to put your children's well-being first, setting aside any feelings of hostility or anger?

Will both of you be willing to meet on a regular basis to discuss problems related to the children?

Are you both willing to remain in the same community or city until the children reach the age of majority (usually 18)?

Will you and your husband be able to provide a room in your homes for the children, rooms that may be vacant half of the time?

Be realistic as you weigh the pros and cons of joint custody as they relate to your particular situation. If you and your husband haven't spoken a civil word to each other in four years, it's unrealistic to expect that you'll suddenly be able to communicate and agree on how the children should be raised.

If you feel that joint custody is a viable option, arrange a meeting with your husband and the attorneys to see if a compromise can be reached. It may take weeks of negotiating before you are able to agree on an arrangement. Once both of you are satisfied with the terms, have one of the attorneys draw up the agreement for your signatures. The following list covers some essential provisions that you may want to include in your agreement:

Both parents are willing to meet regularly in order to discuss matters related to the children's well-being—their educational and religious training, the need for disciplinary action, problems at school, etc.

Either parent may seek emergency health care for the children without obtaining the other parent's consent. Non-emergency health care decisions shall be made jointly.

Each parent is to inform the other immediately of any change of residence or phone number.

State who is to mediate any disputes which may arise between the parents.

State exactly how the financial obligation of raising the children is to be satisfied. Who will be responsible for the children's necessities, day care, clothing, health insurance, etc.?

How will the agreement be modified if either spouse remarries or moves to a different area?

Which parent will claim the children as income tax deductions? What about the head of household exemption?

Specify how the children's time will be divided between the parents.

CHILD SUPPORT

The court will require that both parents be responsible for the support of their children until they reach the age of majority. When determining the amount of the child support, it will consider each parent's financial situation as outlined in the financial declaration and budget that were previously submitted to the court at the beginning of the divorce process as well as the needs of the children. Normally, the non-custodial parent will be ordered to pay a specified amount to the custodial parent for the support of the children. The court is concerned that the minors be afforded the necessities of life, including adequate housing, food, clothing, and personal items (not necessarily a supply of new deck shoes and an Apple Computer).

If at all possible, work out an agreement with your husband ahead of time as to the amount of child support to be paid. Child support will probably be negotiated at the same time as the custody arrangement. No matter how amicable your relationship, have everything in writing and signed. It often happens that the husband makes generous offers at the time of the divorce that are never put in writing, and later circumstances cause him to renege on his promises. While his primary concern at the time may be the well-being of the children, you must consider the likely possibility that he will remarry, taking on additional concerns and financial obligations. As with any critical legal matter, the negotiation should take place in the presence of your attorneys, who will be able to advise you on essential elements that should be contained in your agreement. You may want to set up a trust for the children. Who will be responsible for paying for the children's medical and dental expenses and college educations? Unlike alimony, child support is not taxable or tax deductible, so this will have to be considered when preparing your agreement.

As is true of child custody agreements, the court will generally accept the amount of child support payments agreed upon by the parents as long as it appears to be fair to both of them and is sufficient to cover the children's expenses. Either parent can later petition the court to modify the amount of child support, although the court will generally consider a change only when it has reason to believe that the original order has become unrealistic or results in undue hardship for one of the parents. For example, if there is a substantial increase or decrease in either parent's income, inflation has diluted the original order, or the children's expenses have increased as they become older, the court will likely consider adjusting the amount of support.

Child support payments are not related to alimony in any way; even if alimony is discontinued, the parent's responsibility to support the children continues. Should your ex-husband fail to pay the support as ordered by the court, your attorney should be notified so that she can arrange for a hearing. If he offers no acceptable excuse for nonpayment, the court will find your ex-husband in contempt of court and he may be incarcerated until payment is made. A bill passed by the House and Senate in 1984 allows courts to garnish wages, impose liens on property, withhold tax refunds, and inform credit bureaus if support payments are 30 or more days late, and these actions are enforceable across state lines. On the other hand, should you refuse to allow your husband visitation rights as ordered by the court (even as retaliation for nonpayment), you may be requested to appear at a hearing and found in contempt.

10
Juvenile Law

Barbara, a single parent, received a call at work one afternoon from a police officer, who informed her that her son Michael had been arrested outside a local toy store after attempting to steal an Atari video game. The officer told her that Michael would remain at the police station until she arrived. In a panic, Barbara drove immediately to the station, where she was directed to the department's juvenile officer. She was informed that Michael, after having been read his Miranda Rights, including the right to have a parent present during questioning, had agreed to talk with the officer. He admitted that he had hidden the video game under his coat and was out the door and headed toward a friend's house when he was stopped by a security guard.

The juvenile officer told Barbara that the store had chosen to prosecute under the state's shoplifting laws and that she and Michael were to report to the Juvenile Probation Department the following Monday at 9 a.m. so that the matter could be reviewed. At that time, a decision would be made as to whether the probation officer would be able to deal with the matter directly or whether Michael would be required to appear before a judge of the juvenile court.

For both Michael and his mother this was a sobering and frightening experience. Having never dealt with the juvenile justice system before, Barbara was unsure of how to proceed. While she was confused and angry over her son's behavior, at the same time she had the natural desire to protect him from a system she didn't understand. Does Michael, at age 12, have the same rights as an adult? Can he be represented by an attorney? Will a juvenile offense go on his record?

THE PURPOSE OF THE JUVENILE JUSTICE SYSTEM

Before the first juvenile court was established in Illinois in 1899, naive minor offenders were cast into the same criminal arena with violent adult offenders. The adverse effects of this practice were obvious: rather than being rehabilitated, the minors were actually being prepared for a life of crime. The juvenile justice system was established to serve the interests of minors as well as of society by protecting and rehabilitating, rather than punishing, minor offenders, and by providing the necessary guidance and discipline to discourage them from becoming adult criminals.[1]

The present juvenile court system handles all cases involving minors, generally defined as those under 18 years of age. (Laws established in some states prescribing a lower age of majority for girls were found to be sexually discriminatory and therefore unconstitutional.)[2] Two types of offenders are recognized by the juvenile courts—the delinquent and the out-of-control minor. The delinquent is one who has violated a state or federal law, such as shoplifting or driving a vehicle while under the influence of alcohol.[3] The out-of-control minor is one who rebels against authority figures and appears to be beyond parental control;[4] he may come to the attention of the juvenile court after repeatedly running away from home or skipping school.

THE PARENT'S ROLE

There are specific things you can do as a parent to protect your child's rights and to influence the court's decision as to whether he will be released or detained and, if found guilty, what rehabilitative or disciplinary measures will be taken. Should you receive a call from your child informing you that he has been arrested, recommend that he not discuss the matter with you over the telephone or with anyone else until you can talk in private. Explain to him that he has the legal right to remain silent. When you arrive at the police station, ask the officer in charge to provide you with the details of the incident and then request that no questioning take place until you and your child have conferred with an attorney.

Whether your child is released to you after arrest will depend on the seriousness of the violation and his prior record. In minor incidents, it is likely that he will be allowed to return home with you. If the violation is of a more serious nature, the child may be taken to juvenile hall, or, should the police feel that the child will receive adequate supervision at home, he may be released to you with the understanding that both of you will appear in court on a particular date. In some states, minors may be referred to a diversion program. These programs, operated either by the court or by the police department, have been set up to provide counseling and supervision for minors charged with less serious offenses. Some programs are residential while others allow the minor to live at home.

Unless the charges have been dropped, you will want to contact an attorney immediately. Select one who specializes in juvenile law (not all attorneys are allowed to represent juveniles in court; some states require special certification). Hiring a competent attorney will increase the chances that the matter will be settled to your satisfaction. Remember that the stakes are high—in some cases, minors are placed in juvenile hall, a foster home, or even prison, and the parents' authority is then replaced by that of the court. To lessen the chances that your child will be removed from the home environment, you must be prepared to demonstrate to the court your concern for the child and your willingness to provide the type and amount of supervision necessary to his rehabilitation.

JUVENILE COURT

Detention Hearing

If your child is not released after the arrest, the court must schedule a detention hearing within 48 hours (excluding weekends and holidays). Because juvenile proceedings are civil, minors are not guaranteed the right to bail. The purpose of this hearing is to determine whether your child should be released (possibly on probation) or referred to some type of correctional facility. (If the court has reason to believe that the child has serious psychological problems, he may be transferred to a hospital psychiatric ward.) In deciding where the child should be placed, the court will consider the seriousness of the violation, whether the minor's release would be a threat to the community, and the willingness of the parents to provide adequate supervision and to cooperate with the court in rehabilitating the child. Although you will be asked certain questions relating to your ability and willingness to supervise the child, all of the legal issues will be handled by your attorney. (If you have not retained an attorney, the court will appoint one and you will be billed for his services.)[5]

Pre-Trial Hearing

If your child was released after the arrest, his first court appearance will be at a preliminary hearing, where he will be given a copy of the charges against him (the petition) and informed by the judge or referee of the juvenile court of his constitutional rights. Even though cases heard in juvenile court are considered civil matters, minors are allowed many of the same constitutional rights as adults who are involved in criminal proceedings. These include: the right against self-incrimination; the right to be represented by an attorney; the right to call witnesses in their defense; the right to cross-examine those witnesses who are called to testify against them; and the right to appeal. Because the courts consider the formalities of a jury trial to be disruptive to the informal setting of the juvenile hearing, the right to a trial by jury is not guaranteed in most states.[6] However, in a few states the courts, upon receipt of a formal request by the minor or his attorney, have recently allowed jury trials—especially in those more serious cases in which the proceedings were to be conducted in a formal setting similar to that of an adult court.

At the pre-trial hearing, the minor must either admit or deny the charges against him. Before he pleads guilty or not guilty, the judge will explain the consequences of a guilty plea. For example, by admitting guilt he will give up certain constitutional rights and the court will take some sort of disciplinary action. If the minor states that he understands the consequences and wishes to admit his guilt, the case will be scheduled for a disposition hearing. If he denies the charges, a date will be set for the trial.

Plea Bargaining

In the majority of juvenile cases, the charges against minors are either reduced or dismissed. This is a result of the process known as plea bargaining. The defense attorney presents to the prosecutor certain favorable information about the minor that may suggest he deserves leniency—perhaps he has no previous record or has made amends for the damage he caused. Although the prosecutor may refuse to dismiss the charges, she may conclude that the violation with which the minor was charged should be changed to a lesser one, given the extenuating circumstances.

The Trial

Juvenile trials are conducted by either a juvenile court referee or a judge. Unless excused by the court, the minor's parents or guardians must be present at all stages of the judicial proceedings. The trial will be private, which means that only the parents, the attorneys, observers authorized by the court, and members of the court staff will be allowed to attend. In rare cases, usually those sensationalized trials of minors accused of serious crimes, members of the media are authorized to attend, generally under the condition that they not identify anyone under the age of 18.

At the beginning of the trial, the court will allow the prosecution to present its case against the minor. The prosecutor will be required to present evidence showing that a violation has occurred and that the minor actively participated. The defense attorney will have the opportunity to cross-examine the prosecution's witnesses and at the conclusion of the prosecution's case will present evidence in the minor's defense. After all the evidence has been presented and the prosecution has completed cross-examination, the judge will render a decision. Should she find that the prosecution was unable to establish beyond a reasonable doubt that the minor did commit the act specified in the petition, she will find him to be not guilty.[7] Should she find that the minor did commit the offense, a disposition hearing will be scheduled.

Disposition Hearing

The purpose of a disposition hearing is to determine what sort of disciplinary action should be taken that will discourage the minor from continuing the type of activity that brought him before the juvenile court. Unlike adult sentencing, the intent is not to punish the minor but to rehabilitate him.

Before the hearing, the court will request that the local agency responsible for minors, usually the Juvenile Probation Department, prepare an investigative report on the minor, covering such matters as previous violations of the law, the minor's ability to adjust to school, the community, and the home, his family situation, and the attitude of the parents. The agency will interview the minor and his parents and perhaps other persons who are in continuous contact with him—friends, relatives, teachers, and neighbors. The report will also recommend whatever remedies the agency feels are suitable.

A copy of the agency's or probation officer's recommendation will be presented to the minor and his attorney before the hearing. During the hearing, both sides will be allowed to respond to the recommendation, stating why they feel it is reasonable or what changes or alternatives should be considered. After reviewing the investigative report and all the evidence, the judge will render her decision.

A number of states have set minimum and maximum sentences for the various violations to ensure that the courts' decisions are consistent. For minor violations, the judge may place the child on probation for a certain period of time or require him to perform some type of volunteer work for the community. Or she may refer the child (and possibly the parents) to counseling. If the minor has committed a serious crime, he may be sent to jail.

In reaching a decision, the court's primary consideration is whether the child would more likely be rehabilitated in the home environment than in some type of correctional facility. If the parents show a willingness to work with their child in resolving problems and to make whatever arrangements are necessary to provide the necessary supervision and guidance, the courts almost always prefer to return the child to the home, as long as he is not a threat to society.

MINORS TRIED IN ADULT COURTS

In some instances, the court will recommend that a minor be tried as an adult, although certain circumstances must exist before such an arrangement can be made. The following conditions must be met in most states before a case will be transferred to an adult court:

> The minor must be at least 16 years of age, and a) be charged with commiting a serious crime, such as murder, arson, armed robbery, kidnapping, or rape, or b) the prosecution must show that he is not a "fit and proper subject to be dealt with under the juvenile law" (evidence to support such a claim may include a degree of criminal sophistication, a history of delinquent behavior, and previous unsuccessful attempts at rehabilitation).[8]

Should either of these situations exist, the prosecution may request that a fitness hearing be scheduled to determine in which court the minor should be tried. Both the prosecution and the minor's attorney will be allowed to present evidence at the hearing (in most cases, the defense attorney will introduce testimony by the parents). Should the juvenile judge rule in the prosecution's favor, the case will be transferred to the adult court for criminal proceedings and the minor will be tried in the same manner as an adult and be subject to the same type of punishment.

SEALING A JUVENILE RECORD

The records of the juvenile court are not part of the official record and are available only to those specified by state statute. After the minor has been discharged from the juvenile justice system, he may request that the juvenile court either seal his record or release it to his custody. This right is available to any person convicted of an offense while a minor who has fulfilled his obligations to the court, whether it be probation, being placed in the custody of a youth authority, or a term in juvenile hall. He may also request that information concerning his arrest or conviction not be released to any individual, organization, or governmental agency.

Though the procedure of sealing a juvenile record is not identical in all the states, the following, taken from the Texas statutes,[9] is fairly standard. The individual who desires to seal his record must file a motion with the juvenile court requesting a hearing. At the hearing, the record will be sealed if the following conditions have been met: two years have passed since the final discharge of the minor from the juvenile justice system; during that two years he has not been convicted of a felony or of specified misdemeanors; there are no pending criminal charges against the individual; and the judge has reason to believe that he has been rehabilitated. Once a file is sealed, any inquiry regarding the juvenile record will be returned with a statement that there is no existing record on the individual. A sealed file may be inspected only if the minor himself files a petition and the court orders it to be opened.

WOMEN AS VICTIMS

11
Sex Discrimination

Discrimination has always existed in the workplace and has often chosen its victims on the basis of their race, color, religion, national origin, or age. Traditionally, sex discrimination has been considered less dastardly than the other forms of discrimination. In fact, for many years sex was viewed by the courts as a valid basis for discrimination.[1] In the case of Bradwell v. the State of Illinois in 1872, the court denied Myra Bradwell admission to the Illinois bar solely because of her sex. When the case was appealed to the U.S. Supreme Court, the ruling of the lower court was upheld.[2] The attitude of the courts has changed gradually as more and more sex discrimination cases have been heard, although, as with other legal issues involving women, it is a matter of two steps forward one step back along the road to equality.

Not until the 1960s and 1970s were women, armed with several new employment laws, able to successfully challenge discriminatory practices to obtain equal treatment. Still, traditional sexist attitudes and prejudices persist in the business world, and statistics show that there continues to be a wide disparity in the incomes of males and females in most types of employment. Sex discrimination occurs either through conscious, overt actions or through subtle actions or policies which may seem perfectly innocent on the surface but have the same adverse effect—the denial of equal employment opportunities for women.

In a 1980 Georgia case, Futran v. Ring Radio Company, the court held that the defendant had discriminated against Ms. Futran, a talk show host, by requiring her to perform certain menial tasks (such as making coffee and cleaning up) which were not required of the male talk show hosts. In addition, the court found that by firing Ms. Futran after she filed a complaint, Ring Radio Company had acted in retaliation, a second violation of Title VII of the Civil Rights Act.[3]

In the case of Hill v. Nettleton, an assistant professor of physical education at Colorado State University brought an action alleging sex discrimination when her contract was not renewed.[4] While the university claimed that the nonrenewal was a result of Ms. Hill's failure to complete a Ph.D., the court ruled that since male assistant professors seemed not to be pressured to obtain higher degrees the degree was not essential for performing the duties for which Ms. Hill and her colleagues were hired. Evidence was presented that the university had acted in retaliation against Ms. Hill's public complaints regarding the disparity in the allocation of funds to women's and men's intercollegiate athletics. She was reinstated at the university.

A third case, Griggs v. Duke Power Company, illustrates a more subtle form of discrimination, that which appears to be unbiased but in effect limits the employment opportunities of a particular group.[5] In this case, a black man challenged a company's hiring policies, which required that job applicants be high school graduates and that they pass an intelligence test. The Supreme Court found that these requirements were unrelated to job performance and in fact resulted in racial discrimination, since they disqualified a substantially higher number of minorities than whites. Although the Griggs case involves racial discrimination, Title VII sex discrimination claims can be based on the same "discriminatory impact theory." Regardless of the *intent* of the employer, if employment policies "neutral on their face" have a disproportionate effect on women, they are discriminatory.

CHECKLIST OF DISCRIMINATORY PRACTICES

The following checklist covers those employment practices that may be a sound basis for a sex discrimination complaint:

—Is advertising for jobs placed in sex-segregated columns? (Remember "Help Wanted—Female"?) Do job titles (such as *salesman* or *repairman*) specify or suggest that only male applicants will be considered?

—Are hiring practices discriminatory? Does your employer interview only men for higher-level positions such as manager and only women for lower-level positions such as clerk or secretary?

—Are interviewing practices for initial employment or advancement discriminatory? For example, are women asked if they are pregnant or intend to become so? Are they asked about marital status, their availability for weekend work, or the number and ages of their children? Questions about height, weight, and strength which set unfair standards (positions with police or fire departments, for example) are considered to be discriminatory. (Obviously, if applicants are required to be 6 feet tall and weigh 190 pounds, few women fit into this classification and such standards would likely be viewed as an attempt to deny employment opportunities for women.) In 1984, the Supreme Court extended the definition of discriminatory employment practices to include those that deny women partnership promotions (as in a law firm) solely because of their sex.[6]

—Are unwelcome sexual advances common at your place of employment? Is submission a basis for employment decisions?

—Are there different standards for men and women regarding business trips, business luncheons, etc.?

—Is the opportunity to work overtime limited for female employees but not for male employees?

—Do women receive less pay than men in positions requiring the same skills and aptitudes?

—Do training practices discriminate against women? Are men trained to be vice-presidents while their female counterparts are trained for middle management?

—Do policies related to sick leave or reimbursement of medical expenses discriminate against pregnant women?

—Do testing practices that lead to promotions overtly or subtly discriminate on the basis of sex? Are women required to reach weight, height, or physical strength standards which are beyond the average for women and beyond that necessary for performing the work satisfactorily?

—Are health insurance, disability payments, or pension or profit-sharing plans denied to women but not to men?

THE FOURTEENTH AMENDMENT

Discrimination complaints have often been based on the Fourteenth Amendment of the U.S. Constitution, which guarantees all persons equal protection under the law. Its provisions, the well worn "Equal Protection and Due Process Clauses," apply to the states as well as to the federal government (through the Fifth Amendment). The interpretation of these clauses has changed as the names on the musical chairs of the Supreme Court have changed. For example, in 1873 the Supreme Court interpreted the Fourteenth Amendment as applying only to racial discrimination, while today the interpretation has been expanded to include sex discrimination.

A widely publicized claim of employment discrimination based on the Fourteenth Amendment was filed by a female reporter for *Sports Illustrated* against the New York Yankees and the baseball commissioner after she was denied entrance to the Yankees' locker room following a World Series game. The argument that the players' privacy should be protected was found to be less persuasive than the reporter's claim that she was at a disadvantage in competing with male reporters if not allowed to conduct the popular locker-room interviews. The court ruled that the reporter's constitutional rights had been violated and that no women reporters would be barred from the locker room.

In a second case based on the Fourteenth Amendment, female teachers were able to prove sex discrimination when they presented evidence that although female teachers outnumbered male teachers three to one, almost all preferential assignments and promotions went to the male teachers.[7]

THE CIVIL RIGHTS ACT, TITLE VII

Title VII of the Civil Rights Act of 1964 prohibits employers from discriminating against anyone because of their race, color, religion, sex, or national origin. A discrimination claim under Title VII can be brought against almost any employer who employs 15 or more persons and who is engaged in commerce or the production of goods for commerce (broadly interpreted by the courts to cover almost all types of businesses). Those subject to Title VII are:

— Private employers with 15 or more employees
— State and local governments with 15 or more employees
— The federal government
— Employment agencies that refer people for possible employment
— Unions and labor organizations with 15 or more members that maintain a hiring hall

Employers who are exempt include:

— Those who hire aliens or non-U.S. citizens
— Tax-exempt private membership clubs
— Religious organizations, when employment is for carrying out religious purposes

- Businesses on or near Indian reservations with respect to preferential hiring of Indians
- Government employers with regard to elected staff positions
- Those who hire individuals for national security jobs

If your employer owns a small business with fewer than 15 employees, you cannot file a discrimination claim based on Title VII. Nevertheless, he is still subject to state (and in some cases, city) employment laws. These vary widely from state to state, so you will need to review the laws or consult with an attorney.

HOW TO FILE A DISCRIMINATION COMPLAINT

If you feel you have been discriminated against and your employer is subject to Title VII, you will need to contact the Equal Employment Opportunity Commission, the watchdog agency of Title VII, which has offices throughout the United States. If there is no EEOC office listed in your city telephone directory, contact the main office in Washington, DC, and it will provide you with the address and phone number of the district office nearest you:

Equal Employment Opportunity Commission
Columbia Plaza Highrise
2401 E Street, N.W.
Washington, DC 20506 (202) 634-7040

The commission is in charge of investigating all complaints to determine if violations have in fact occurred. Most states also have agencies that administer state antidiscrimination laws. The names of these agencies vary, but your state Attorney General's office can direct you to the right place.

Whether or not you hire an attorney is up to you. It is not a requirement for filing a complaint or a lawsuit, but you should be aware of the fact that the various filing procedures and time limitations can become confusing and that in many cases only an attorney with experience in this area will be able to help you through the maze of federal, state, and local laws and regulations. At the very least, it is recommended that you consult with an attorney before filing a complaint; she should be able to advise you on the antidiscrimination laws that apply to your case and to outline the steps you will need to take. If you decide to pursue the matter on your own, you will need to be well organized. If possible, have your co-workers sign notarized statements attesting to the discriminatory practices and start a documentation file for copies of all correspondence, forms, documents, and filing dates and requirements.

Employees are required to follow these procedures when filing a discrimination complaint under Title VII (federal employees, although covered by Title VII, must follow different procedures—see page 123):

1) If your state or city has no antidiscrimination laws, you must file a Charge of Discrimination, a written complaint, with the EEOC within 180 days after the act of discrimination. Whether or not it is written on an official EEOC form, your complaint must include your name, address, phone number, the names and addresses of all other parties involved (your employer, union, or employment agency), the date and place of occurrence, and a description of the discriminatory act. In order for the EEOC to investigate the matter, you must sign the complaint and have it notarized. There seems to be some preference by the EEOC that the charge be filed in person, but this is not mandatory. If you send your complaint by mail, fill out a return receipt request so you will have evidence that it was received. The returned receipt should be kept in your documentation file.

2) If your state or city has its own antidiscrimination laws, you must first file a complaint with the agency that enforces those laws (each one has a specified time limit for filing). The agency has jurisdiction over the complaint for a period of 60 days. Your complaint to the EEOC must be filed within 300 days of the discriminatory act or within 30 days after the state or local agency has notified you that it has ended its proceedings, whichever occurs first. You may want to file charges with the EEOC and the local or state agency at the same time, requesting the EEOC to automatically assume jurisdiction 60 days after receipt of the complaint.

3) When the EEOC assumes jurisdiction it will notify your employer, and any other parties involved, of the charges and may request additional documents and evidence from you, your co-workers, and your employer. Once its investigation is completed, the EEOC will determine whether the charge is valid according to the law. If it finds reasonable cause to believe you have been discriminated against, all parties will be notified and the EEOC will attempt to resolve the dispute by informal conference. If the parties are able to agree on measures to correct the discriminatory practices and on compensation for past violations, the case will be closed. If the other party is able to prove that the discrimination was legally valid, that is, that the practices are necessary to the operation of the business, you will lose your case and the EEOC will send you a right-to-sue letter (notification that proceedings against your employer have concluded and that you have the right to file a lawsuit on your own in the federal district court). On the other hand, if the other party is unable to justify the discriminatory acts and a settlement cannot be agreed upon, the EEOC

may sue the other party on your behalf. (The Department of Justice will sue if you are an employee of a state or local government.)

Because of the large volume of complaints the EEOC receives, it may be a year or more before it can bring a lawsuit on your behalf, so you may want to request a right-to-sue letter and proceed on your own. This request can be made after the EEOC has had jurisdiction over your complaint for a period of 180 days. Likewise, if the EEOC fails to act upon your complaint during the 180 days, you can request a right-to-sue letter.

4) You may file a lawsuit on your own after obtaining a right-to-sue letter from the EEOC or the Department of Justice. The suit must be filed within 90 days after receipt of the letter so if you decide you want legal representation, do not request a right-to-sue letter until your attorney is prepared to go to court. In your suit, you can name as defendants only those named as respondents in your EEOC complaint, and the discriminatory practice must be closely related to the one mentioned in the original complaint. You have the right to request that the EEOC make available to you the information uncovered during its investigation of your complaint.

In some instances you may be able to bring a class action if your employer has discriminated against other women as well. Class actions are lawsuits brought by one or more persons (or an organization, such as the EEOC) who represent or act on behalf of a particular class of employees. Many such cases have been successful in putting a stop to employment practices that discriminate against women. However, the courts require that certain conditions be met before they will allow a class action.

5) Should you lose your case, you will probably be ordered to pay your employer's attorney's fees. If the court rules in your favor, your attorney's fees and court costs will likely be recovered, and the court will decide what measures should be taken to stop the discriminatory practices and how you should be compensated. Depending on the circumstances, the court may order your employer to pay you for lost wages, to hire or rehire you, or to provide insurance, profit-sharing, or pension plan benefits.

Federal employees, although covered by Title VII, must first consult with their government agency's Equal Employment Opportunity counselor (within 30 days of the discriminatory act). The counselor will act as mediator in attempting to resolve the problem through informal methods. If the matter is not resolved, you can submit a written complaint to your agency within 15 days of the final consultation with the EEO counselor and an investigation will be conducted. Should you be dissatisfied with the disposition, you may request a formal hearing within 15 days. If the problem is still not resolved to your satisfaction, you may file an appeal with the EEOC (within 20 days) or file a civil action in district court within 30 days of the final action by the agency. You have the right to be represented by an attorney at any stage of these proceedings.

THE PREGNANCY DISCRIMINATION ACT

The newest and the most long-awaited amendment to Title VII of the Civil Rights Act is the Pregnancy Discrimination Act, which prohibits discrimination on the basis of pregnancy or childbearing. Basically the amendment states:

— A written or unwritten policy of employment which excludes applicants or employees because of pregnancy, childbirth, or related medical conditions is a violation of Title VII.

— Disabilities caused or contributed to by pregnancy or childbirth shall be treated as a disability caused by any other medical condition.

This amendment protects women against being fired, refused employment, denied promotions, or forced to take a leave of absence by their employers merely because of pregnancy. Pregnant women must be allowed to work at their jobs as long as they are able. Any woman unable to work for pregnancy-related reasons is entitled to sick leave (and in certain instances, disability benefits) on the same basis as employees unable to work for other medical reasons. Health insurance as a benefit of employment must cover expenses for pregnancy-related conditions on the same basis as expenses for other medical conditions, as long as these conditions are covered by the insurance policy. Jobs must be held open for the return of female employees who are on sick leave for pregnancy on the same basis as for employees on sick leave for other reasons. Finally, the method of calculating vacations, pay increases, and seniority accrual must be the same as that used for employees whose medical conditions are not pregnancy-related.

The courts interpret discrimination on the basis of pregnancy or childbearing as being a form of sex discrimination. If you feel you have been discriminated against in this manner, you will need to file a complaint with the Equal Employment Opportunity Commission and follow the procedures outlined in the section "How to File a Discrimination Complaint" on pages 121-24.

THE EQUAL PAY ACT

It is hard to believe that women, since they first entered the business world, have never received wages equal to those of their male counterparts. Statistics show they are still underpaid by as much as 40% in most work arenas; that is, the average woman earns $.60 for every $1.00 earned by her male counterpart. This is particularly distressing when you consider that 53% of the female population are in the labor force. A common argument offered in defense of this disparity is that the majority of women are in lower-paying jobs, such as clerical or secretarial, and thus their wages cannot be compared with those of men in higher-level positions. But this argument does not hold up when one considers that the same disparity exists in women's and men's wages when they are in identical, higher-paying positions (attorneys, computer systems analysts, engineers, physicians, and school administrators).[8]

The Equal Pay Act (EPA) prohibits sex discrimination only as it applies to equal pay for equal work. It is much more specific and narrowly drawn than Title VII, in which sex discrimination was tacked on as an afterthought to racial discrimination. The EPA was enacted in 1963 as an amendment to the Fair Labor Standards Act and thus is applicable to nearly all private employers as well as federal, state, and local governments. Unlike the Fair Labor Standards Act, the EPA also covers executive and administrative positions as well as labor unions. The basic standard applies to virtually any establishment engaged in interstate commerce, which is broadly interpreted to encompass almost any type of business. Those workers who are *not* covered by the EPA are:

- — Employees working for recreational establishments in operation less than eight months a year
- — Employees in the fish industry who catch, cultivate, process, can, or pack fish
- — Employees of small newspapers with a circulation of less than 4,000
- — Employees of small agricultural farms
- — Employees of independent telephone companies who are switchboard operators

The word *pay* in the Equal Pay Act has been interpreted by the courts as including all forms of payment such as vacation pay, holiday pay, overtime pay, and regular pay. By statute, the act requires that the equal wages be paid at the highest pay rate of comparable jobs, not the lowest; in other words, your employer cannot reduce your male co-worker's wages, rather than increase yours, to comply with the EPA.

If you feel you have a grievance in this area, take a look at the four factors that the EPA states must exist in order for your employer to be considered in violation of the law. The act stipulates that an employer may not pay a woman less than a man if their jobs require equal *skill*, *effort*, and *responsibility* under *similar working conditions*. Although the definitions of these terms vary somewhat from state to state, most courts interpret them in the following manner:

Equal skill has been interpreted to mean that which is substantially equal, not necessarily identical. The courts have consistently looked at job performance and job tasks, rather than titles, to measure skill. Factors that the court may view as important include the amount of training or education that is necessary to perform the tasks satisfactorily. For example, the court may look at your job descriptions to determine if both you and the male employee perform tasks that would require an MBA. If only your position requires the degree, it could be said that your job requires greater skill and that consequently you should receive a greater salary.

Equal effort is viewed by the courts as being based on both quantitative and qualitative measurements. When evaluating your own job, remember that the effort may be mental as well as physical. In the case of Marshall v. Central Kansas Medical Center, the court stated that the extra effort expended by the male janitors, who were responsible for cleaning larger areas of the medical center, was offset by the fact that the housekeepers were required to perform additional tasks. Consequently, it found that there was no justification for paying the women less than the men.[9]

Equal responsibility is harder to decipher. Many courts look at the employees' financial or supervisory responsibilities and the amount of independent judgment and discretion that the positions require. In Usery v. Richman, the court ruled that the higher wages paid to a male cook were justified since he was found to have greater responsibility for ordering meat, training new employees, and preparing more difficult meals than the female cook with equivalent skills.[10]

Similar working conditions may refer to physical location or work hours. Only a few courts have attempted to interpret this area, but the majority have found indoor and outdoor conditions to be dissimilar, while day and night conditions have been found to be either similar or dissimilar, depending upon the jurisdiction. (This raises the question of night differential paid to many night-shift employees.)

One of the more interesting cases involving wage discrimination based on sex was brought before an Oregon court in 1981.[11] Women employed as guards in a county jail system filed suit under Title VII alleging that they had been paid substantially lower wages than male guards because of their sex. The lower court found that the women had no justifiable complaint since the jobs were not equal according to the standards of the Equal Pay Act, which are deferred to by Title VII. The Supreme Court reversed the ruling of the lower court, stating that although the four preconditions of the Equal Pay Act had not been met, the fact that the jobs were *similar* was sufficient to show intentional sex discrimination. By stating that the equal work standard of the EPA need not necessarily be satisfied in order for an individual to bring a sex-based wage discrimination claim under Title VII, the Supreme Court may have increased women's chances of proving discrimination in similar, though not equal, work.

The federal agency that enforces the Equal Pay Act is the Equal Employment Opportunity Commission. To bring your employer's pay discrimination to the attention of the EEOC, you must notify the agency by way of a written complaint letter and follow the steps outlined in the section "How to File a Discrimination Complaint" on pages 121-24. The only difference between filing a Title VII complaint and an EPA complaint is that under the EPA you do not have to wait 180 days to file a lawsuit in the district court. You can bring a suit immediately, although you lose this right if the EEOC decides to sue on your behalf. Also, the EEOC is allowed to file class actions for EPA violations.

Because wage discrimination is so narrowly defined by the Equal Pay Act, recognizing pay disparity only in *equal* jobs, you may want to file a Title VII complaint as well. The EPA offers fewer remedies for victims of wage discrimination for the obvious reason that women rarely hold positions equal to those of men, a result of sex segregation, which channels women into lower-level positions and men into higher-level jobs. Title VII has been interpreted by the courts to be much broader, prohibiting employers from paying women less than men when they hold *similar* jobs and from discriminatory hiring practices that result in sex segregation.

When your employer is notified of your complaint, he may very well consider retaliating in some way. Be that as it may, you have the right to be paid a fair salary, and any act of retaliation on his part, such as transfer, demotion, or loss of your job, is prohibited under the EPA.

Before filing a complaint, consider the fact that the EPA specifies four defenses that, if proven by the employer, may be found to justify disparity in pay of male and female employees. These are not valid defenses, however, if it is found that any of the systems used to set wages are either directly or indirectly based on the employees' sex.

1) *Seniority.* The Supreme Court does not interpret seniority as merely the length of time you have been employed but also considers the conditions of your employment and your compensation.

2) *Merit.* If an employer can show that a male employee earns more than a female because his responsibilities are greater, the EEOC or the court will likely consider the pay disparity justifiable. But if sex is in any way a factor in determining merit, the policy will be considered discriminatory. In some cases, employers have asserted that their merit systems are based on the completion of training programs, but such programs are generally disallowed by the courts as a valid method of determining salaries, especially if females are automatically excluded from them.

3) *Quantity or Quality of Production.* If your employer defends the disparity in the pay scale on the basis of quantity or quality of production (that is, your ability to produce), he must be able to convince the EEOC or the court that he uses only one standard of measurement for all employees.

4) *The Catchall—Any Factor Other Than Sex.* Although employers have come up with various ingenious defenses to discriminatory compensation policies, the courts have defined this category very narrowly. One argument rejected by the courts is the "market force theory," in which unequal pay is said to be justified by the fact that women will generally work for less pay than a man. Another is that it costs more to employ women than men.

Should you file a complaint against your employer, be sure to document everything so that you will be able to present evidence to the EEOC or the court to support your charge. Keep a file of correspondence and documents, including salaries of male and female employees, written company policies regarding pay scales and methods of determining when and on what basis pay raises are given, as well as written evaluations of your job performance. Be prepared to defend yourself against all of the arguments discussed above.

12
Sexual Harassment

Margaret, a supervisor of nurses at a Veterans Administration hospital, became irritated when the work-related phone calls from her male supervisor became more frequent and sexually suggestive. When her supervisor made it clear that she could be promoted to a newly vacant position only by submitting to his sexual demands, she complained to the administrator of the Veterans Administration. Not only did the administrator fail to take any disciplinary action, but her supervisor retaliated by refusing to provide her with information she needed to perform her job and increased his sexual demands. When she sought another, lower-paying position at the hospital in an attempt to avoid the problem, she was allowed to transfer but the harassment from her supervisor did not stop. Finally, Margaret brought a sex discrimination suit against the V.A. administrator. Even then, she continued to receive the phone calls—this time they were threats.[1]

Deborah, the only female traffic controller at the Washington Air Traffic Control Center, found it increasingly difficult to do her job because of continual verbal sexual harassment by her co-workers. When the degrading comments, insults, and propositions continued, she complained to her supervisor, who suggested that the problem would be solved if she would just submit to her co-workers' sexual advances. Deborah talked to another crew's supervisor about the possibility of transferring to his crew. The supervisor's response was that he was sure the transfer could be arranged if she would grant certain sexual favors. When complaints to her employer brought no results and she had exhausted all of the administrative remedies, she brought a suit claiming sexual harassment and sex discrimination. Three months later Deborah was fired by the Federal Aviation Administration for allegedly participating in an illegal strike against the FAA.[2]

These and various other forms of sexual harassment have been prevalent in the workplace since women first began earning wages. But as with other acts of which women are the victims, such as rape and spouse abuse, both society and the judicial system have preferred to ignore the issue, and if that was impossible, to treat the women as though they had somehow encouraged such behavior. Sexual harassment has always been considered a trivial form of discrimination, if not an acceptable one, and women have been expected to ignore it or to learn to live with it.

Victims of sexual harassment have inevitably found themselves in a no-win situation. Since most of them are in lower-status jobs and their employers are almost always men, they are extremely vulnerable to male sexual aggression and coercion. They can either remain silent in an unbearable work environment or complain and take the risk of losing their jobs (which is usually the case, since they, unlike their supervisors and employers, are considered expendable). Most of those who decide to remain silent eventually quit their jobs.

It was not until the 1970s that working women became more outspoken about the issue and began challenging sexually discriminatory behavior. Sexual harassment became an explosive topic, and talk shows, legal journals, and newspaper columns began exploring the obvious injustices of such practices. Eventually, strong public reactions to sexual harassment led to congressional hearings and civil service investigations as well as the issuance of guidelines by the Equal Employment Opportunity Commission. And in 1976, for the first time a court ruled in favor of a victim of sexual harassment, stating that sexual harassment is in fact a violation of Title VII of the Civil Rights Act.[3]

DEFINING SEXUAL HARASSMENT

Whether or not an act is considered sexual harassment depends on the place and the circumstances. A comment made at a social gathering, such as "I'd feel better if you sat a little closer," can be interpreted as a form of harassment when made in the workplace, say at a board of directors meeting. Statements or actions that undermine a woman's role at her place of employment, affect her ability to do her work, or threaten her job are forms of sexual harassment.

Until sexual harassment became recognized as a violation of Title VII, the courts had problems defining the term, and consequently cases dealing with the issue were handled inconsistently. In 1980, the EEOC, the enforcement agency of sex discrimination matters, issued its guidelines regarding sexual harassment. These guidelines are not regulations but rather interpretations of the law, which are given great deference by the courts. The guidelines define sexual harassment in the following manner:

> Unwelcome sexual advances, requests for sexual favors, and other verbal or physical conduct of a sexual nature constitute sexual harassment when (1) submission to such conduct is made either explicitly or implicitly a term or condition of an individual's employment, (2) submission to or rejection of such conduct by an individual is used as the basis for employment decisions affecting such individual, or (3) such conduct has the purpose or effect of unreasonably interfering with an individual's work performance or creating an intimidating, hostile, or offensive working environment.[4]

The key word in the first line of the definition is "unwelcome." The victim of sexual harassment is unwilling to cooperate or to submit. (1) and (2) refer to actions which affect or threaten to affect the victim's job in some way. This includes hiring policies as well as penalties for those already employed. If the victim does not comply, the harasser may retaliate by refusing her a job, firing her, demoting her, or refusing her a promotion, benefits, or training for which she is qualified. Generally, there must be proof that there has been some adverse change in your employment status for the behavior to be considered harassment. In the majority of cases, this means that the woman has been fired, although demotions and denials of promotions have been considered sufficient by the courts.

The third item in the EEOC guidelines refers to more subtle behavior that does not result in an obvious change in your employment status. This covers such things as continual sexist comments, jokes that denigrate women, and propositions. Even though such behavior is recognized by the guidelines as creating an "intimidating, hostile, or offensive working environment," this form of harassment is difficult to prove in the courtroom. Sexual coercion is easier to prove, since such demands and advances in some way threaten your economic security. It is another thing to produce evidence that your work environment has become unbearable, unless there are other women employees who are willing to substantiate your charges.

The EEOC guidelines clearly state that sexual harassment is determined by the *effect* of the behavior on the victim and her work environment rather than the *intention* of the harasser. In other words, he cannot plead ignorance or suggest that he is not responsible since his intentions were harmless. The guidelines also spell out that an employer is responsible for, and can be held liable for, acts of sexual harassment in the workplace initiated by any of his employees when he or his supervisors are aware of the behavior, or *should* have been aware, unless he can show that he took "immediate and appropriate corrective action."[5]

Unfortunately, the courts have not always followed the guidelines when deciding cases. Some courts have required that it be proven that the employer actually approved of the behavior or that the official policy of the company allows such behavior. Other courts have adopted the position that only passive approval by the employer be shown, or at least knowledge of the behavior. The victim often must prove that the employer had knowledge of the harassment and failed to take action. Employers have gotten off the hook in some cases simply by presenting to the court a written company policy prohibiting sexual harassment. In a few cases, however, employers have been held liable for sexual harassment by their supervisors even when they had no knowledge of it.

As you can see, like other areas of the law the outcome of a case is dependent to a great degree upon the discretion of the court and its interpretation of the law, or in this case, the EEOC guidelines. The following are examples of how the individual courts are dealing with the issue of sexual harassment.

In Tomkins v. Public Service Electric & Gas Co., Ms. Tomkins was denied a promotion and later fired after she rejected the sexual advances of her supervisor and reported the incident to her employer. The court found that the denial of promotion was not a discriminatory act under Title VII and so dismissed that part of the complaint against Ms. Tomkins' supervisor, but found that by ignoring Ms. Tomkins' complaint and firing her, the company had acted in retaliation and in violation of Title VII. The case was appealed, and the decision of the lower court was reversed when the Court of Appeals ruled that the sexual harassment was a valid cause of action under Title VII.[6]

In Miller v. Bank of America, Margaret Miller filed a complaint under Title VII when her refusal to have sexual relations with her supervisor resulted in her dismissal. Even though Ms. Miller had a witness to such behavior, the court regarded the bank's written policy, which did not condone such actions, as more persuasive evidence. It ruled that the bank was not responsible for the supervisor's behavior since Ms. Miller failed to report the incident to her employer. However, the appellate court reversed the decision of the lower court, finding the termination of employment an act of discrimination and holding the employer liable for the actions of its supervisors.[7]

FILING A SEXUAL HARASSMENT COMPLAINT

Many victims of sexual harassment, fearing the consequences of reporting the incident to their employer, decide to keep quiet and when the situation worsens end up leaving their jobs. And while it's true that many women who have filed complaints have been branded as troublemakers and treated unfairly by their supervisors and employers, as well as their co-workers, sexual harassment will continue unless more women start challenging such discriminatory behavior.

As a victim of sexual harassment, there are certain procedures you should follow in filing a complaint. The first step is to attempt to resolve the problem informally. You may, depending on the circumstances, want to confront your harasser with your complaint and demand that he stop the discriminatory behavior. If this method proves unsuccessful, write a letter to your employer, with a copy to the harasser, informing him of the problem and requesting that something be done to put a stop to it. (You will need to keep copies of all correspondence, as it may later be used as evidence that you notified your employer before filing a complaint.)

Some businesses and most unions have their own grievance procedures, which may or may not prove satisfactory to you. In some cases, the victim is not taken seriously, or it will be said that she waited too long to file her complaint. In others, these procedures lead only to a reprimand or to the victim's being demoted or transferred. And there is always the possibility that she will be threatened with slander or libel suits. In any case, prepare yourself for the possibility that your supervisors and co-workers may react strangely to you and in fact may avoid all contact with you. After all, if sexual harassment is common at your place of employment, you will be opening up a can of worms and the guilty parties will want you fired or transferred as soon as possible.

Regardless of who will be investigating the matter, you will need evidence to support your complaint. You should have a list of the occurrences along with the dates and circumstances and the names of those who witnessed the behavior. If at all possible, arrange to have witnesses corroborate your charge. Often, other victims are willing to support such a complaint and to provide details of their own experiences with the harasser once someone else has decided to take action. In addition, you may want to consider recording one of your encounters with your harasser. Or if you have any correspondence relating to the matter or any documents that might support your claim, have them ready.

Once your evidence is gathered, you will probably want to consult with an attorney before proceeding, as procedures may vary depending on the circumstances. She will be able to advise you and to inform you of any state antidiscrimination laws that may apply to your situation. If the internal grievance procedure proves unsatisfactory or if no such procedures are available, you will have to decide whether you wish to take legal action. If you decide to pursue the matter, you will need to file a complaint with a state or local agency, assuming that either your state or city has its own laws regarding sexual harassment. At the same time, you can file a complaint with the Equal Employment Opportunity Commission, informing them that you have simultaneously filed with a state or local agency, and request that the EEOC automatically assume jurisdiction once the agency has completed its investigation. You must file within 180 days after the internal grievance procedure has been completed. If neither internal grievance procedures nor state or city laws apply to your situation, you can file immediately with the EEOC (or within 180 days of the incident). The procedures, time limits, and remedies are the same as those outlined in chapter 11 (pp. 121-24).

The EEOC has 180 days after receipt of your complaint to complete its investigation. If it fails to act on the complaint within that time period, you can request a "right-to-sue letter," which authorizes you to file a civil suit on your own. Even if the EEOC investigates and determines that your case is invalid, it will still provide you with a right-to-sue letter. If you decide to take the matter to court, you must file your suit within 90 days of receiving the letter. As with other sex discrimination complaints, your attorney or the EEOC may be allowed to file a class action and represent all of the complainants at the same time.

The decision to bring a sexual harassment suit is a difficult one to make. The harsh reality is that most women find themselves, rather than their harassers, treated as the guilty party, the troublemaker. They are often faced with skepticism and insensitivity on the part of their employers, their co-workers, and even judges. All too often, the courts have trivialized the problem of sexual harassment, and their rulings have on many occasions shown their inclination to view it as a personal matter not serious enough to warrant litigation. In addition, it is often difficult to find an attorney who is willing to take on a sexual harassment case, since the chances of winning are slight. Apart from all of these drawbacks, one must consider that a lawsuit takes a great deal of time, money, and commitment.

Nevertheless, the situation is improving as more and more women are refusing to be forced out of their jobs through intimidating, sexist behavior and have committed themselves to the task of eliminating sex discrimination from the workplace. As more sexual harassment suits are being brought and women dedicated to correcting discriminatory practices continue to enter the legal profession in large numbers, the courts are beginning to recognize how widespread and serious the problem is and the degree to which working women have been exploited. And if recognition of the problem causes the courts to reevaluate their attitudes toward victims of sexual harassment, perhaps this most humiliating form of discrimination will no longer be commonplace.

The following organizations offer further information on sexual harassment:

Working Women's Institute
593 Park Avenue
New York, NY 10021

Alliance Against Sexual Coercion
P.O. Box 1
Cambridge, MA 01239

Women Organized Against Sexual Harassment
2437 Edwards St.
Berkeley, CA 94702

13
Rape

There was a knock at the door. It was 8 o'clock at night and Anne was alone. Peering out the window, she saw a man wearing political buttons and carrying campaign literature. Anne, who had only recently moved to the neighborhood, remembered having seen him in front of one of the houses down the street only a few days before and so opened the door, thinking he must be one of her neighbors. The man introduced himself and asked if he could take a few minutes of her time to discuss several political issues related to the upcoming election. Once they entered the living room, he threatened Anne with a gun and forced her to submit to sexual intercourse while he held the weapon to her head. Then he tied her up and threatened to return if she called the police.

Every day there are women who find themselves in situations similar to Anne's. Rape is the fastest growing violent crime in the United States. In fact, according to the Justice Department's Bureau of Justice Statistics, in 1983 every crime included in the National Crime Survey showed a decline except rape, which increased.

Most women, either consciously or unconsciously, live in fear of rape. This fear often influences their decisions regarding where they live, what parts of town they're willing to go to when they're alone, and what times of the day or night they're willing to leave their homes. They are uneasy about taking walks in their own neighborhoods, going from their cars to their offices or homes, and driving alone on long stretches of highway. To some extent, women have become prisoners; they are not able to move about as freely as men do.

Whenever women have been victimized, whether through discrimination, sexual harassment, wife beating, or rape, society has tended to view the matter as a personal problem, to be resolved in private. This attitude results from a number of misconceptions about female victims that have existed for centuries and have only recently been challenged. The most obvious myth related to rape is the traditional belief that women are to blame for men's sexual aggression, that they instigate such behavior by their provocative clothing and actions or by having the audacity to walk unaccompanied down a street at night instead of staying at home. Beyond this, it has been generally accepted that when a woman says "no" she really means "yes" and that more often than not she eventually will submit.

Other widely held misconceptions involve the rapist himself. Until statistics proved otherwise, it was assumed that most rapists were unknown to their victims, to some degree mentally deranged, and driven by an uncontrollable sexual urge. In fact, the majority of reported rapes are committed by men the victims know—acquaintances, relatives, or friends. Most rapists are of the same race and age group as their victims, and are often from the same neighborhood and of the same social status. Furthermore, the majority appear to be normal, functioning members of society. Research has shown that rape is not motivated by uncontrollable lust but rather by a deep-seated hostility toward women and a desire to overpower and degrade someone weaker than themselves. Rape is a crime of violence rather than of passion. This fact becomes obvious when one considers that most rapes are planned in advance and that the victims are often elderly or disabled women and young children.

Anyone who has read case histories is overcome with the brutality and psychological injuries that are inflicted upon the victims of rape. They are humiliated and degraded, often beaten and tortured, and sometimes murdered. Almost all are left with permanent emotional scars. With these things in mind, let us look in the light of day at the legal realities of rape.

DEFINING RAPE

Rape is a crime in all states, although some classify it as sexual assault or unlawful sexual intercourse. While it was once considered a capital crime, punishable by death, sentences for convicted rapists now range anywhere from a year to life, and only in rare cases is the death penalty imposed. Some state statutes specify various degrees of rape, each with its own minimum and maximum sentences. These are determined by such factors as the amount of force used, the mental capacity of the victim, the presence of intoxicants, and threats of bodily injury or death. Rape was defined by English common law as the unlawful carnal knowledge of a female by force and against her will, a definition that is still used today. The three basic elements of this crime are: carnal knowledge, the absence of consent, and the presence of force.

Carnal Knowledge

According to case law, carnal knowledge has come to mean bodily knowledge or actual physical contact of the sex organs and penetration of the female by the male "no matter how slight." In the past, this definition was limited to genital copulation, but presently many states have revised their laws to include oral and anal contact and the use of objects. Neither the completion of the sex act nor emission is necessary from a legal standpoint, although rape may be more difficult to prove without evidence of semen. In Neal v. the State of Georgia,[1] the defendant appealed his rape conviction, using the argument that no evidence had been presented that semen was found in the vagina of the victim. The court denied the appeal, stating that the statute did not require the emission of semen as evidence that rape had occurred but only evidence that force had been used.

Consent

The second element, the absence of the victim's consent, refers to three conditions. In order to prove rape, it must be shown that: 1) either the woman was legally capable of consenting and did not or she was legally incapable of giving consent, 2) that she resisted as much as was possible under the circumstances, and 3) that her resistance was overcome by force or threat of force. According to the law, those who are incapable of consenting to sexual intercourse include women who are extremely intoxicated, drugged, unconscious, mentally incompetent, or below the age of consent (specified by state law). If a woman is legally incapable of giving consent, the act of sexual intercourse is rape.

In the case of females who are below the age of consent, the act is rape even if consent was given, as the courts generally assume that underage females are too young to understand the possible consequences of the act. Sexual intercourse with a female who is below the age of consent is called statutory rape.

If a woman is insane or mentally deranged, she is considered incapable of consenting. The determination that a victim of rape is legally incapable of consenting is based on evidence that she lacks the ability to understand the nature of the act and its possible consequences. In Commonwealth v. Carter,[2] the defendant appealed a rape conviction, claiming he was unaware of the fact that the victim, a patient at a state home for the mentally retarded, was so deranged as to be legally incapable of consenting. The court ruled that the defendant should have assumed that the woman was incapable of consenting since she was institutionalized.

Rape cannot occur if there is no force or threat of force, unless a woman is legally incapable of giving consent. In addition, when deciding whether a woman consented to the sexual act, the court will rely on evidence that the victim resisted as much as was possible under the circumstances. If her life or safety was not threatened and she offered no physical resistance, it may be determined that she in fact consented. Furthermore, even if force is used, the victim must, in most cases, have resisted up to the point where she was in fear of serious bodily injury or death.

Force

To prove that rape has occurred, it must be shown that the victim's resistance was overcome by force or a threat of serious bodily injury or death. Usually, the courts recognize that threats may be inferred by a man's conduct or actions as well as by his words. When determining whether force was used, the courts consider such things as the suspect's height, weight, and strength compared to those of the victim, the degree of bodily injury that was threatened, and the presence of weapons at the scene. In Michigan, the courts require physical force, the threat of force or of future retaliation, or evidence of an unethical medical examination or treatment. Kentucky uses the term *forcible compulsion* and requires that the attacker overcame resistance by placing the victim in fear of death, physical injury, or kidnapping.

In People v. Dorsey,[3] a 5-foot, 130-pound woman was raped by a 5-foot, 7-inch man weighing 220 pounds. The victim testified that she was confronted in an elevator that her attacker had stalled. The defendant used no physical force and made no threats until after the act was completed, when he told her he would retaliate if she called the police. The victim did not cry out for help, as she felt no one would hear her. The defense argued that since no physical force had been used, the act was not rape, but the court ruled in favor of the victim, stating that in view of their difference in size and strength and the fact that the victim was trapped in a stalled elevator with no way of retreating, force was *implied* and the victim had offered reasonable resistance.

In another, rather bizarre case, Fitzpatrick v. the State of Nevada,[4] the defendant was charged with forcible rape and extortion. According to the testimony, Michael Fitzpatrick, who had recently been released from prison, told the fiancée of one of his former fellow inmates that he would arrange to have the man killed by members of a crime syndicate unless she would agree to pay him $1,000 and have sexual intercourse with him. The Supreme Court ruled that the threat against the victim's fiancé constituted constructive force sufficient to prove rape and that under the circumstances the victim could not be expected to offer physical resistance.

Resistance

Because it is so often difficult or impossible to prove that the victim did not consent to sexual intercourse, the courts generally require some type of evidence showing that she offered a certain degree of resistance. Traditionally, most courts would allow a rape conviction only if the victim could demonstrate that she had resisted "to the utmost" of her ability, but this requirement no longer stands in the majority of states. The degree of resistance required varies from state to state, although, generally, the victim must have offered as much genuine resistance as could be reasonably expected under the circumstances. The degree of force used, threats of bodily injury or death, the presence of weapons, and the degree to which escape would be possible are all considered when determining the amount of resistance required to prove rape. In most states, active rather than passive resistance is required, although the courts generally agree that active resistance is not necessary if the crime involved a deadly weapon or the victim had reason to believe that her cries for help or physical resistance would only jeopardize her life. If it is shown that physical resistance would have been futile, the victim need have offered only the amount of resistance that would demonstrate her refusal to consent.

Unfortunately, many courts continue to view the victim's spoken refusal to submit as insufficient resistance. Consequently, in order for a rape conviction to be sustained, she often must present evidence that suggests she resisted and that the resistance was overcome by force or violence. The most convincing evidence, of course, is proof that the victim suffered physical injuries.

Many states recognize several degrees of rape, such as "forcible rape—resistance required" and "forcible rape—resistance prevented by threats." The type of rape charge to be brought against a suspect is determined by such factors as the amount of force or violence that was exhibited or the condition of the victim at the time of the rape (intoxicated, unconscious, or mentally ill). The amount of resistance offered by the victim is another determining factor. Each type of charge carries its own minimum and maximum sentences.

ACTS OF SELF-DEFENSE

Whether or not a woman should attempt to defend herself against possible rape or physical injury is a difficult question to answer. In the past, women were often warned against using self-defense, the argument being that most women are brought up to be nonaggressive, are not trained in self-defense, and are not physically strong enough to protect themselves against men. Apart from this, there is the possibility that a weapon may be forced out of a woman's hand and used against her or the attempt to use a weapon might incite the attacker to greater violence. On the other hand, some studies have found that a high percentage of women who do defend themselves are able to avoid rape. Obviously each situation is different, and every woman confronted by a rapist must make the decision for herself based on the specific circumstances.

Generally, a victim has the following rights regarding self-defense:

— She may legally resist the force of a rapist with like force. In other words, if the victim is held at gun point, she may legally use a gun to protect herself.

— She may use a deadly weapon only if she has reason to believe that she is in immediate danger of being killed or seriously injured. In many states, the victim must be able to show that she had reasonable cause to believe serious injury or death was impending.

— She may use only the degree of force that is necessary to prevent the assault. If no weapon is used by the attacker and no threat of physical harm is made, or if the victim fails to escape when she has the opportunity to do so safely, she may not use deadly force against him.

— She may not use force in retaliation, that is, when she is no longer in fear for her life or safety.[5]

When deciding whether a victim's act of self-defense was legal, the court considers several factors: the amount of force and violence displayed by the attacker, the point at which the victim used force against him, and the degree to which the victim believed she was in imminent danger of death or serious injury. What has made it especially difficult to justify a woman's use of self-defense is that the courts' standard of meeting deadly force with deadly force is based on *men's* perception of a life-threatening situation. A petite, unarmed woman who has no self-defense skills may very well consider the fist of a 6-foot, 200-pound male a deadly weapon. Yet the courts often fail to take a woman's perception of danger into consideration.

RAPE BY THE HUSBAND

In the majority of states, rape of a woman by her husband is not a crime. Despite the fact that many states have revised their rape laws in recent years to cover sexual attacks by spouses, the reality is that the law offers little protection for female victims. Alabama, Louisiana, South Dakota, Vermont, and West Virginia refuse to recognize spousal rape charges under any circumstances. And even in states that do have marital rape laws, the majority require that the woman be living apart from her husband, legally separated, to have arranged for protection orders, or to have initiated divorce proceedings (or a combination of these) before she can press charges. Some states do not recognize rape even when a woman is sexually attacked by her husband when she is living apart from him and has already filed for divorce. "Legal rape," as it is often referred to, generally extends to those who live together while unmarried. Most states, at least with regard to rape laws, view the cohabitating couple as legally married. In other words, the courts in the majority of states consider it legally impossible for a man to rape a woman while they reside together.

Only in the following states is marital rape a crime:[6]

Arkansas	Iowa	New Jersey
California	Kansas	North Dakota
Connecticut	Massachusetts	Oregon
District of Columbia	Minnesota	Virginia
Florida	Mississippi	Washington
Georgia	Nebraska	Wisconsin
Illinois	New Hampshire	Wyoming

In these states, a husband can be prosecuted even if he and his wife share the same residence.

That marital rape is excluded from most states' rape laws is not surprising when one considers that U.S. legal codes are based on English common law, which viewed women as the property of their husbands. Many of our laws continue to reinforce the stereotype of women as submissive, dependent, and second-class citizens. According to common law, a married woman is assumed to have consented to have sex with her husband under any and all conditions and to submit to his will at all times. Apart from this, since common law viewed the husband and wife as "legally one," with the husband as superior, a wife could not be called to testify against him, let alone bring charges against him.

Only in recent years has the obvious injustice of allowing women to be physically abused and raped by their husbands been challenged. In 1978, the subject of marital rape received national attention with the highly publicized Rideout trial in Oregon. Greta Rideout was the first woman in the United States to bring marital rape charges while residing with her husband. When the jury acquitted him and the couple were later briefly reconciled, the news media had a heyday, many accounts falsely construing the acquittal as proof that a rape charge could not successfully be brought against a husband.

In State v. Smith,[7] the New Jersey Supreme Court held that the rape statute allowed the husband to be charged with marital rape. At the time of the attack, the wife was living apart from her husband; in fact she had lived in another city for nearly a year. Her husband broke into her home, threatened and beat her, and then forced her to have sexual intercourse.

Before a victim of marital rape can press charges, generally she must move out of her home or convince her husband to move. In addition, she often must request a protection order, which prohibits the husband from threatening or abusing her. These court orders usually are issued only to women who are legally married and petitioning for divorce. In many states, the husband and wife must be legally separated before charges can be brought. Even in states that recognize marital rape, it may be necessary to file assault charges instead, if these requirements are not met.

Should a woman be successful in her attempt to bring charges against her husband, additional obstacles confront her as she becomes involved in the legal proceedings:

— As is true of battered spouses, those who bring spousal rape charges are often taken less seriously than those who are raped or attacked by strangers. Once again, when women are victimized in their own homes, the problem is often considered a personal matter to be resolved outside the courtroom.

— The police are hesitant to respond to domestic violence calls, which is understandable, as such situations are usually extremely volatile and dangerous, and women often refuse to press charges against their spouses.

— Prosecutors often are unwilling or unable, because of the strict requirements, to charge husbands with rape.

— Juries tend to be skeptical when a woman presses charges against her husband, unless she has suffered serious physical injury.

The bottom line here of course is the traditional "woman as property" concept, which persists in our laws and in the judicial system. Such attitudes are slow to change, but the situation is improving somewhat as some states are beginning to recognize the need to pass legislation to protect women against rape and other physical abuse by their husbands. The next step of course is to ensure that these laws are enforced.

Rape crisis centers and battered women's shelters have been set up in most cities; they are listed in your telephone directory, and most have 24-hour hotlines. For additional information, contact:

National Clearinghouse on Marital Rape
Women's History Research Center
2325 Oak Street
Berkeley, California 94708
(415) 548-1770

WHAT TO DO IF YOU ARE RAPED

Rape is a terrifying and painful experience that leaves its victims feeling degraded, traumatized, helpless, and angry. At a time when she is most disoriented, the victim is expected to remain calm and rational. The fact is that rape is the most difficult felony to prove, and thus the woman must be as composed as possible so that she can provide the information necessary to capture and prosecute the rapist. Every victim of rape must judge for herself how best to escape from her assailant. Once she is out of immediate danger, she may want to consider screaming as loudly as she can to alert neighbors or passers-by, who may be able to identify the rapist for the police. By calling out, she may also dispel any doubt on the part of the police or the court that she was actually attacked.

In order to preserve any evidence that may exist, it is imperative that the victim do nothing to alter the scene of the attack. She must not change her clothing, shower, or clean, move, or touch any item that may later be used as evidence. And she must instruct anyone who comes to her assistance to refrain from disturbing any items that may contain fingerprints.

If you have been raped, get to a telephone as soon as possible and call a rape crisis center or women's center immediately. Most communities have at least one organization set up to aid rape victims (you will find the number listed in your telephone directory or the operator will assist you). Most rape crisis centers have 24-hour hotlines, and their counselors are extremely helpful to the victim, offering much-needed emotional support as well as advice on the medical and legal aspects of the crime. Often the center will arrange for one of its workers to stay with you during the police investigation and accompany you to a hospital and to court.

It would be unwise to attempt to handle the matter by yourself. You will need someone by your side for emotional support as well as a person who will defend your rights and see to it that the police investigation is thorough and proper. You will probably want to arrange for a friend or a member of your family to stay with you during the police investigation. At this point, you may also want to call your attorney (if you do not have an attorney you can call, the rape crisis center will recommend one). Although if you decide to press charges the district attorney or prosecutor's office will be representing you in court, you may still want to discuss the matter with a private attorney. He can observe the police investigation to ensure that your rights are protected and that none of the evidence is mishandled or destroyed and advise you as to whether you should pursue prosecution if your attacker is apprehended.

If you decide to report the rape to the police, you should do so immediately after making your other calls. The rape crisis center or your attorney can explain how reports of rape are handled by the police in your community. In making your decision, there are several things that should be considered: 1) in some states, it will be assumed that you are willing to press charges against your assailant if you report the rape to the police; in others, an investigation will be made but you need not press charges unless you sign a formal complaint; 2) if a rape victim fails to report the incident immediately, she often faces skepticism on the part of the police and the court as to whether the rape actually occurred; 3) if you decide not to contact the police and later change your mind, the chances of your attacker being apprehended are slim.

A high percentage of rapes are never reported, which is not surprising when one considers the following:

- The police, prosecutors, and the courts have traditionally been insensitive and unsympathetic in their dealings with rape victims.
- Rape is almost always difficult to prove.
- Rape is one of the least punished crimes; even if apprehended, there is a good chance that the rapist will not be convicted.
- The majority of victims are raped by someone they know, which makes it even more difficult to prove lack of consent.
- In many cases, victims of rape have been subjected to humiliation and vicious cross-examination on the witness stand.

On the other hand, it is also true that the majority of rapists go on to assault other women unless they are incarcerated and that only by pursuing convictions will increased sexual assaults against women be prevented. Somewhat encouraging is the fact that many states have revised their rape laws and others are in the process of doing so; if these laws are actually enforced and if the police authorities and courts continue to be pressured to treat rape victims with more sensitivity, it should become less difficult to prosecute and convict rapists.

The Medical Examination

Before the police begin their investigation, they should arrange to have you taken to a hospital or doctor's office for a medical examination. Of course if you have suffered serious physical injury, the first person to arrive at the scene of the attack should immediately call for an ambulance, in which case the police will prepare their report after you have been treated and are capable of responding to their questions. You may request that a female police officer be present during the examination and that a friend or a counselor from the rape crisis center accompany you to the hospital.

The medical examination will generally consist of the following:

— The doctor will ask you specific questions about the rape and any injuries you may have.

— She will document your physical condition in a medical report, identifying any scratches, wounds, or bruises, and any internal injuries.

— She will conduct several tests and a pelvic examination to check for the presence and activity of sperm, internal injuries, venereal disease, and pregnancy.

— She will administer medication or injections for the prevention of venereal disease and pregnancy.

— She will check for any other physical evidence that may later be used in prosecution, such as scrapings from under your fingernails.

Because some of the tests require laboratory analysis, you will not be immediately informed of the results. You should schedule an appointment with your own doctor to verify the hospital's findings and for any further treatment of injuries that may be necessary. Request that the hospital and your doctor provide you with copies of their reports.

The Police Investigation

The purpose of the police investigation is to obtain whatever evidence is available from the victim, the scene of the attack, and any witnesses in order to apprehend the suspect. All of this information will appear in a detailed written report which will later be used by the district attorney or prosecutor.

This process can be extremely difficult and frustrating for the victim, who has just been traumatized, humiliated, and possibly physically injured and now must relive the experience and respond to hours of questioning. This is only the first step in the legal process: from this moment until the completion of the trial, the victim will be confronting a male-dominated legal system whose authorities cannot possibly understand women's fear of rape or the feelings of the victim. In some cities, special units have been organized to investigate sex crimes. Often these officers are specially trained to conduct investigations in a proper and professional manner and to be sympathetic in their treatment of rape victims. This, plus the fact that many of these units are staffed by female officers, represents a positive change in the way police are dealing with victims of rape. If no such crime unit exists in your community, you have the right to request that a female police officer be present during the investigation.

It is important to remember that, should the case end up in court, whatever information you volunteer to the police during the investigation becomes a part of the written report that will be used at the trial and that the officers will be called to testify as to their observations. The more information you can provide the police, the better the chance that they will be able to apprehend the rapist and that he will be prosecuted. Most rapists have established patterns of operation—they may return to the same neighborhood, attack only at a particular time of day or night, approach their victims in a certain manner, or carry a particular weapon. A "60 Minutes" segment on rape showed how one rapist always removed the bedroom screens several days before he assaulted his victims. You may be able to supply information that conforms to a pattern of a certain suspect in other rapes and thus aid the police in identifying him.

The police may ask you to reenact the assault. You may be taken back to the scene of the attack if it occurred in a place other than your home and asked to recall the event in as much detail as possible. The types of questions you may be asked at this point are:

— What time did the attack occur?
— Give a description of the surroundings—the type of weather, the visibility, etc.
— Exactly where did the rape occur?
— Did the rapist threaten to injure or kill you?
— Was he carrying a weapon? Can you describe it?
— Can you describe the rapist—his height, weight, color of hair and eyes, distinctive features or speech patterns, race, clothing, etc? Is he someone you know?
— Did you notice any other persons in the vicinity?
— Did the rapist take any personal item of yours with him when he left?

Apart from questions relating directly to the rape, the police may inquire about other subjects of a more personal nature—regarding your use of drugs and alcohol, the type of clothes you were wearing at the time of the attack, any hostile feelings you may have toward men in general, your past sexual relationships, any contact you may have had with the rapist before the attack, any previous reports of rape or other crimes, or any history of mental illness in your family. Not every investigation will include all of these questions, but in some areas it is standard procedure. You can see why it is recommended that you have a friend, and preferably your attorney as well, with you during questioning. A common complaint made by victims of rape is that they, rather than the rapist, are treated as the guilty party—the one who *provoked* the attack. And the questioning by the police is only a hint of what will likely occur in the courtroom if the assailant is arrested. You will have to remind yourself throughout the process that you are not the one on trial, although it may seem otherwise at times. You are not required to answer any questions the police may pose regarding your past sex life, as it has nothing to do with the fact that you were raped, but apart from those questions which you feel are improper and no one's business but your own, do your best to be cooperative and to furnish the police with whatever information they feel will aid them in arresting the rapist.

The police will collect whatever physical evidence can be found. In almost all cases, the law requires evidence that supports the victim's testimony. The following are examples of the types of evidence that may be used to prosecute a suspected rapist:

— the victim's bruises, scratches, blood, etc.
— the victim's clothing, bed sheets, etc.
— overturned or damaged furniture or any other physical damage that suggests violence and force were used
— hair, blood, or skin specimens and fingerprints of the rapist
— any articles left behind by the rapist, such as a button, a piece of clothing or jewelry, or a weapon
— results from the medical examination which indicate the presence of semen and internal and external injuries

The more evidence that is collected the better the chance the rapist will be apprehended, prosecuted, and convicted. Not every bit of evidence will necessarily be admitted in court; for any number of reasons, the judge may refuse to admit certain items as evidence.

The police will question those who may have witnessed the rape, often going from door to door in search of anyone who was in the vicinity who may be able to identify the rapist or his car or who heard or saw anything out of the ordinary. Once the police have concluded their questioning and the collection of evidence, they may ask you to sign a complaint indicating that you want to press charges. Request that you receive a copy of the police report and that photographs be taken of any physical injuries you incurred as well as the scene of the attack, especially if it suggests that a struggle took place. If the police do not take photographs, ask a friend or your attorney to. If you are asked to take a polygraph test, check with your attorney or the rape crisis center to see if your state laws require you to take it. In many states you are not under any legal obligation to comply, although you may want to take the test if there is little evidence to corroborate your account of the attack.

The police may also request that you go through mug shots of those who are suspected or known sex offenders or that you observe a lineup in an attempt to identify the rapist. In some cases, the police will prepare a composite sketch of the rapist from your description. If a suspect is apprehended, the police will question him and if there is sufficient evidence to suggest that he committed the crime, he will be arrested.

THE DECISION TO PROSECUTE

Because rape is considered a crime against the state, such cases are handled by the district attorney or the public prosecutor, who represents the interests of the state. Whether or not a suspected rapist is prosecuted depends on the decision made by the prosecutor, which to a great extent is based on his own discretion. Prosecutors are not required to prosecute every case; the American Bar Association defines the prosecutor's duty as one of seeking justice, not merely convicting. Although you may want to consult with your own attorney and request that he be present at the trial, the presentation of the case in court is the responsibility of the prosecutor.

In making the decision as to whether a suspect should be prosecuted, the district attorney or prosecutor will consider the following: 1) does he believe that the suspect is guilty? 2) is there sufficient evidence to prove his guilt? 3) does he anticipate any difficulties in the courtroom, such as a witness being unable or unwilling to testify, or certain evidence not being admitted? and 4) would prosecution be within the public interest? Even if he is convinced of the suspect's guilt, the prosecutor must objectively analyze the evidence to determine whether there is a good chance a jury will convict him. If the suspect's constitutional rights were violated during or after the arrest (for example, if his Miranda Rights were not given before questioning), he may automatically reject the case, in spite of the fact that there is sufficient evidence to prove his guilt. In addition, the prosecutor must base his decision in large part on the degree to which the victim is willing to cooperate—will she be able and willing to present convincing and consistent testimony before a jury? is she strong enough to withstand the emotional stress of a trial and cross-examination in particular? and is she determined to pursue the matter, despite possible delays and postponements of hearings? After weighing all of these considerations, the prosecutor must decide if prosecution is in the public's best interest; that is, is it likely to result in conviction or would it be a waste of the taxpayers' money to pursue the matter?

Rape is one of the most difficult crimes to prove. A great many offenders are never apprehended, but even when they are, a large percentage are never prosecuted. And of those who are prosecuted, very few are convicted. It is especially difficult to convict a rapist when he is an acquaintance of the victim—a present or former boyfriend, a boss, or a neighbor. When victims know their rapists, juries frequently come to the conclusion that the woman must have been agreeable to sexual relations or that she may have had a motive for wrongfully accusing him of rape. And if she was raped by someone she had gone on a date with or had a drink with in a bar, someone she invited into her apartment, or a boss whom she agreed to work with after regular hours, the chances are slim that a jury will convict him. It all comes down to the matter of consent. A jury is much more sympathetic toward a woman who was accosted by a stranger than one who was *allegedly* raped by someone she knows. Unfortunately, this means that for many women who report rape, conviction is doubtful, since most rapes are committed by men who are acquainted with their victims.

Should the decision be made to prosecute, the next step is to determine what charge should be brought against the suspect. Most states recognize different types of charges, each with its own maximum and minimum sentence. The normal practice is to charge the highest offense substantiated by the evidence, but the prosecutor may consider bringing a lesser charge for one or more of the following reasons: a more serious charge may take a much longer time to reach trial, since there is usually a backlog of cases to be heard, while a lesser charge usually results in an earlier trial; by the time a higher charge is brought to trial, witnesses may have left town, died, decided against testifying, or have forgotten or become confused about the details of the incident; and a jury is much more likely to convict when the sentence is shorter, particularly if the defendant has no previous record.

During your discussions with the prosecutor, be sure that he explains to you exactly what he expects will transpire in the courtroom. He should outline the evidence he plans to present, the types of questions he will ask you, and those he expects the defense to ask during cross-examination. The prosecutor undoubtedly will inquire about your prior sexual relations, and in this case it is advisable that you cooperate. In order to prepare the case, the prosecutor will need to have as much information as possible so that he can anticipate those aspects most likely to create doubt about the defendant's guilt. He will want you to be prepared for the types of questions the defense may raise and will need to weigh the likely impact that your testimony regarding your past sex life will have on a jury. Even in those states that restrict the admissibility of testimony related to the victim's prior sexual relations, some evidence may still be admissible, depending on the circumstances of the case and the discretion of the judge.

GOING TO COURT

Pre-Trial Procedures

The prosecutor's investigation is only the first step in bringing a case to trial. Generally, these procedures are followed once the suspect has been arrested:

The suspect is informed of the charges and of his right to have an attorney represent him. The judge sets bail, and the defendant is given the opportunity to make application for release upon payment of the bail.

The purpose of the PRELIMINARY HEARING is to establish the factual basis for the rape charge and, in some states, to screen cases before they go to the grand jury. In some jurisdictions, the grand jury takes the place of the preliminary hearing. If a preliminary hearing is required, the prosecutor will present only the amount of evidence necessary to bind the case over, so as not to reveal facts that may further the defense attorney's case. Generally, the standard of proof is less strict than at trial, so it may be necessary to have only the victim testify and to establish the identity of the defendant. If a witness for the prosecution will be unable to attend the trial, she likely will be asked to testify at the preliminary hearing so as to preserve the evidence.

GRAND JURY proceedings either follow or replace the preliminary hearing, and are similar to a trial. The purpose is to ascertain whether there is probable cause to believe the defendant committed rape. The standard of proof is usually greater than that of the preliminary hearing but less than that of the trial, where guilt beyond a reasonable doubt must be proven. Witnesses may be called. If the grand jury finds sufficient evidence for a trial, it issues an indictment.

At the ARRAIGNMENT, the defendant must enter a plea of guilty or not guilty. At this stage, the prosecutor and the defense attorney may consider plea negotiations, whereby they discuss the possibility of dismissing or reducing the charges against the defendant. If agreement is reached that the defendant will plead guilty to a lesser charge, there will be no trial and the judge will impose a sentence. If the defendant pleads not guilty, a trial date will be set.

The Trial

All criminal trials proceed in the same manner. Once the jury has been selected, both the prosecutor and the attorney for the defense will make opening statements, giving a brief summary of the case and what they intend to prove. The prosecutor presents his case first. Generally, "background witnesses," including those who witnessed the rape, are called to testify as to the location, time, date, and special circumstances of the crime, followed by the testimony of medical experts (including the physician who examined the victim), the police officers who investigated the crime, and the victim herself. The prosecutor will introduce as evidence any items discovered during the investigation that corroborate the victim's charge—items of clothing, a weapon, fingerprints, and police and medical reports. The defense attorney will have an opportunity to cross-examine each of the witnesses for the prosecution, attempting to discredit their testimony by pointing out inconsistencies or conflicting statements.

When the prosecution has concluded its presentation, the defense will present its case. As witnesses are called or recalled for cross-examination, the defense attorney will endeavor to prove the innocence of the defendant in one of three ways—by showing that 1) the victim was mistaken in her identification of the rapist, 2) the victim consented to sexual intercourse, or 3) there was no sexual intercourse between the parties (the ulterior motive theory). In most cases, the defendant will testify, although he has the right to remain silent. When all the evidence has been presented and the prosecution has cross-examined, the prosecutor and the defense attorney will give their closing arguments to the jury, each attempting to show how the evidence proves or fails to prove the elements necessary for a rape conviction. Then the judge will instruct the jury on the law as it applies to this particular case, and the jury will decide whether the defendant is guilty or not guilty.

Most women find the following aspects of the trial the most difficult to deal with:

Publicity. Unless the prosecutor requests that the trial be closed to the public and that your name and address not be given to the media, the case may be publicized and your identity disclosed on news programs and in the newspapers. The judge may or may not grant the request.

Skepticism. From the time the rape is reported until the final day of the trial, a victim often is made to feel as though *she* is the guilty party. After surviving the often humiliating questioning by the police, the prosecutor, and the defense attorney, she may be unfortunate enough to have the case heard by a jury that concludes she must have somehow provoked the defendant or, if he is an acquaintance, that she falsely accused him to get back at him for some reason. Unless a victim has suffered serious physical injury, juries are reluctant to convict.

Inadmissibility of Previous Offenses. In most cases, a defendant's previous criminal record will not be admitted as evidence, even if he has been accused or convicted of numerous sex crimes in the past. The courts do not admit such evidence simply to prove the defendant's criminal nature, although they may admit it if it shows a specific plan or scheme of attack that conforms to the present crime or if the identity of the rapist is at issue. When defendants are convicted, however, their prior criminal records are almost always considered in sentencing.

Admissibility of Evidence of the Victim's Prior Sexual Activity. Although many states have revised their rape evidence rules to prohibit questions concerning the victim's sexual history, for any number of reasons the judge may allow such questioning. Some of these rules simply are not enforced. Even when they are, certain exceptions are made if the judge finds the information relevant to the case. For example, if the victim was raped by someone she knows, she can be questioned about previous relations with him, or if the prosecution has produced evidence of semen, pregnancy, or venereal disease, it is likely that the defense will be allowed to question the victim about her sex life in order to show that she could have had intercourse with some other man prior to reporting rape. In states that restrict such questioning, it is common procedure for the judge to conduct a private hearing away from the jury to determine whether the evidence should be admitted.

CIVIL SUITS

Apart from criminal prosecution, the victim has the right to file a civil suit against the rapist as well, suing for damages resulting from the rape. These may include compensation for physical injuries, mental anguish, and expenses (such as lost wages and medical bills). Civil suits may also be brought against a third party whose negligence contributed to the rape, such as a landlord, hotel owner, or employer. An example of this is Connie Francis' highly publicized lawsuit against Howard Johnson's, in which she was awarded $1.5 million in damages. The court found the hotel's locks and security system to be insufficient and contributory to the rape. The disadvantages of filing a civil suit are that they often take years to resolve and you will have to pay an attorney to represent you in court.

The following organizations offer further information and assistance for rape victims:

National Center on Women and Family Law
799 Broadway
New York, NY 10003

National Center for Prevention and Control of Rape
600 Fishers Lane
Rockville, MD 20857
(301) 445-1910

National Women's Health Network
2025 I St., N.W., Suite 105
Washington, DC 20006
(202) 223-6887

Center for Women Policy Studies
2000 P St., N.W.
Washington, DC 20036

National Criminal Justice Reference Service
P.O. Box 6000
Rockville, MD 20850
(202) 862-2900

14 Battered Women

According to English common law, upon which our present legal system is based, wives were considered the property of their husbands. Because men were viewed as the head of the family, the provider and protector, they were allowed by law to discipline and punish their wives and children as they saw fit. Although the law did not actually condone physical violence against a spouse, it offered little protection to the battered wife.

It was not until the early 1970s that the issue of battered women was brought to national attention by feminists and various women's organizations. For the first time the problem was identified as a legal issue, rather than a personal matter to be resolved behind closed doors. Wife beating is a criminal offense in every state, although it may be classified as assault and battery rather than spouse abuse or wife beating. The terms and definitions vary from state to state, but the crime generally involves a forceful and violent attempt to cause bodily injury. Most states classify assault in several degrees, such as assault with a deadly weapon, aggravated assault, and assault with intent to commit murder. Although assault is actually a threat of physical attack, and battery the carrying out of the threat, the two terms are often combined in legal usage. Some states have recently enacted legislation that designates wife beating or spouse abuse as a separate crime category; in other states battered women have recourse only through the various assault and battery laws, which do not refer to the relationship of the perpetrator and the victim. In those states that do recognize wife beating, the offense also applies to former husbands and present and former boyfriends.

The problem with these laws, as with others relating to crimes against women, is that they are rarely enforced. Traditional attitudes concerning women, especially married women, are reflected in our laws and in the justice system, which results in reluctance on the part of police officers, prosecutors, the courts, and members of society to interfere in "family matters." Crimes involving the family unit are considered less serious than those perpetrated by strangers, evidenced by the few cases in which husbands have been prosecuted for beating their wives. Even when they are prosecuted, few are convicted, and almost none of these cases reaches the state supreme courts. The preference toward nonintervention has cost more than a few women their lives.

Not all the blame can be put on the legal system, however. The victims themselves make enforcement of the law difficult. For various reasons, they often refuse to get help, to take legal action, or to follow through on a complaint. So the wife beater continues to beat his wife, secure in his belief that no one will interfere or come to the victim's assistance. He is truly the master of the house.

How prevalent is wife beating? Because the crime is seldom reported and national crime statistics are unavailable, it is impossible to determine with accuracy. Even in states that recognize wife beating as a separate crime, there are problems in defining terms. What constitutes *violence* or *abuse*? How does one differentiate between a *domestic disturbance* and *spouse abuse*? The most reliable statistics resulted from a national survey conducted in 1976 by Murray Straus, Suzanne Steinmetz, and Richard Gelles.[1] Based on the responses of a representative sample of American couples, the researchers estimated that within any 12-month period almost 2 million wives are beaten by their husbands. These figures do not reflect the incidence of less severe abuse such as slapping or pushing but only the more violent assaults, which, according to the study, occur on the average of two to three times a year. Straus goes on to say that the actual number may well be as high as 50 or 60% of the population, allowing for unreported and less severe assaults.

THE VICTIM

The problem of spouse abuse is not limited to families of a particular race or social or economic class. It occurs among the poor and the wealthy, among whites, blacks, and other minorities. No matter what their background, the victims are reluctant to report the abuse to the police, to seek assistance elsewhere, or to leave the home. Why do so few women take steps to put a stop to the abuse? First, and foremost, they are fearful that the legal system, as well as their relatives, friends, and neighbors, will react with indifference or hostility if they complain. Out of shame, embarrassment, fear of retaliation, or a lack of knowledge of the remedies available to battered women, they often resign themselves to their role as victim. Many women, having been conditioned to believe that the wife is solely responsible for the well-being of the family, blame themselves for the abuse and are too ashamed to admit that their marriages have failed. Apart from this, the majority of battered women feel they have nowhere else to go and would be unable to make it on their own. If a woman has children, has not been in the work force for a number of years, has no funds of her own and no marketable skills, she is likely to remain in the home and keep her mouth shut. Finally, some victims, having grown up in homes where acts of violence were commonplace, don't even consider the possibility of leaving their homes and marriages, since they assume that physical abuse is a natural part of the husband-wife relationship.

The feelings of the battered woman are unique when compared with those of victims of other crimes. She is locked into a relationship with a man on whom she is dependent emotionally, financially, and legally. She is frightened and desperate, seeing no way to escape. She often experiences an overwhelming sense of guilt—what has *she* done to cause these violent reactions in her husband? We might ask ourselves why it is that the victim so often blames herself or attempts to rationalize her husband's behavior. Wife beating and burglary are both crimes. Would she take responsibility for the actions of a burglar who broke into her house and made off with her possessions, or blame herself for his criminal tendencies? Why are excuses made for the criminal just because he resides with the victim? We often find the same response any time the victim is a woman, a man the perpetrator, and the act specifically directed toward the female sex, whether it be sex discrimination, sexual harassment, rape, or wife beating.

SELF-DEFENSE

It is not uncommon for a battered wife to take matters into her own hands and to fight back against her husband. Often this occurs after years of being beaten and intimidated, when she has reached the limit of her endurance. The battered woman has the same legal rights regarding self-defense as the victim of rape (these are outlined on page 142). Although laws vary from state to state on the matter of using a deadly weapon, generally, when a victim is clearly in danger of being killed or seriously injured, she can use whatever force is necessary to protect herself.

Nevertheless, the number of battered women being convicted of murdering their spouses is increasing.

Studies on domestic violence indicate that once a pattern of abuse is established, the chances of a dispute ending in homicide increase dramatically. It has been estimated that one-eighth of all murders in the United States are committed by the victim's spouse. Obviously, the best defense is to take whatever steps are necessary to remove yourself from the abusive environment before the violence increases to this point (many victims have been even more severely beaten after attempting to defend themselves). Depending on self-defense tactics to protect yourself is extremely risky business.

THE OPTIONS

What can you do if you are a battered wife? A number of options are available, imperfect though they may be, and only you can decide which will work best in your situation. Most women who take action against their husbands are not one-time victims: in most cases, they have been beaten or slapped around for years and decide to take action only when the violence increases to the point where they fear for their lives or the safety of their children. The short-term options boil down to staying in the violent home or fleeing to safety (or persuading your husband to move out, which is very unlikely). If the battered wife leaves the home, she leaves her possessions and her financial stability behind, while her husband enjoys the comforts of home and the condolences of his friends.

Leaving the Home

It may be best for you to leave the home as soon as it is safe to do so, taking your children with you (leaving the children with your husband places their safety in jeopardy and may lessen the chances of your being awarded custody if you later file for divorce). However, the move must be planned in advance if it is to be permanent. Most women who do leave the home return time and time again, hoping that the situation will improve, or because they have no place to stay on a permanent basis or no way to support themselves. The result of course is that the husband's abusive behavior is reinforced. The message is clear: he can continue to abuse his wife without interference and his wife will always return.

Contact the local battered women's shelter or a women's support group and make arrangements to rent an apartment if you can afford it. You will need a job or some other means of financial support, as well as the moral support of your friends and relatives. This will be an extremely difficult transition—no matter how violent and stressful the home environment was—so you will need a network of supportive friends to help you through the ordeal. If you can afford an attorney, make an appointment and discuss your problem and the legal options available to you. (Be careful in your selection of an attorney; unfortunately, a great many of them hold the traditional beliefs about women discussed earlier and they may try to dissuade you from pursuing the matter.) If you can afford therapy, consider it as well, not to find out what it is about *you* that provokes your husband to violence but to work through the anger, the depression, and the feelings of insecurity that have resulted from your violent and destructive home environment. If finances are a problem, consider free counseling services or those whose fees are based on the amount of your income.

Remember, no one will come to your assistance unless *you* take the first step. The decision is yours—can you and your children survive the situation as it is or should you seek a solution? In deciding whether to move out of the home, there are several factors to consider:

— Once a pattern of abuse is established, the assaults almost always become more frequent and more severe, unless the wife takes action.
— It is unlikely that the problem will be resolved as long as you and your husband continue to live together.
— Children brought up in violent homes tend to become perpetrators or victims of physical abuse themselves when they become adults.

It *is* difficult; it *is* frightening; it *is* the unknown—the only sure thing in your life at this point is that if you return to your husband he will continue to intimidate and abuse you. You deserve better.

Shelters

Most larger communities have at least one battered women's shelter (or crisis intervention center) that has been set up to offer moral support, legal advice, referrals, medical assistance, and temporary living quarters for the battered woman and her children. Most shelters operate 24-hour hotlines, and their addresses are kept strictly confidential. These shelters have been quite successful in their attempts to aid victims of violent homes, providing assistance in obtaining job training, employment, and welfare benefits (a woman who is still legally married may be denied these benefits because of her husband's income).

Unfortunately, a number of shelters have had to close their doors because of a lack of funding. Although the subject of federal funding for shelters has been receiving more and more attention in Congress, it remains a controversial subject and bills introduced by Congressman George

Miller and Senator Alan Cranston to establish federal funding have been unsuccessful. Most shelters receive around 25% of their funding from the tax on marriage licenses, a very small percentage from the federal government, and the remainder from the local community, through private fundraising, walkathons, bake sales, and donations.[2] State funding from divorce court filing fees and marriage licenses is being challenged in some states, such as Illinois.

State funds are provided on an ongoing basis in such states as New Jersey, New York, Washington, Illinois, and Virginia. In other states, the lack of funding has forced shelters to limit their services to women on welfare or only married women. In California, some shelters are reducing their expenses by placing battered women in the homes of volunteers. This system seems to be working quite well, offering a comfortable, safe alternative to the abusive home environment. Some of the battered women are able to contribute toward food and rent, while others who cannot contribute financially become shelter volunteers themselves once they are back on their feet financially and emotionally.

If your community has no shelter, contact a women's organization, a social service agency, or a counseling center. Some states have emergency welfare programs for battered women who have left their homes. The problem is that these women often must wait as long as a month before they are eligible for benefits. Check with the state welfare office to see if such a program exists in your area.

Protection Orders

For those women who feel they are not ready to move out of the family home or to press criminal charges against their husbands, there are several half-way measures that can be taken to put a stop to the abuse. Protection orders (or restraining orders) can be issued by a civil court judge demanding that your husband refrain from further abusing, threatening, or in any way harassing you, your children, or other members of the family. In some states, the order may require that he leave the home (even if the lease or title is in his name), provide financial support for you and your children, or pay for your medical bills, moving expenses, and any lost wages.

The types of protection orders available to the battered woman vary from state to state. Sometimes vacate orders are issued to evict the husband from the home. In some states, immediate, temporary protection orders can be issued for an emergency; they can be obtained within a few hours, often at night and on weekends. These orders, called "ex-parte" orders, can be issued without the husband being present, although a hearing will be held at a later date to determine whether another, longer-term protection order should be issued. Normally, it takes weeks before an order is in effect, since the husband must be served notice and a hearing date set. In some states, the husband may be required to deposit a sum of money with the court (called a peace bond), which he forfeits if he violates the order; peace bonds are rarely used, however, and are almost never enforced.

Many states have provided for protection against abuse in their divorce statutes, allowing the wife to obtain an order prohibiting her husband from abusing or harassing her or her children while she is seeking a divorce. In addition, most states have revised their laws to disallow the husband from claiming desertion when the wife has left the home because of physical abuse. In the past, the desertion defense was often used by husbands in divorce actions, and the availability of this defense kept many women from leaving the violent home.

Not all states allow protection orders to be issued, and of those states that do, many will issue them only to a married woman or to a married woman who has filed for divorce. In some states, a spouse or any blood relative who resides with the abuser can seek a protection order. Many states are vague about the eligibility of a woman who resides with but is not married to or otherwise related to the abuser; sometimes the couple must live together in a "close relationship" or have minor children before the woman can request a protection order.

In some states, a woman can request a protection order on her own; in others, she will need an attorney's assistance. A petition must be filed in the family court, at which time a hearing will be scheduled (usually several weeks from the filing date). Both you and your husband are required to appear at the hearing, where you will have an opportunity to present evidence of the abuse (bruises or other signs of injury as well as witnesses who can testify on your behalf) and your husband the chance to respond to the complaint. The judge will determine whether a protection order is warranted. If either partner fails to appear, the judge usually will decide in favor of the spouse who is present (a default judgment).

Unfortunately, even if a battered wife succeeds in obtaining a protection order, she has no guarantee that it will be enforced. If the husband violates the order, he may be in contempt of court or guilty of a misdemeanor, for which he may receive a short jail sentence, a fine, or a term of probation. In reality, a violation rarely results in any form of punishment for the abuser. The police are reluctant to become involved in domestic matters, preferring to dismiss the incident as a family problem rather than placing the husband under arrest. If the order is violated, it is generally up to the wife to see that it is enforced; she or her attorney may have to contact the court to arrange for another hearing and then submit evidence that the order was violated. Judges, however, are as reluctant as police officers to punish the offender. Only in extreme cases are jail sentences imposed. Typically, the offender is given only a warning or a term of probation. Some states do allow the police to make an arrest without a warrant even if they did not witness the attack, but they must have verification that a valid protection order exists before they can proceed. This is why it is recommended that the wife, as well as the police station in her area, have a copy of the order.

Calling the Police

In deciding whether or not to call the police, you must consider what effect such intervention is likely to have. If they are called but refuse to take action against your husband, you may be beaten even more severely after they have gone. On the other hand, a call to the police can be the first step in putting a stop to the violence.

At the very least, the officers' presence may give you the opportunity to leave the home without fear of a violent response from your husband. Only if you agree to press charges, however, are the police authorized to arrest your husband. If you remain in the home and refuse to press charges, there is nothing the police can do to help you, except respond to your next call.

Although the police are required to respond to all complaints of spouse abuse, they are reluctant to become involved in "family disputes" and in the past have been severely criticized for their insensitive treatment of the victim and their hands-off attitude toward the abusive husband. The ineffectiveness of police procedures is not surprising when one considers the following:

- — Some police officers consider wife abuse a civil rather than a criminal matter, a personal rather than a social problem. Consequently, they may discourage the wife from pressing charges, recommending instead that she "try to work it out."
- — Some police officers hold traditional beliefs about women, that the wife should be subservient to her husband, that the well-being of the family is her responsibility, and even that a husband has the right to physically abuse his wife or that she gets some type of satisfaction from being beaten. Many women have reported that police questioning focused on what they did to *provoke* their husbands rather than on the injuries they incurred during the attack.
- — In a large number of cases, the wife refuses to press charges or changes her mind once a complaint is filed. Understandably, the police are not anxious to intervene in such a volatile situation only to have the wife refuse to pursue the matter.
- — A significant number of the police officers assaulted or killed every year are those who were intervening in a family dispute. This fact illustrates the great risk the officer takes when he responds to a

spouse abuse complaint as well as the extreme violence that battered women are subjected to.

It is well known that the police have offered very little protection to the battered woman in the past. But progress is being made in many parts of the country as a number of states are adopting "Prevention of Domestic Violence" laws and police departments are organizing special units of officers (many of them women) to deal with complaints of spouse abuse and rape. In New Jersey, for example, police officers receive special training and are encouraged to take a more active role in resolving family conflicts. They advise victims on the legal remedies available to them and may accompany them to a hospital for treatment of injuries or to a battered women's shelter. These officers are granted immunity from damage suits related to any action they have taken in a "good faith effort" to enforce the law. As police officers become more knowledgeable about the causes of domestic violence and more sympathetic toward the victims of this crime, we can expect that battered women will finally receive the protection and assistance they desperately need.

Each state has its own provisions regarding arrests. Some require that the officers have a warrant, unless they have witnessed the assault or have reason to believe that a felony assault has been committed (one that results in serious injury or that involved the use of a deadly weapon). In many other states, the police are allowed to make arrests without a warrant if they have probable cause to believe an assault has been committed or that a protection order has been violated. A recent study conducted by the Police Foundation with the assistance of the Minneapolis Police Department showed arrest to be a strong deterrent to recurrent spouse abuse. Its findings indicated that only 10% of the offenders who were arrested committed assault within the next six months, as compared with 16% of those who were merely given a warning and 22% who were ordered to leave the house for a few hours in order to "cool down."[3]

Criminal Prosecution

Criminal charges can be brought against your husband in either of two ways—as a result of an arrest made by the police or by your filing a complaint with the prosecutor's or district attorney's office. The prosecutor's office is required to investigate every complaint and to determine whether charges should be brought against the offender.

As is true of all other criminal charges, the burden of proof is on the complainant, so you must have evidence to support the charge. This evidence may include a medical report and photographs documenting the degree of injury, the police report, and witnesses who are willing to testify on your behalf. Should the prosecutor find sufficient evidence to sustain a charge, the court will issue either a warrant for arrest or a summons informing the offender that he must appear in court on a particular date. Only on rare occasions, however, do abuse cases ever reach trial. Prosecutors have been as reluctant as the police to take action against the abusive husband. If the attitude of the courts is that domestic disturbances are a private rather than a legal problem, the police and the prosecutors are likely to follow suit, as their attempts to enforce the law will run up against a brick wall once the case gets to court. The courts traditionally have perceived their primary responsibility to be the preservation of the family rather than the protection of a family member from physical abuse.

Even if the prosecutor thinks the wife has a strong case, it is unlikely that it will ever be heard in court. The prosecutor may agree to postpone or refrain from prosecution upon certain conditions—that the offender agrees to move out of the family home, that he have no contact with the victim, or that he undergo counseling. If he fails to comply with the terms of the agreement, he can be prosecuted. Many cases are resolved through plea bargaining, whereby the prosecutor and the defense attorney agree that the defendant will plead guilty to the charge if the prosecutor will recommend a lenient sentence. Generally, the offender gets off with a warning or probation (the order should contain provisions for the wife's protection). If he fails to adhere to the terms of probation, he can be imprisoned without a trial. Even if the case does end up in court and the judge finds him guilty, it is unlikely that the offender will receive a jail sentence or even a fine. In most cases, he will simply be warned against further abuse or perhaps be placed on probation or given a suspended sentence.

The courts' tendency toward lenient treatment of defendants in spouse abuse cases results not only from their outdated attitudes toward women but also from the recognition that imprisonment may be detrimental to the offender and the victim as well as to society. If the husband is convicted and imprisoned, he will be unable to support his wife and children, and he may very well lose his job and have difficulty finding another after his release. A woman who is shut off from her husband's income and who has no way to support herself and her children may be forced to go on welfare. The battered woman must consider this possibility before filing a criminal charge.

Diversion Programs

Diversion programs have been established in a number of cities throughout the country as an alternative to the traditional method of handling criminal complaints of spouse abuse. Under this system, the case is dealt with informally and outside of the courtroom. The diversion program attempts to resolve the problems of the battered family through mediation and education, rather than merely to punish the offender.

Upon recommendation of diversion, a hearing may be scheduled to determine whether the case is an appropriate candidate for referral. Generally, only misdemeanor cases are diverted from the criminal justice system. The court may dismiss the charge if the program is successfully completed.

One 30-week diversion program in Cook County, Illinois has separate programs for the offenders and their wives.[4] Attendance is mandatory for the men, voluntary for the women. The purpose of the men's group is to educate the offenders in regard to the underlying causes of violence, the relationship between violence and the use of alcohol or drugs, and the ways in which patterns of violence evolve. The group discusses individual problems of the offenders, nonviolent ways of expressing anger and hostility, and methods of dealing with stress. The support group for women attempts to help them clarify and deal with the problem and to outline the viable alternatives that exist for the battered woman.

In some states, spouse abuse cases may be referred to mediation programs, in which the husband and wife together attempt to resolve their problems outside of the courtroom. Criminal proceedings will be suspended only if both spouses agree to mediation. After determining the causes of the conflicts and physical abuse, the couple draws up an agreement stipulating what is and is not appropriate and acceptable behavior and how they will attempt to resolve their differences. The court supervises the case and may dismiss the charges against the offender if the agreement is not violated over a certain period of time. If the offender violates the agreement, prosecution will resume.

While some of these programs have been relatively successful, courts have been accused of diverting cases simply to keep them out of the criminal justice system. By reducing felony charges to misdemeanors, they often can transfer cases to mediation or other diversion programs, thereby decreasing their case loads.

Civil Suits

Traditionally, because the courts considered a husband and wife "legally one," a woman could not sue her spouse. Most states have eliminated interspousal tort immunity and now allow a battered wife to sue her husband for injuries she sustained and property damage. She also may be awarded money damages for mental anguish, medical expenses, and lost wages. Civil suits can be brought in addition to criminal prosecution. Very few women have filed assault charges against their husbands, however, for obvious reasons—1) in most cases, the wife has little to gain from a civil suit, unless her husband is fairly well off financially; 2) she will have to hire an attorney to represent her (many women cannot afford this expense); 3) she must have strong evidence to support her complaint and may well be subjected to skeptical and sexist attitudes in the courtroom; 4) it could be a matter of several years before the case is settled.

In a few states, crime victims compensation is available to battered women. Certain conditions are attached to such programs, though (such as that the victim must be living apart from her husband), and the availability and amount of compensation are subject to funding decisions made by state legislators.

For further information and referrals to local shelters and women's groups, contact:

National Coalition Against Domestic Violence
1500 Massachusetts Ave., Room 35
Washington, DC 20005
(202) 347-7017

National Clearinghouse on Domestic Violence
P.O. Box 2309
Rockville, MD 20852
(301) 251-5172

National Center on Women and Family Law
799 Broadway
New York, NY 10003

Center for Women's Policy Studies
2000 P Street, N.W., Suite 508
Washington, DC 20036
(202) 872-1770

National Organization for Women
Task Force on Battered Women
1917 Washtenaw Avenue
Ann Arbor, MI 48104

Community Services Administration
1200 19th St., N.W.
Washington, DC 20506
(202) 254-5840

U.S. House of Representatives
Select Committee on Children, Youth, and Families
George Miller, Chairman
Room H2-385 House Office Building Annex 2
Washington, DC 20515

PURELY FINANCIAL

15
Wills

We all try to avoid thinking about death, especially our own, which is probably the primary reason so many women postpone writing their wills. For many, the thought of writing a will brings to mind their own mortality, a subject they have happily avoided up to that point. In fact, the writing of a will does not suggest that you are approaching the end of the road, but rather that you are responsible enough to organize your business and personal affairs so that *some* day your property will be distributed according to your wishes.

Wills are not just for the wealthy and the elderly but for any person who owns some kind of property or who has minor children. A will may be written by anyone who is of sound mind and of legal age (over 18 in most states). Even if you are single and own no real property (such as a house), you should have a will. Almost everyone has a bank account, a car, and some personal possessions—these are all part of your estate. Those old family photographs or the antique furniture your grandmother gave you may not bring much in a garage sale but may have a great deal of sentimental value to a member of your family. If you own real property or have minor children, it is even more important that you write a will to specify who should receive your property after your death and in what proportions, and who should be guardian of your children should you and your husband die before they reach legal age.

WHY YOU NEED A WILL

Do you want to have a say in how your property will be distributed after your death? Would you want Uncle Charlie to be your son's guardian? Would you like your daughter to be guaranteed a college education, or part of your savings to go toward your sister's law school tuition? Would you want your jewelry and other personal possessions to be sold, or to be given to your close friends and members of your family? Would you like a particular charity to receive a portion of your estate?

All of these matters can be resolved by writing a will. A will is simply a document outlining how you wish your property to be distributed after your death; it has no legal significance during your lifetime. There are numerous advantages to writing a will:

- You can express exactly how you wish your property to be distributed after your death.
- You can designate a person to be guardian of your minor children.
- You can appoint a trustee to manage your children's share of the estate until they reach legal age.
- You can designate who will be your executor, or personal representative (the person who will administer the estate according to the provisions of your will).
- You can avoid having unnecessary expenses deducted from the assets of your estate during probate.
- You can lessen the chances that your relatives will squabble over your personal property after your death.

IF YOU LEAVE NO WILL

Should you die without a will, your property will be distributed according to your state's laws of intestate succession. These laws determine not only who is eligible to be a beneficiary but the portion of the property they will receive. Although these laws vary somewhat from state to state, the usual procedure is to distribute half of the property to the surviving spouse and half to the deceased's children (in some states, the surviving spouse receives only a third). If there are no children, all of the property may go to the surviving spouse, or a part of it may pass to the deceased's parents. In the case of a widow's death, her children will probably be the sole beneficiaries, and if any of the children have died, their children will receive that share of the property. The property of a single woman with no children is usually passed to her parents, or, if they are deceased, to her sisters and brothers. In most cases, the court will attempt to locate more distant relatives, should all close relatives be deceased. However, if there are no surviving relatives of a certain degree of relationship, the assets of the estate will become the property of the state.

As you can see, by not having a will you allow the state to have the final say on how your property is to be divided, which likely will not coincide with your wishes. The laws of intestate succession do not take into consideration the age or financial need of a particular beneficiary; nor do they provide for persons who are not related to you. Consequently, if you die without a will, those who were closest to you or who are in most need of financial assistance may receive nothing. Furthermore, if you leave no will or your will is found to be invalid for some reason, the sister who hasn't spoken to you in 15 years may receive your entire estate (if she is your closest living relative). Or, if you'd always planned for your best friend to have your prized Persian rug or to leave $10,000 to the American Cancer Society, instead these will be passed on to your relatives.

Apart from the fact that your property will not be distributed according to your wishes, there are numerous other disadvantages in failing to write a will:

— The intestate process is likely to be more complicated and time-consuming than the probate of a will.

— The court will appoint an administrator to settle your estate. This person has the same responsibilities as an executor but is legally required to post a bond to protect the estate against losses due to mismanagement (executors do not have to post the bond as long as the will waives this requirement). The bond, usually a percentage of the estate's value, is deducted from the assets of the estate.

— The court will appoint a guardian for your minor children, not necessarily the person you would have chosen, and certain expenses will be deducted from the estate to cover the guardian's bond and the cost of providing court supervision.

— The court will supervise the sale of any property, and distribution of property is often delayed because the administrator must have the court's approval before proceeding with any transaction.

— The estate may be subject to substantially higher estate taxes than would have been the case if a will had been written.

HOW TO PREPARE YOUR WILL

The first thing you must do is compile a list of your assets, anything that has a monetary value. This should include any real estate you own, automobiles, bank accounts, stocks and other investments, and all of your personal possessions, such as jewelry, furniture, and silver. Also include personal items of sentimental value that you would like to pass on to others. Then determine how you would like your property to be distributed after your death. For the most part, you can name whomever you wish to be beneficiaries and can designate that they receive whatever portion of the property you choose. However, in the majority of states, the law provides certain protections to the surviving spouse. Generally, a surviving spouse cannot be disinherited, despite the will's provisions to the contrary. Should the surviving spouse receive less of a share through the will than he or she would have received according to the laws of intestate succession, a petition can be filed with the probate court. In most states, the spouse is entitled to one-third of the estate, although it may be as high as one-half. In addition, a number of states recognize any property transferred during the two years prior to death as a part of the deceased's estate; thus the surviving spouse's share of the estate would be increased by one-third or one-half of that amount. These laws protect the surviving spouse against fraud, as, for example, when a husband sells or gives away property in an attempt to keep his wife from obtaining it after his death.

Remember, as you are determining who should get what, that unless your primary objective is to have the last laugh, it is probably wise to inform the disinherited of your decision so that they will be less likely to contest your will later. Bitter family squabbles over the distribution of property can often be avoided if you anticipate problems at the time you write your will. Nothing will dissipate the assets of your estate like a contested will.

Types of Wills

Some states recognize holographic wills, those which are written entirely in the handwriting of the testator (the person whose will it is). Although this form of will is not witnessed, certain requirements must be met before it will be admitted to probate. These requirements vary somewhat from state to state but generally include: that the will be dated and signed at the end by the testator and that the entire will be in the testator's handwriting with no typed, printed, or stamped material on any of its pages. Because holographic wills are so informal and require no witnesses at the time they are signed, it is sometimes difficult to get them admitted to probate. To ensure that the will is valid, the court will usually request verification that the handwriting in the will is actually that of the testator. There is also the problem of interpretation of holographic wills. What may have been clear to the testator could be vague or open to several interpretations once the will reaches probate, and thus her wishes may not be carried out. For these reasons, it is suggested that you consider preparing a formal, witnessed will.

This second type of will must meet very strict requirements, but its validity is much less likely to be challenged during the probate proceedings and therefore the testator's wishes are generally carried out without much difficulty. You can prepare such a will yourself, but there are a number of advantages in hiring an attorney to assist you:

— A competent attorney will be knowledgeable of the latest revisions of the laws and can ensure that your will meets all of the state requirements. Few laypersons have such expertise. Once a will is admitted to probate, it is presumed that the testator knew the law, and failure to comply with the law may cause the will to be invalidated, in which case your estate would be administered as if you had died intestate.
— A good attorney will ensure that your will states precisely how your property is to be divided, using the proper legal terminology.
— He may be able to advise you on alternative ways of distributing your property that will avoid unnecessary expenses and excessive taxes (if your assets are substantial, you may want to consult a tax attorney or an estate planner).

Most attorneys charge a very moderate fee for drafting a will. If your estate is small and the provisions you wish to include simple and straightforward, you may be able to use a preprinted form, which simply requires you to fill in the blanks. Otherwise, your attorney will have the will drawn up at his office.

A formal will should include the following items:

— the full name and permanent address of the testator and the date of the will's execution
— a declaration that the document is the testator's last will and testament
— a listing and description of all the items that make up the estate, along with the names of the beneficiaries and the exact portions of the estate they are to receive
— the name of the person who will serve as executor of the will
— the name of the guardian for minor children
— the name of the person appointed to be trustee, the name of the beneficiary, and the specific terms of the trust
— the signature of the testator at the very end of the will (Provisions appearing below the signature will not be recognized by the probate court and may cause the entire will to be invalidated.)
— the signatures of the witnesses, their permanent addresses, and the date of execution

Failure to satisfy these requirements may invalidate the will, causing your property to be distributed according to the laws of intestate succession.

Selecting an Executor

The person you name as executor will take custody of your estate after your death and will be responsible for managing your property until it is distributed according to the provisions of your will. (The duties and responsibilities of the executor are described in detail under "Probate" at the end of this chapter.) By writing a will, you have the authority to appoint as executor the person you feel is the most honest and reliable and the one most capable of handling your estate. Generally, the only legal requirement is that your executor be of legal age and of sound mind. Many married women select their husbands to be executor, but you may choose any of your relatives or friends, your attorney, or even a bank. You are not limited to one person; two or more executors can be named. If you select only one executor, you may want to consider naming an alternate, in case your first choice is unable or unwilling to assume the responsibility at the time of your death. Should you designate only one executor and she for some reason cannot carry out the duties, the court will appoint someone at the beginning of the probate proceedings. Of course you should discuss the duties of the executor with the person you have chosen to be sure she is willing to assume those responsibilities.

Executors generally receive some type of compensation for their services. You may want to specify a particular amount in your will; the probate court will usually comply with your wishes. If no such provision is made in your will, the executor will receive an amount set by the probate court (or occasionally by state law), which is usually a percentage of the dollar value of the estate, although this figure may be increased if the administration turns out to be especially complicated or time-consuming. This amount is deducted from the estate's assets.

Witnesses

You are required to sign your will in the presence of either two or three witnesses, depending upon which state you reside in. Although you need not divulge the contents of the will to the witnesses, you must declare that the document is your will. The witnesses sign their names under an attestation clause, and for later verification that the will has not been altered in any way, you should be sure the pages of the document are numbered and that you and your witnesses initial each page. Should there later be any questions regarding the will's authenticity, the witnesses may be called to testify before the probate court that all the legal requirements were met.

Choose carefully those who will serve as witnesses. In some states, the beneficiaries of a will are not allowed to be witnesses. This restriction may also apply to the executor, trustees, and the spouses of those who may benefit from your estate.

Guardians and Trustees

If you have minor children, your will should designate a guardian who would care for them in the event that both you and your husband die before they reach legal age. The guardian may also be responsible for managing property left to the children (until they reach legal age), although you may ask another individual to handle those responsibilities if you wish. In most cases, the courts honor the parent's choice, as long as the arrangement appears to be in the children's best interests. If you leave no will, or make no provisions for your children's guardianship in your will, the court will appoint someone to raise them and manage their inheritance.

Generally, those appointed to manage the property of minors have little say on how funds are to be allocated or invested, as all transactions are closely supervised by the court. If you wish, you can specify in your will that your child's share of the property be held in trust until she reaches a certain age. Under this arrangement, the title to property is transferred to a trustee, who manages the property for the child according to your instructions. Trusts can be set up in any number of ways to serve different purposes. You may direct that the trust fund be used solely for the child's education or that it be invested in a certain manner or according to the trustee's best judgment, and that the property pass to the beneficiary in a lump sum or in installments. Unlike the court-appointed guardian, the trustee may be given the authority to use his own discretion in allocating and investing funds if you so choose, and there is no limit beyond that expressed in the will on the length of time the money can be held in trust. Of course, you can set up a trust for anyone you wish, not just your children.

Guardians and trustees receive compensation for their services, which is taken out of the estate's assets. You may specify an amount in your will, and the court will usually comply with your wishes. If no provision is made in your will, the guardian or trustee will receive an amount set by state law or by the probate court.

When selecting a guardian, you will want to consider only those who would be willing to take on the responsibility of raising your child, and whose values are similar to your own. Religious beliefs and age may also be important considerations. Since your child's guardian would be responsible for her until she reaches legal age, your 68-year-old mother may not be the wisest choice. Remember also that when the matter of guardianship is brought up in probate court, the judge often will consider the preference of the child if she is old enough and mature enough to make an intelligent decision.

The person you appoint as trustee or guardian of your child's property should have experience in financial matters—this may be a relative, a friend, or a bank or trust company. You can name more than one trustee.

Taxes

Depending upon the value of the property you own and the manner in which it is to be passed on to others, a portion of it may be subject to federal estate and gift taxes. Federal estate taxes are progressive, which means that the larger the estate, the higher the taxes. According to the Economic Recovery Act of 1981, any property passed to your spouse is exempt from federal estate tax, regardless of its value. In addition, no federal estate tax is imposed on a certain amount of property that is passed to others (this limit is increased every year: in 1984, $325,000; in 1986, $500,000). Excluding these exemptions, all other property, including personal property, is subject to both federal estate tax and federal gift tax (it is also subject to state gift and estate taxes in some states).

All of these taxes are deducted from the assets of the estate, while inheritance taxes are paid by your beneficiaries. The tax rates for inheritance taxes are determined by the amount of property each beneficiary receives and his or her relationship to you. Those beneficiaries who are not members of your immediate family pay a higher rate.

Because tax laws are complex and frequently revised, it is strongly recommended that an attorney (preferably a tax attorney) assist you in the preparation of your will, especially if your estate is large and involves trusts and complicated holdings. Intelligent tax planning may well result in substantial savings to the estate. A knowledgeable attorney can advise you on the various ways in which tax liability can be decreased or avoided.

Storing the Will

You should have an original and one copy of your will, both signed by you and the witnesses. The copy should be kept at your home, preferably in a fireproof safe rather than under your mattress. It should be safe from fire, theft, and vandalism, and yet readily accessible to members of your family. You may want to leave the original with your attorney (most of them have fireproof safes) or, in some states (such as New York), the court will store your will for a small fee. Should you move to another city, be sure to take both copies of the will with you. Your primary beneficiaries and your executor should always know where your will is located.

OTHER METHODS OF TRANSFERRING PROPERTY

There are a number of ways to transfer property other than through the provisions of a will. All of these transactions should be carefully planned out in advance, with the assistance of a knowledgeable attorney. If you plan wisely, there are several advantages to transferring property through other means: 1) the property or proceeds go directly to your beneficiaries according to the terms of the agreement (since this property is not considered a part of your estate, it need not go through probate), and 2) in some cases, you can avoid or decrease taxes.

Joint Tenancy

Joint tenancy with right of survivorship is a form of ownership in which a title to property is in two or more individuals' names, usually, though not necessarily, wife and husband. When one of the owners dies, her or his share is automatically transferred to the other. The property is not subject to probate, and the surviving joint tenant becomes the sole owner, even if the deceased specified otherwise in a will. There may be more than two joint tenants, and they need not be related.

Tenancy by the Entirety

A title to property may be held by husband and wife as "tenants by the entirety." This form of ownership has the same effect as joint tenancy with right of survivorship—when one of the spouses dies, the surviving spouse becomes sole owner of the property. The difference is that tenants by the entirety may transfer ownership of their share of the property only with the permission of the spouse, while joint tenants may sell their share at any time and to whomever they choose without the consent of the other owner.

Life Insurance

The proceeds of a life insurance policy are paid directly to the beneficiary by the insurance company upon the death of the insured. The provisions of a will have no effect on the insurance policy and cannot change or revoke the terms of that contract. Since probate court has no jurisdiction over these proceeds, your beneficiary is likely to receive the benefits much sooner than if you had transferred property to her through your will, and in some cases your estate's tax liability can be minimized. You may cancel the policy, borrow against it, or change the beneficiary at any time. Of course there are a number of different kinds of insurance policies, and you should seek expert advice on which type would be of most benefit to you and your heirs.

Trusts

As discussed earlier, trusts set up in a will take effect upon the death of the testator. A second type of trust, called an *inter vivos* or living trust, can be set up to take effect during the owner's lifetime. The advantages of the *inter vivos* trust are that the property is not subject to probate and that such an agreement, if drawn up correctly, may result in a considerable savings in tax dollars. In addition, the *inter vivos* trust may be set up for the owner's benefit, as well as that of her beneficiaries. She may transfer property to a trustee simply because she prefers not to be involved in its management, and the trust can be set up to be in effect for a certain number of years or until her death. She may specify that she receive a set amount of income during her lifetime and that the property remain in trust for a beneficiary after her death or that the property revert to her estate for distribution according to the terms of her will.

You will need the assistance of an attorney when drawing up a trust agreement, as there are variations among the states regarding what constitutes a revocable or an irrevocable trust. A revocable trust generally allows you to change the terms of the agreement or to revoke the trust and resume control over the property. An irrevocable trust cannot be changed or revoked. Your estate may receive no tax benefits whatsoever if the trust is found to be invalid or it is discovered that you retained some measure of control over the property placed in trust. A competent attorney can point out the advantages and disadvantages of the *inter vivos* trust (it is not always wise to transfer property through a trust rather than through a will) and will see to it that your trust meets the state requirements.

Gifts

Some women prefer to transfer a portion of their property as gifts during their lifetime rather than through their will. If a woman is married, there is no limit on the value of gifts she may give to her spouse tax-free. And anyone may give as much as $10,000 a year to as many individuals as she chooses without it being subject to gift taxes (these limits are occasionally revised so be sure to check with your attorney before transferring property). The same rate is used for calculating federal gift and federal estate taxes, and the $10,000 is included in the total amount allowed to be transferred tax-free (in 1984, $325,000; see "Taxes" earlier in this chapter). In other words, as of 1984, you may transfer property with a value up to $325,000 during your lifetime or through your will without incurring taxes. Anything over that amount will be subject to both gift and estate taxes.

UPDATING OR REWRITING YOUR WILL

Your will should be reviewed on a regular basis to be sure it still reflects your wishes and is up to date. At that time you may want to confer with your attorney to see if there have been any changes in the laws that could affect your estate (such as tax laws). You may need to revise or rewrite your will in the following circumstances:

— there is a change in the laws that could adversely affect the value of your estate or increase your tax liability
— there is a substantial increase or decrease in the value of your estate
— you marry or divorce or your husband dies
— your executor, a trustee, or a beneficiary dies
— you give birth to a child or adopt one
— you move to another state

Should the value of your estate increase to the point that it may be subject to substantially higher tax rates, you may want to consider some of the alternative methods of transferring your property that were discussed earlier. If you marry or remarry, you may want to leave a portion of your property to your husband; or if you divorce, you probably will want to delete your ex-husband's name as beneficiary. You may need to rewrite or at least revise your will if you move to another state, as the laws differ somewhat from state to state. Your will will be probated according to the laws of the state in which you resided at the time of your death, so you should consult an attorney to be sure it is in order and meets the requirements of that state.

If significant and extensive changes are necessary, you probably should write a new will. In order to make it clear that your new will is your *last* will and testament, be sure it explicitly states that it "revokes all previous wills."

You need not write a new will if the changes are minimal. Instead you may write a codicil, which is simply an amendment to a will. For example, if you previously named your sister to be executor of your will and later decided that someone else would be better able to handle those responsibilities, you need only write a codicil naming the new executor. Because the codicil becomes a part of your will, it must be executed with the same formalities as the will. Never attempt to change your will by crossing out or adding items; any such alterations may invalidate the entire will.

PROBATE

Probate proceedings, which are held in the county where the deceased last resided, involve the court's validation of the will, if one was left, and the administration of the estate (additional proceedings in another state may be necessary to probate property owned in that state). This procedure may be relatively inexpensive and take a minimum amount of time, or it could be complicated, costly, and time-consuming (sometimes administration of an estate takes several years), depending upon the size of the estate, the complexity of the transactions required, and whether or not the will is contested. The court will determine whether the document is the genuine last will and testament of the testator and if it meets all the legal requirements of the state. In some cases, the witnesses will be called to testify as to its validity. If the court is satisfied that the will is authentic, and that the testator was of sound mind and of legal age and not acting under anyone else's influence at the time the will was written, it will authorize the executor to assume her responsibilities in administering the estate. (If there is no will, the court will appoint an administrator to settle the estate.) The executor is generally required to post a bond to protect the estate against losses due to mismanagement unless the will specifically requests that this requirement be waived (the cost of the bond is deducted from the estate's assets).

The specific responsibilities of the executor usually include the following:

— compiling an inventory and appraisal of all the assets of the estate
— collecting, preserving, and occasionally investing or selling the assets
— arranging for temporary financial support of the deceased's dependents during the period of administration
— paying all outstanding debts (sometimes the executor must negotiate the sale of property to pay off debts)
— preparing and filing estate, inheritance, and income tax returns
— preparing an accounting of the estate's income and expenses
— distributing the remaining assets to the beneficiaries according to the provisions of the will

All of these transactions are supervised by the probate court. Usually, the executor must obtain permission from the court before selling property, although the amount of authority given to the executor depends to a great degree on the terms of the will. Testators often stipulate in their wills that the executor be given the authority to use her own discretion in administering the estate, and the probate court in most cases will agree to such an arrangement. The executor may need to hire certain specialists to assist her in settling the estate—such as attorneys or accountants. These fees are paid by the estate.

16
Social Security

The Social Security system, established in 1935 under President Franklin D. Roosevelt, was designed to provide supplemental retirement income for U.S. citizens, who at that time were struggling to recover from the Depression. The plan was that a portion of the money contributed by workers during the first years of the program's existence would be paid out to those who had reached the age of retirement, while the others would receive credit for later benefits. The Social Security system has become more complicated over the years and now provides benefits not only for the retired, but for disabled workers, children of disabled or deceased parents, widows and widowers, those on Medicare, and, in certain cases, divorced spouses. As the system has expanded, so have the options for women. The Social Security laws have been continually revised, the most recent revision having occurred in January 1984.

The time to think about retirement income is not at age 65, when you call the Social Security office to find out what monthly benefit you're entitled to, but in your twenties, when most women first enter the labor force. If you postpone making plans, you may later find the promised freedom and joy of retirement to be an illusion. We're all familiar with the dismal statistics regarding older women—the majority of them are widows who live alone on inadequate retirement income; many of them live in poverty. Women who are dependent on their husband's income and Social Security benefits are in a particularly precarious position, but even women who have worked outside the home all their adult lives may be at a disadvantage since their average income is much lower than that of men (and thus their retirement benefits are less). Most women who reach retirement age must rely entirely on small monthly Social Security checks to support themselves. Had they been knowledgeable of how the Social Security system works and of alternative sources of retirement income, many of them could instead be enjoying a life of independence and financial security.

HOW THE SYSTEM WORKS

Nearly every woman in the United States is, or will be, entitled to Social Security benefits, either as a worker in the labor force or as a dependent of a worker. Social Security benefits are determined by the amount of money you earn (or your husband earns) over a period of years; the higher your income the higher your benefits will be. To be eligible for benefits, you must accumulate a certain number of "work credits." At the end of each pay period, your employer deducts Social Security tax from your pay (the 1984 tax rate is 6.7% of your wages), contributes an equal amount, and deposits the total either monthly or quarterly. The Social Security Administration keeps an account of your earnings.

To receive the maximum retirement benefit, you must have paid the maximum contribution allowed. The problem is that this amount continues to increase. In 1954, the highest wage bracket was $3,600. The 1984 figure is $37,800. This means that in 1984 any earnings over $37,800 are not subject to Social Security tax. The exemption from taxes applies only to the individual's income, not the combined income of a wife and husband. For example, if you earn $24,000 annually and your husband earns $18,000, you have a combined income of $42,000, but since each of you earned less than $37,800, all of your income would be taxed at 6.7%.

When you become eligible for benefits, you must apply at the local Social Security office; you do not automatically start receiving monthly checks in the mail. Delays are not uncommon, so it's a good idea, in the case of retirement benefits, to apply three months before you intend to retire. Otherwise, you may not receive all the benefits that are due you. The monthly payments are retroactive for only 12 months. When you go to the Social Security office, take the following items with you:

— your Social Security card

— a copy of your birth certificate

— your marriage license or a copy of the final divorce decree (if you are applying as a dependent spouse)

— the Social Security number of the person whose work record qualifies you to receive benefits (if you are applying as a dependent)

— a copy of your discharge papers (if you are a veteran)

Contact your local Social Security office whenever you have questions relating to your eligibility or benefits (the address and phone number are listed in the telephone directory under "United States Government—Department of Health and Human Services"). If you lose your Social Security card, you will have to fill out an application for a duplicate at that office. Likewise, you will have to visit the office to apply for a new card if you change your name. Your new card will have the same Social Security number as your old one, but your account will reflect your new name. If you fail to report the name change, you risk losing benefits you accumulated under your previous name. In addition, if you feel an error has been made in the calculation of your monthly payments, contact the Social Security office. If the problem is not resolved to your satisfaction you can pursue the matter with the Office of Hearings and Appeals. You can also take the case to federal court. An attorney may represent you in either situation.

TYPES OF BENEFITS

As a Worker

As a worker in the labor force, you are earning credits toward monthly retirement income as well as protection for your husband and children. Your earnings for each year of employment are averaged together, and a computation based on this figure will determine the amount of your monthly payment. Many women interrupt their careers, of course, usually to raise young children, and these women, as well as those who prefer to work part-time, are penalized under the Social Security system. When the zero earnings for years you were not employed (or the low earnings for part-time work) are averaged in with your annual income for other years, the amount of your benefit will be significantly less than if you had remained in the work force throughout your adult life. Unfortunately, women who work in the home receive no credit for Social Security benefits. Add to this the fact that the median pay of women workers is 40% less than that of men and it should come as no surprise that women's benefits are almost always less than men's.

If you retire at age 62, your benefit is permanently reduced, since you will receive a greater number of monthly payments. By waiting until age 65 to retire, you will receive full benefits (this age limit will increase gradually, beginning in the year 2000). If you are married, you can receive retirement payments based on either your own work record or that of your husband (as long as he is eligible for Social Security). A woman who has worked continuously in relatively high-paying jobs will probably receive larger monthly payments by claiming the worker benefit rather than the dependent benefit (which is 50% of her husband's benefit, if she retires at age 65); a woman who interrupted her career for a number of years or who earned much lower wages than her husband would probably receive higher payments by claiming as a dependent spouse. The Social Security office can tell you which payment would be greater, and you are entitled to receive the larger amount. Your husband has the same options: if both of you are eligible for Social Security, he is entitled to retirement benefits at age 62 or older based on either his or your work record.

If you retire before your husband does, you can claim the worker benefit and then later change over to the dependent spouse benefit, when your husband retires. However, if you start receiving payments before the age of 65, both the worker and the dependent benefits will be reduced.

As a Wife

Because a woman chooses to work in the home rather than in the labor force does not mean she is automatically ineligible for Social Security benefits. If her husband is eligible for Social Security benefits, both she and her children are covered because of his work record. When she reaches the age of 65, a wife is entitled to receive 50% of the benefit her husband is eligible for at 65. If she wishes to receive payments before the age of 65, they will be less than the full benefit. A wife is also entitled to benefits, at age 62, if her husband becomes disabled or retires. Or, if she has children under the age of 16 or a disabled child, she is eligible to receive payments at any age if her husband is retired or has become disabled.

As a Widow

A widow who has no dependent children is entitled to benefits at age 60, although payments will be less than if she waited until 65. At 60, she will receive 71½% of her deceased husband's benefit; at 65, she will receive 100%.

If a widow has children under the age of 16 or a disabled child, she is eligible for benefits at any age. These payments will continue until the children reach the age of 17 or until the disabled child is no longer in the mother's care.

A disabled widow is eligible for benefits at a lower age. At 50, she will receive 71½% of her deceased husband's benefit.

A widow who qualifies for benefits on her own work record has several options available to her: she can take reduced retirement payments at age 62 and then at 65 receive the full widow's benefit, or she can take the widow's benefit at 62 and at 65 receive her full retirement benefit. Those who start collecting reduced widow's benefits before 62 will receive a reduced retirement benefit at 65.

In most cases, widows who remarry are no longer eligible to receive the widow's benefit. However, benefits are not affected if the widow remarries after the age of 60, or the disabled widow remarries after the age of 50. A widow who remarries has the option of claiming the dependent spouse benefit rather than the widow benefit, if her new husband's work record qualifies her for a larger monthly payment.

As a Divorcee

A divorced woman can claim benefits on the basis of her ex-husband's work record if she is at least 62 years old, has not remarried, her marriage to her ex-husband lasted at least 10 years, and her ex-husband has begun receiving retirement or disability payments. As of January 1985, she is entitled to retirement benefits if the divorce has been final for at least two years, she is at least 62 years old, and her ex-husband is eligible for benefits (even if he is not yet receiving monthly payments). If the ex-husband dies, she is eligible for benefits as long as she is at least 60 years old, the marriage lasted at least 10 years, and she has not remarried (disabled divorcees are eligible at age 50).

Until January 1984, a divorced woman who remarried lost all Social Security benefits based on her ex-husband's work record. Now, she can continue receiving payments if she remarries after the age of 60 (or after 50 if she is disabled). Of course, she may be entitled to higher payments if she claims benefits as a dependent spouse of her new husband.

Disability and Survivors Insurance

Once a woman enters the work force, she need meet only minimal requirements to qualify for disability and survivors insurance. The number of work credits she needs to be eligible for these benefits is less than she needs for retirement benefits. Eligibility is determined by a sliding scale based on the employee's age—a younger woman needs fewer work credits than an older woman.

A worker can file a disability claim if she has some "medically determinable" physical or mental impairment that makes it impossible for her to work and that could result in death or last for a period of a year or more. The disability payments begin after five months and continue as long as she is disabled. If she has received the payments for a period of two years or longer, she may also be eligible for Medicare.

When a married woman becomes disabled, her husband may be eligible for payments if he is at least 62 years old. He may be entitled to benefits before that age if he has children who are 15 or younger or a disabled child. The woman's unmarried children may be eligible for payments as well, if they are 17 or younger, disabled, or under the age of 20 and attending elementary or secondary school. These benefits also apply to adopted children and stepchildren.

Your husband and children are protected by survivors insurance if you have earned enough work credits for eligibility. If you were to die, they could apply for monthly payments. Should there be no children, your husband would have to be at least 60 years old (or between the ages of 50 and 60 if disabled) to be eligible for benefits based on your work record. Upon your death, your husband or children could also receive a small lump-sum payment.

Medicare

If you qualify for monthly Social Security benefits on your own or your husband's work record, you will automatically be eligible for Medicare hospital insurance at 65. (Insurance covering medical expenses must be applied for, and you must pay monthly premiums.) If you don't qualify for monthly benefits, you will have to pay for this coverage. As mentioned earlier, those who have collected disability payments for at least two years may be eligible for Medicare at an earlier age. It is a good idea to apply for Medicare several months before you reach 65 to be sure you are immediately eligible for benefits.

OTHER SOURCES OF RETIREMENT INCOME

Pensions

Some women are covered by a pension plan instead of, or in addition to, Social Security, either as a worker or as a dependent spouse. Federal employees and those who are in the military or the Foreign Service earn retirement benefits through public pension plans and may also be eligible for Social Security. Some state and local government employees are not eligible for Social Security benefits but are covered by various pension plans. If you receive a public pension for employment that is not covered by Social Security, you may have your dependent spouse or widow's Social Security benefits reduced (the same goes for your husband, if his

Social Security payments are based on your work record). Those who become eligible for a public pension after June 1983 will have their Social Security payments reduced by two-thirds the amount of the pension. Your Social Security benefits will not be reduced, however, if they are based on your own work record.

Many businesses provide private pension plans for their employees. Sometimes a certain portion of an employee's check goes toward the pension fund; in other cases, the employer makes a contribution. The amount of deductions taken from the employee's wages is determined by such things as her salary, her age, and her approximate retirement date. Most private pension plans require that the employee work for her employer for a minimum of 10 years before she is fully vested, that is, eligible to receive full benefits. If she leaves her job before the tenth year, she may receive a portion of the benefits.

There are many kinds of pension plans, and they vary in their benefits and coverage. You should be familiar with the provisions of the plan, and you have the right to request from your employer a summary that outlines when and under what circumstances benefits will be paid, and the amount you have vested. Not all pension plans provide benefits for a surviving spouse.

IRAs (Individual Retirement Accounts)

Although the Social Security system was established to provide *supplemental* retirement income, it is the sole means of support for the majority of women over the age of 65. Not only is such income insufficient to meet most women's financial needs, but there is already a growing concern that by the time the baby boom generation reaches retirement age in the first years of the next century the Social Security system may be bankrupt. And not everyone has access to an adequate pension plan. It is essential then that women plan wisely for their retirement years, investigating every available option, so that they will be financially secure in their later years.

One of these options is the IRA, a retirement plan established by the government for the individual wage earner. The plan was designed to encourage workers to save for their retirement by allowing them to defer tax liability until they reach retirement age, when they most likely will have a smaller income and thus will pay a lower rate of taxes. Any woman who is employed is eligible to open an IRA, even if she already is participating in another retirement plan (those who are self-employed may also qualify for a Keogh account). You are allowed to deposit up to $2,000 of your annual earnings each year. If both you and your husband work, each of you can contribute up to $2,000 a year, or if you are a homemaker without an income and your husband contributes to an IRA, the maximum amount that can be deposited is increased to $2,250. The annual contributions you make to an IRA are not subject to federal income taxes in the years the money was earned, which can result in substantial savings. For example, if you deposit the $2,000 maximum and you are in the 30% tax bracket, your potential savings is $600 (30% of $2,000).

There are several important advantages to opening an IRA:

— Money deposited in an IRA is not subject to federal income taxes until it is withdrawn.
— Interest earned on your account is not subject to federal taxes until it is withdrawn.
— After deducting from your income the amount you deposited in an IRA, you may be in a lower tax bracket.
— When you begin receiving distributions from the plan at age 59½ or later, your income will likely be much less than it was during your years of employment; thus you will probably be in a lower tax bracket.
— You can start withdrawing from your account after the age of 59½ even if you are still employed.
— You can receive your distribution in a lump sum or in increments, depending on your needs.
— Many institutions will accept an IRA for collateral for loans, mortgages, etc.

As you might expect, there is a catch, a price you must pay for entering and enjoying the game. The catch is that you will be penalized should you withdraw any amount from your IRA before reaching the age of 59½. There will be a surcharge imposed on any money withdrawn (10%, as of 1984), and of course the amount you withdraw will be added to that year's income, resulting in increased taxes and perhaps a higher tax bracket. Only in the case of disability or death is the penalty waived.

The manner in which withdrawals are made is determined by the type of account you have. Should you prefer to delay withdrawals after reaching 59½, you may do so until you are 70½, when they become mandatory. For example, if you plan to work until reaching the age of 65, it would be wise to postpone withdrawing from your account until you are ready to retire; otherwise, your tax liability will increase. Once you begin withdrawing from your account, you must annually take out at least the minimum amount the program requires, which depends on your age. This amount is calculated according to a life-expectancy table similar to the actuarial tables used by insurance companies. A rollover provision allows you to receive a lump sum payment and reinvest it within 60 days without taxation. Otherwise, any money withdrawn from the account will be taxed as if you had earned it in the year the withdrawal was made.

The tax benefits of the IRA apply primarily to federal income tax. If your state has an income tax, your entire earnings (including any amount deposited in your IRA) may be subject to taxation. Check with a bank, a savings and loan institution, or an accountant to see if your state allows the IRA exemption.

You can open an IRA at any number of financial institutions—a bank, savings and loan association, brokerage firm, insurance company, or an authorized limited partnership. How the funds in your account will be invested is up to you, but you should consider such factors as the age at which you want to retire, how much retirement income you'll need, and how much you wish to deposit in the IRA each year. Some types of investments earn a fixed rate of return (such as Certificates of Deposit), while others pay the prevailing interest rate. You will want to discuss all the options with someone who is knowledgeable in this area.

17
Consumer Concerns

Many women purchase more items on credit than with cash—items such as furniture, clothing, appliances, and even houses and automobiles. It's the American way of life—buy now, pay later. Credit cards, which generally are easy to obtain, make shopping a lot more convenient and enjoyable, since you're not obligated to hand over your hard-earned dollars at the moment of purchase. If you want it, you can buy it—on time. Besides the fact that easy credit has resulted in a large number of consumers becoming overextended, the only problem with the credit system is that sometimes disputes occur over a credit purchase—the creditor refuses to remove a charge on your bill for a purchase you didn't make, you receive a bill stating that you owe $420 for a purchase paid off the month before, or a creditor refuses to extend credit, even though your credit history is impeccable and your income and financial assets are substantial.

Even if you operate on a cash-only basis, you will likely run into problems sooner or later—the hair dryer you purchased doesn't work, the furniture you ordered seven months ago still hasn't arrived, you find that the "new" tires you purchased at the service station are actually retreads, or you encounter an unethical salesperson or buy faulty merchandise based on misleading advertising.

In either case, you should be aware of your legal rights as a consumer and of the laws that protect you against unfair and illegal business practices. You should not feel that you are at the mercy of merchants and creditors. Become familiar with the laws and be ready to take action if you are treated unfairly.

CREDIT

Establishing Credit

Until recently, it was nearly impossible for women to obtain credit on their own. Since all credit was in the husband's name, divorced women and widows, after 20 or more years of marriage, were automatically denied credit when it was discovered they had no "credit history." Even those who were financially independent were considered poor credit risks—after all, there was always the chance they might quit their jobs to have a baby or to care for young children.

Then, in 1974, the Equal Credit Opportunity Act (ECOA) was enacted, a federal law prohibiting creditors from discriminating against credit applicants on the basis of race, age, religion, national origin, sex, or marital status. The Federal Reserve Board, which is responsible for interpreting this area of the law, issued "Regulation B," rules that describe in detail the rights of the consumer and those practices prohibited under the ECOA:

1) Credit cannot be denied on the basis of gender or marital status.
2) You are entitled to the same credit rates as any other person with a similar credit rating.
3) A co-signature on a loan cannot be required unless the same requirement is imposed on other persons having the same credit qualifications. (It will be required, however, if a husband or other person has an interest in the property used as collateral.)
4) Creditors cannot demand your husband's signature on a credit application if the account is to be in your name only and you have sufficient income or other assets to qualify. (However, he must sign for a joint account or if you live in a community property state; see page 91.)
5) You have the right to open an account under whatever name you go by—your birth-given first and last names or a combination of your birth name and your husband's surname (Jane Williams, Jane Brown, or Jane Williams-Brown).
6) Creditors cannot revise the terms of a credit agreement or terminate an account solely because you have changed your name or your marital status. Nor can they demand that you fill out another credit application unless you are unwilling or unable to pay your debt,

or the original credit agreement was based on your husband's income and your income alone is insufficient.

7) Creditors cannot ask you if you are planning to have children or inquire about birth-control methods. However, they can ask you about your dependents.
8) Credit applications sent by mail cannot solicit information regarding your sex or title (Ms., Miss, Mrs.). If you are applying in person, you are not legally required to indicate a title on the application.
9) A creditor cannot inquire about your marital status unless you are opening a joint account, you live in a community property state, or you are relying on your husband's property or income to support the application.
10) A creditor cannot inquire about your husband unless any of the conditions listed in item 9 apply or your application is based in part on spousal or child support payments made by your ex-husband.
11) A creditor cannot demand disclosure of income in the form of spousal or child support. On the other hand, he cannot refuse to consider spousal and child support as part of your income if you list them on your credit application, as long as you can show that these payments are consistently made.
12) A creditor cannot disqualify you because you work part time or are a housewife. He must consider as income any pension and other retirement benefits listed on your application.
13) A creditor is not allowed to discourage you from applying for credit by suggesting that your application will probably be denied because of your sex or marital status.

Once the completed application is in the hands of the creditor, he has 30 days in which to notify you of the action taken on the application. If your application is rejected, your creditor must notify you in writing, providing you with the specific reasons for the denial of credit (or informing you that such a statement will be sent if you request it within 60 days), a written statement outlining your rights under the ECOA, and the name and address of the federal agency that enforces the act.

Even though most women now have a less difficult time establishing credit, increasing numbers of those who are married are opening checking, savings, and credit accounts in their own names. And they are wise to do so. It is important that every woman establish credit in her own name so that she will have her own credit history.

It used to be that even joint accounts were listed only in the husband's name. This discriminatory practice became illegal with the enactment of the Equal Credit Opportunity Act. The Federal Reserve Board adopted a rule that requires creditors to report credit information in both the wife's and the husband's name if the account is used by both and it was established after June 1, 1977. For accounts established before June 1, 1977, creditors must either report credit information separately for the wife and the husband or allow them to decide how they wish it to be reported. In community property states, however, even though credit information must be reported separately, the husband's credit history may be considered by creditors when a woman applies for an individual account.

Remedies for Discriminatory Credit Practices

The Informal Complaint. If you feel a creditor has discriminated against you, attempt to resolve the problem informally:

1) Collect all information relating to the credit application, including correspondence and documents, the name of the creditor or his representatives, any notes you have made and the dates on which you spoke with the creditor, and a copy of the credit denial.
2) Send a complaint letter to the creditor, requesting that he reevaluate your application. Explain your reasons for believing the credit denial was a violation of the ECOA.
3) Submit a complaint letter to the head of the company, describing the specific violation, the applicable law, and the action you wish him to take. Send the letter by certified mail, return receipt requested. The receipt may later be used as evidence that a complaint was sent and received.

Federal Enforcement Agencies. If you receive an unsatisfactory response from your creditor, or no response at all, your next step is to contact the federal agency responsible for enforcing the ECOA. If you were denied credit, the creditor must provide you with the name and address of the appropriate agency. Each of these agencies oversees a particular group of creditors (these appear on page 201).

You will need to submit to the agency a written statement of facts as well as copies of all correspondence and documents relating to the incident. The Federal Trade Commission, which has overall enforcement power, investigates creditors who are suspected of violating the law. Although none of the federal agencies handles individual cases, they do investigate creditors who repeatedly discriminate against a particular group of consumers. If the creditor is notified by the agency, he may contact you in an attempt to resolve the problem; otherwise, the agency will advise you of your right to bring legal action on your own. You may also be referred to the U.S. Attorney General, who may decide to bring a civil lawsuit against the creditor if it is determined that many other consumers have been similarly discriminated against (this is called a "pattern and practice" suit).

In addition to federal laws, most states have their own laws protecting women against discriminatory credit practices. The remedies include private civil actions and complaints filed with state agencies that conduct public hearings on consumer complaints (such as state banking agencies and consumer commissions). Contact the office of your state attorney general for a copy of the state laws and the name and address of the enforcement agency. You may not pursue your rights under both state and federal law in this instance.

Civil Suits. Your last resort is to hire an attorney and bring a civil action against the creditor. The ECOA allows you to sue for actual and punitive damages in federal court regardless of the size of the loan or the amount involved. You must file the suit within two years of the violation. The damages you may be able to recover are:

1) actual damages (such as the lost opportunity to buy your dream home)
2) punitive damages up to $10,000 (these are imposed to punish creditors who intentionally or maliciously violate the law, such as those who consistently deny credit to women solely because of their sex). Governmental agencies are not liable for punitive damages.
3) equitable relief, such as when the court orders that your previous credit rating be restored
4) attorney's fees and court costs

If the creditor has discriminated against a number of women in a similar manner, one or more of them may be able to file a class action. In this case, punitive damages cannot exceed $500,000 or 1% of the creditor's net worth, whichever is less.

If you bring suit against your creditor, you will follow the same procedure as you would in any other civil lawsuit. File a complaint with the court that has jurisdiction over such matters (in this case, the federal district court in your area). The court clerk will provide you with the correct forms and set a court date. You will be required to pay a filing fee. Present your attorney with all the evidence you've collected (copies of correspondence, documents, and your notes). If there are any witnesses who would be willing to testify on your behalf, contact the court clerk and arrange to have them subpoenaed.

Credit Agreements

For many years, consumers who wished to buy on credit had a very difficult time trying to comparison shop for the best credit terms. Each creditor told a different story and had a different method of expressing financial terms and rates. Since no standard method was used, consumers were often confused and unsure of exactly how much they would have to pay for a particular purchase after all the various charges were added on. The Truth in Lending Act has simplified such transactions for the consumer by requiring that creditors disclose all credit terms and amounts before an account is opened or credit is extended so that the consumer knows exactly how much she is paying for credit.[1] They must itemize all charges, and the cost must be clearly stated in writing. In addition, the "finance charge" (the amount you must pay for the privilege of buying on credit, such as interest) and the "annual percentage rate" (the annual cost of the credit expressed as a percentage) must be stated on a credit agreement in a more conspicuous manner than the other credit terms.

There are two basic types of credit—open-end credit and closed-end credit. Open-end credit generally allows you to pay the bill either in full or in monthly installments according to the terms of the credit agreement. In this type of account there are usually repeated transactions between creditor and consumer. Credit-card accounts are an example of open-end credit.

Closed-end credit involves a particular amount that is repaid in equal monthly installments (such as the purchase of furniture or an automobile). The agreement or contract must include the following items:

1) Cash price
2) Cash down payment
3) Unpaid balance (the cash price minus the down payment)
4) Additional charges (all charges that are not included in the finance charge). These must be clearly identified, such as "Delivery Fee - $25."
5) Prepaid finance charges or deposits (the unpaid balance would be reduced by this amount)
6) Total amount financed (unpaid balance before interest is added)
7) Finance charge
8) Repayment schedule (including balloon payments, if applicable)
9) A description of the early repayment penalty (if applicable)
10) Identification of the method of computing rebates for finance charges in the case of early repayment
11) Description of any security interest retained by the seller (this allows the seller to repossess the property or goods if the buyer fails to make payments)

12) Insurance. This must be stated as a separate cost if such is offered by the creditor.
13) Annual percentage rate (the interest rate, or cost of credit, expressed as a percentage)

The Truth in Lending Act applies to credit purchases and loans made for personal use that are subject to a finance charge and payable in more than four installments. It covers credit-card issuers, auto dealers, banks, savings and loan associations, department and other retail stores, credit unions, and consumer finance companies. If you are seeking a loan for a home you plan to use as a primary residence, the transaction is covered by the Truth in Lending Act. As a homebuyer, you have the right to cancel the financial agreement within three days after it is signed (although you may still be bound by a contract for sale, which is a separate agreement). Those who offer services rather than products and regularly extend credit, such as plumbers and doctors, are not required to comply with the Truth in Lending Act.

Any time you buy on credit, read the entire credit agreement carefully and watch out for hidden finance charges. If you do not understand any of the provisions, ask the creditor to explain them to you.

Credit Cards

In 1970, the Truth in Lending Act was amended to provide additional protections to the consumer. One of these pertains to the cardholder's liability when her credit card has been stolen, lost, or used without her authorization. The cardholder's liability is now limited to $50, unless the unauthorized charges were made after she notified the credit-card company, in which case she is not liable for any amount. The $50 liability does not apply in the following circumstances:

1) the cardholder is not notified of the $50 liability
2) the creditor failed to send a stamped envelope to be used in reporting a stolen or lost credit card
3) the creditor does not provide a means of identifying the cardholder (such as a signature, fingerprint, or photograph)

If your credit card is lost or stolen, contact the company immediately to avoid being liable for unauthorized charges. It is best to call first and then report the loss in writing (most companies issue forms for reporting such incidents).

Avoid sending your credit-card number through the mail for mail-order purchases, as this may result in unauthorized charges. Credit-card scams have become very popular in recent years. Congress is considering an amendment to the Truth in Lending Act that would restrict disclosure of a cardholder's credit-card number. If the amendment is passed, fraudulent use of a credit card (possessing a stolen card or forging the cardholder's signature) would be a federal offense, allowing damages to be awarded for illegal charges over $1,000.

Another provision of the Truth in Lending Act prohibits companies from mailing out unsolicited credit cards. The only time an unauthorized credit card can be sent is when the individual already holds a card from the company and it is soon to expire.

Credit-card companies send monthly bills to the cardholders, who usually have the option of paying in full or in monthly installments. If the bill is paid in installments, a finance charge will be added on (some credit-card companies also charge annual membership fees). The Truth in Lending Act requires that the annual percentage rate appear on both the credit application and each monthly statement and that every statement include a description of the purchase billed.

Billing Errors

Billing errors occur frequently. You are charged for an item you didn't buy, you are overcharged for an item you did buy, your account was not credited for an earlier payment, or the bill reflects an unwarranted finance or late-payment charge. What can you do?

The Truth in Lending Act protects consumers against inaccurate and unfair billing practices. The first step is to notify your creditor in writing within 60 days of receipt of the bill. Describe the error that has been made, including the dollar amount, provide your name and account number, and include copies of documents related to the transaction. Send the letter by certified mail, return receipt requested, so you will have proof that your creditor received the complaint.

The creditor must respond to your letter within 30 days and notify you of his decision within 90 days. During this time you must continue to pay on the undisputed charges, but are not required to pay the amount you are questioning.

If the creditor fails to respond to your letter, he forfeits the right to collect the amount in dispute, as well as finance charges attached to that amount, up to $50. If it is determined that an error was made by your creditor, your account must be adjusted to eliminate the charge as well as any finance charges computed on that amount. If the error was yours, you will have to pay the amount questioned as well as finance charges accumulated during the time you made no payment, but the creditor cannot increase your debt or require payment in full because you questioned the charge.

Remedies for Violations of the Truth in Lending Act

Enforcement of the Truth in Lending Act is divided among the Department of Justice and the federal agencies that oversee the various types of creditors. These include:

Department stores, other retail stores, consumer finance companies, all nonbank credit-card issuers, and all other creditors who are not responsible to another federal agency	Federal Trade Commission Equal Credit Opportunity Washington, DC 20580 *or* the FTC regional office in the region in which the creditor conducts his business
National banks	Comptroller of the Currency Consumer Affairs Division Washington, DC 20219
State member banks of the Federal Reserve System	Federal Reserve bank serving the district in which the member bank is located
Insured banks that are not members of the Federal Reserve System	Federal Deposit Insurance Corporation regional office in the state in which the bank is located
Savings and loan institutions	Federal Home Loan Bank Board district office
Federal credit unions	National Credit Union Administration regional office
Creditors subject to the Civil Aeronautics Board	Director, Bureau of Enforcement Civil Aeronautics Board 1825 Connecticut Ave., N.W. Washington, DC 20428
Federal land banks, production credit associations, etc.	Farm Credit Administration 490 L'Enfant Plaza, S.W. Washington, DC 20578

Because of the large number of consumer complaints, the Federal Trade Commission has concentrated primarily on national creditors. Nonetheless, you should file a complaint with the enforcement agency if your credit problem has not been resolved to your satisfaction. If the creditor is suspected of intentionally violating the Truth in Lending Act, he may be prosecuted by the Attorney General (the maximum penalty for a criminal violation is $5,000 and/or one year in prison), although this rarely occurs.

You may bring an individual civil suit in federal court within one year of the violation (or a class action if there were similar violations involving other consumers). The creditor may be liable for twice the amount of the finance charge (a minimum of $100 and a maximum of $1,000) plus court costs and reasonable attorney's fees. Charges can be brought in a U.S. district court as well, regardless of the amount of damages claimed.

The Credit Bureau

If you have purchased items on credit, your local credit bureau has a file on you. This file includes your address, your place of employment, your annual salary, your credit history, and perhaps even your political affiliation. The Fair Credit Reporting Act, passed by Congress in 1970, protects the consumer against unfair and unethical practices and invasion of privacy by consumer credit reporting agencies. Its provisions include the following:

1) If you are denied credit on the basis of a negative credit report, the creditor must provide you with the name and address of the credit bureau that supplied the information.

2) You have the right to see your credit file for a small fee, or at no charge if you are questioning an adverse report that resulted in a denial of credit within the past 30 days.

3) The credit bureau must investigate all complaints, delete any information that is found to be inaccurate, and notify creditors who have recently requested the credit information that an error was made.

4) If the credit bureau does not remove records you feel are inaccurate, you have the right to send them a written statement of 100 words or less explaining your side of the story. The credit bureau must keep your statement on file and include it in its reports to creditors.

5) The credit bureau must follow reasonable procedures to assure accuracy of credit reports and must delete negative information after a period of seven years (with the exception of bankruptcy, which can be kept on file for 10 years). No time limitations apply for credit transactions involving $50,000 or more or for employment reports when the consumer has an annual salary of $20,000 or more.

6) The information in your credit report can be released only under the following circumstances:
   —with your written consent
   —in response to a court order
   —when requested by an individual who has a legitimate business need relating to a credit transaction, employment, licensing, or insurance.

The Federal Trade Commission has administrative enforcement power over most creditors who violate the Fair Credit Reporting Act (department and other retail stores, consumer finance companies, etc.), but the process of investigation is slow. In some cases, it issues "cease and desist" orders (court orders demanding that creditors stop those actions which are in violation of the law) or seeks penalties up to $10,000, but it generally does not investigate complaints by individuals unless the violation affects the public in general.

If you decide to bring a civil suit, you may be awarded punitive damages for *willful* noncompliance or actual damages for *negligent* noncompliance. In other words, unless you can show that the credit bureau intentionally violated the law you will be able to recover only actual damages if you receive a favorable judgment. Attorney's fees are sometimes recovered as well. You must bring action within two years of the violation.

Harassment by Bill Collectors

The Fair Debt Collection Practices Act, which became effective in 1978, prohibits collection agencies from harassing you for nonpayment of your debts (such as threatening you, using abusive language, or calling your employer or relatives). It also guarantees you certain rights: to be left alone once you notify the collection agency in writing, and to question and verify a disputed debt. In addition, you cannot be sued in any jurisdiction except the one in which you reside. The Act applies only to collection agencies, not to companies or individuals who attempt to collect debts owed to them.

The Federal Trade Commission is authorized to enforce the Fair Debt Collection Practices Act, but you may also bring a suit against a collection agency for actual damages up to $1,000 and attorney's fees and court costs. In addition, some states have their own laws prohibiting harassment by bill collectors, but these laws generally allow only minimal damages to be recovered. The state attorney general's office can tell you about the laws that apply in your state. If your state has no such laws, the Fair Debt Collection Practices Act applies.

Garnishment of Wages

Title III of the Consumer Credit Protection Act (usually referred to as Truth in Lending) prohibits the collection of debts by "force or fear" and restricts the amount of wages that can be garnished (deducted from your paychecks to pay off debts). Garnishment of a weekly wage may not exceed 25% *or* the difference between your weekly disposable income and 30 times the minimum hourly wage. In the case of bankruptcy, tax debts, or child support payments, however, the percentage that can be garnished may be as high as 50%. Most states have adopted the Consumer Credit Protection Act or have similar laws regarding garnishment.

DEFECTIVE PRODUCTS AND SERVICES

What should you do if you bring your new color television home from the store and it doesn't work? Or the furniture you ordered arrives in damaged condition? As you might have guessed, the law provides certain protections and rights to consumers who have purchased a defective product or paid for unsatisfactory services.

Warranties

The Magnuson-Moss Warranty Act (also referred to as the Federal Warranty Act) has established specific standards that must be met in written warranties covering consumer products used for personal, family, or household purposes. The Act includes the following provisions:

1) You have the right to inspect the written warranty before you purchase the product.
2) The language and terms of the warranty must be clearly stated.
3) If the company has agreed to repair the product, it must do so within a reasonable period of time.
4) If a product is defective, the consumer has the right to receive a refund or a replacement without charge.
5) The warrantor may not limit an "implied" warranty by a written warranty.
6) Unless the warranty includes a statement limiting the amount in consequential damages that can be recovered for breach of warranty, there will be no limit.
7) The terms of the warranty apply only to the first purchaser.

In addition to a written warranty, several "implied" warranties apply to most transactions. These are outlined in the Uniform Commercial Code and in most state commercial codes (the UCC applies to sales of goods priced over $500). The implied warranties guarantee that the product will meet the reasonable expectations of the consumer—that it meet certain minimum standards and do what it is manufactured to do (for example, a washing machine will wash your clothes or a refrigerator will keep food cold). In most states, unless there are clear and specific written disclaimers, implied warranties exist, even though they do not appear in the written warranty.

Remedies

If the merchandise you have purchased is damaged or defective, there are several legal remedies you can pursue. Before you call an attorney or file a lawsuit, however, attempt to resolve the problem informally (unless the defect resulted in personal injury—in this case, you should contact an attorney immediately).

1) Contact the company immediately and request a replacement or a refund.
2) Send a letter of complaint, along with copies of receipts, cancelled checks, and other documents, asking the store to take immediate action.
3) If the company fails to take action, contact the Better Business Bureau, your local consumer protection agency, or the organization that handles individual complaints on that particular type of creditor.

You can also bring an action in small claims court if the amount of damages you are claiming does not exceed the small claims limit (these vary from state to state). Chapter 4 discusses the procedures involved in filing a claim in small claims court.

The Federal Trade Commission is empowered to regulate the Magnuson-Moss Warranty Act by informal dispute-settlement procedures. It may bring an action against a warrantor or refer the matter to the Attorney General if the violation affects a large group of consumers.

You can bring suit for damages yourself in either a state or federal court, but the law requires that the warrantor first be given an opportunity to correct the breach of warranty. (Before bringing suit, consider whether the amount in dispute justifies all the time, expense, and trouble of going to court.) To file suit in federal court, your claim must be at least $25 and you must comply with certain procedural guidelines. Class actions can also be brought if there are at least 100 named plaintiffs. In this case, the Act provides for damages up to $10,000 for each violation plus court costs and attorney's fees.

If you sue under state law, the Act requires that the federal disclosure standards and warranty content standards, rather than those of the state, be applied unless the state laws offer greater protection to the consumer.

Automobile Repairs

Donna was driving to her parents' home for the Christmas holidays when one of the tires on her car blew out. Fortunately, she was a pro at changing tires, but the spare was in poor condition so she drove into a service station off the freeway to have the deflated tire repaired. While she waited, the mechanic checked under the car and then informed her that her car was in desperate need of new shock absorbers as well as a new tire (the old one was beyond repair). When she reached her parents' home, she related the incident to her father. He flew into a rage. It seems he had replaced the shock absorbers only a few months before. Donna learned a valuable lesson about auto repairs.

Not all mechanics are out to bilk the unsuspecting woman driver, but there are enough unscrupulous ones out there that you should be aware of your rights and know when your car needs repairs (and when it doesn't) and what you should expect in the way of a guarantee and service. Problems with car repairs are a major consumer complaint. Who hasn't experienced having to return their car to the mechanic time and again for the same repair? Choosing a mechanic is similar to choosing a doctor or an attorney—the results may be with you for a long time. Prevent future problems by shopping around. Ask your friends if they know of a reliable, honest mechanic. Ask those who drive the same make of car as yours where they have repairs done. Should you notice an expensive-sounding noise coming from the engine, solicit the advice of several garages and request a written estimate of the cost of repair. Do they agree on what the problem is and how it can be eliminated? Keep a list of all repairs (and the dates they were done) and retain a copy of all estimates, receipts, work orders, guarantees, and warranties, and take replaced parts with you after a repair (in case you must document a complaint later).

Many states now require that owners of automobiles be advised in writing of the estimated cost of repairs and that the owner sign the estimate before any repairs are done. Should the mechanic later realize that the estimate is too low, he must notify the owner and obtain her authorization before the work begins. The adjusted amount must be noted on the company's copy of the estimate.

Before you approve the estimate, inquire about a guarantee or warranty. Every provision should be in writing and you should read the entire document. How long is it in force? What exactly does it cover? If you were to have problems with your car later and end up in court, would the guarantee or warranty protect you? Or would you have no recourse but to testify that "the mechanic *said* the guarantee was good for a year."

The Magnuson-Moss Warranty Act protects consumers against illegal and unenforced warranties. It requires that the manufacturer or dealer either reimburse the owner or replace a newly purchased car if they are unable to repair it after a reasonable period of time. The Act also specifies what provisions must appear in a written warranty and allows the consumer to bring suit for breach of warranty (see "Warranties" on p. 204).

If you have been victimized by a dishonest or incompetent mechanic, or the car dealership refuses to honor a warranty or service contract, there are several methods of remedying the situation. These are your options:

1) Speak with the manager or owner of the business. Explain the problem and request that immediate action be taken.
2) If your car is new, contact the manufacturer.
3) Contact your local or state agency responsible for licensing automotive shops.
4) Contact the Department of Consumer Affairs in your state, a local or national consumer group, or the Better Business Bureau (particularly if your car has a defect common to others of the same make).
5) You may bring an action in small claims court if the amount of your claim does not exceed the small claims limit (see chapter 4).
6) You can bring a civil action in federal district court for damages as well as attorney's fees and court costs.

DECEPTIVE TRADE PRACTICES

In 1964, a national conference on uniform state laws developed and approved the Uniform Deceptive Trade Practices Act. Many states have adopted the Act outright while others have used it as a model for their own state laws. The business practices covered are twofold: misleading trade identification and false or deceptive advertising.

The Act defines deceptive trade practices as those in which the merchant:

1) passes off goods or services as those of another
2) causes confusion as to the source of sponsorship or certification of goods or services
3) causes confusion over affiliation or association with another person, organization, company, etc.
4) uses deceptive representations of geographic origin of goods or services
5) represents that goods or services have sponsorship, approval, characteristics, uses, or guarantees that they do not have

6) represents that goods are new when they are reconditioned, altered, or deteriorated
7) represents that goods or services are of a particular standard, quality, grade, style, or model when they are of another
8) disparages goods, services, or business of another by false or misleading representation of fact
9) advertises goods or services when they are not intended to be sold as advertised
10) advertises goods or services intending not to supply a reasonable public demand (unless the ad states there is a limited quantity)
11) makes false or misleading statements of fact concerning the reason for or amount of a price reduction
12) engages in any other conduct that creates likelihood of confusion.

Although the UDTPA, as well as most state statutes, covers a broad area, the remedies are generally limited to injunctive relief (stopping a particular business practice by court order) and in some cases attorney's fees.

18
Bankruptcy

In these times of high interest rates, plastic money, and easy credit, it is not uncommon for a woman to go from a financially sound position to near poverty in a relatively short period of time. Businesses continue to fold at a high rate, jobs are lost, illnesses and accidents occur, and many women are in the unfortunate position of being single parents who receive no financial help from their ex-husbands; others are simply poor managers of money. As a result, a number of women are finding themselves in a desperate situation, seeing no hope of keeping up with the monthly bills that continue to pile up. If you are in debt, you can take some solace in the fact that you are not alone. Many Americans are in the same predicament.

What can you do when your debts far exceed your assets and there's no relief in sight? You may want to consider bankruptcy—but only after carefully considering all the other options. Bankruptcy should be your last resort. The bankruptcy laws are quite reasonable and can offer much-needed protection to the debtor, but they should not be abused. Your debts can be eliminated through bankruptcy only once every six years. Before you panic and run to an attorney with bills in hand, ask yourself a few questions:

—Have you attempted to negotiate an agreement with your creditors that will allow you to make lower monthly payments or to pay your debts at a later date? Your creditors should be willing to discuss alternative methods of payment; after all, their only concern is that you pay off your debt, and most of them would prefer to receive smaller payments over a longer period of time than to become involved in bankruptcy proceedings.

—Have you considered obtaining a loan from a credit union or a debt consolidation loan from a bank or finance company to pay off your debts?

—Have you investigated the possibility of refinancing your home and taking out a second mortgage to pay your creditors? (Obviously, your decision will be influenced by prevailing interest rates.)

—Have you consulted a consumer counseling service? Many communities have nonprofit organizations that operate specifically to help consumers with their financial problems.

—Is there a chance that your financial situation may improve within a few months?

If your situation remains hopeless after exhausting all of the other options, it's time to take drastic action. When you reach the point where your mental or physical health is in jeopardy and you're sinking fast, there's no point in digging a deeper hole for yourself. Sometimes the only realistic remedy is to file for bankruptcy and get yourself back on a sound economic footing.

As is true of all other major decisions, there are advantages and disadvantages to declaring bankruptcy. It does not eliminate all of life's problems; in fact, it most likely will create a few. Consider all the pros and cons and then make your decision *before* the sheriff repossesses your car.

The advantages:

1) Bankruptcy can eliminate most of your debts or restructure the terms of payment to allow you a reasonable time to satisfy your creditors.
2) Once you have filed, your creditors will not be allowed to harass you or to bring suit against you for nonpayment of your debts.
3) You will be allowed to keep a certain amount of property and cash to keep you going until your situation improves.

The disadvantages:

1) Your credit rating will take a nose dive. Even when you are back on your feet, it may be difficult for you to obtain credit.
2) Filing bankruptcy may well be very embarrassing for you and your family. And some of your friends and acquaintances may feel that

you jumped ship, took the coward's way out, by reneging on your promise to pay your debts.

3) You will be required to meet with your creditors face to face, to undergo questioning about your finances, and to appear in court.

You are not required to have an attorney represent you in bankruptcy proceedings or to file the bankruptcy forms for you, but there are a number of strong arguments for seeking legal assistance. The bankruptcy laws are very specific regarding which debts are dischargeable (allowed to be eliminated) and what property you are allowed to keep, but you have the option of adhering to either the state or the federal exemption list. You may need professional advice from a bankruptcy attorney on which list would work best for your particular situation, what steps you can take to retain a greater portion of your property, how to complete the forms that must be filed with the court, and whether to file a Chapter 7 or a Chapter 13 bankruptcy (these are discussed below). Legal fees for these services do vary but generally are not excessive, and you should consider that a $500-$2,000 fee may be well worth it if your attorney can guide you through the process and save you much more in exempt property than you would have had by filing on your own. If you decide you do need an attorney's assistance, select one who specializes in bankruptcy.

CHAPTER 13

If you have a steady income and there is a good chance that with careful planning and budgeting your financial situation will improve in time, you may be much better off to file a Chapter 13 rather than a Chapter 7 bankruptcy. In this type of bankruptcy, your unsecured debts cannot exceed $100,000, and your secured debts, $350,000 (see "Debts" later in this chapter). Under Chapter 13, the debtor proposes a plan to the bankruptcy court to make partial or complete payment to her creditors over a specified period of time (usually one to three years, unless she can show cause for extending the plan to five years). This system allows her the time to reorganize her finances and to continue ownership of most of her assets while protecting her against harassment by her creditors. Some debts may be discharged or can be renegotiated with the creditors, but others cannot be discharged, such as spousal and child support and secured debts (those for which the debtor has pledged her property if she fails to make payment).

These are the steps you must take to file a Chapter 13:

1) Complete the bankruptcy petition. Once it is filed, an automatic stay will go into effect (this prohibits your creditors from attempting to

collect payment). All bankruptcy forms are available from the clerk of the local bankruptcy court or from office supply or stationery stores. You will be required to pay a minimal filing fee.

2) Within 10 days of filing the petition, you must file a Chapter 13 Statement of property, debts, budget, and income, which includes a list of your creditors and their addresses (see "Debts" and "Property" later in this chapter). A budget plan detailing how you will repay your creditors over a specified period of time is submitted to the court. The plan must be based on your ability to pay and yet provide for a fair distribution of payment to your creditors. All debts of a similar nature must be treated equally. For example, you are not allowed to pay off in full a personal unsecured loan from an uncle while paying Bank Americard only 10% of the debt.

If the plan provides for less than full payment to unsecured creditors, the court must determine whether they would benefit more if your estate were liquidated under Chapter 7. (You can convert from a Chapter 13 to a Chapter 7 at any time.) If a secured creditor objects to the plan he is given the right to repossess property to satisfy the debt or to retain a lien on the property and receive property or cash with a value equal to the secured debt. You cannot reduce monthly house payments if the debt is secured only by your house, but the court may agree to reduce monthly payments on debts secured by property other than your house. Wages owed to someone in your employ must be paid in full; tax claims can be paid in installments.

3) Once all of the forms have been submitted to the court, your creditors will be notified of the bankruptcy and informed of the date of the confirmation hearing. The purpose of this hearing is to allow your creditors and the trustee appointed by the court to ask you questions relating to your assets and debts and the manner in which you have managed your finances (this process is called "discovery"). The trustee is responsible for administering the plan, and you are required to provide him with all records and documents relating to your assets and liabilities. Creditors are allowed to question you and to protest the proposed plan of repayment, but antagonistic questions can be objected to by your attorney. A creditor may file a written motion requesting a response, and if the court approves it you will be required to provide the information. You may have to submit to other examinations if creditors who were not acknowledged in the bankruptcy forms file an "application of any party in interest."

4) Once the court has approved or "confirmed" the plan, you must turn over to the trustee the amount of your income needed to meet the terms of repayment.

5) When you have paid off all your creditors according to the plan, the court will grant a discharge of all of those debts.

CHAPTER 7

The woman who is deeply in debt with little hope that her financial situation will improve may find that her only recourse is to file a Chapter 7 bankruptcy (also referred to as "straight bankruptcy"). Unlike a Chapter 13, which can be filed only by the debtor, a Chapter 7 can be filed in behalf of a debtor by her creditors (this is called a forced or involuntary bankruptcy). Under Chapter 7, all non-exempt assets (those not protected under state or federal law) are liquidated and distributed as final payment to creditors having priority (such as the government) and to unsecured creditors (such as credit-card companies, department stores, and doctors). All debts owed to secured creditors are eliminated, although the creditors have the right to repossess the property used as security or collateral.

These are the steps involved in filing a Chapter 7 bankruptcy:

1) Fill out the bankruptcy petition, Schedule A & B (Statement of Liabilities and Statement of Property), a Summary of Debts and Property (which summarizes the information provided in Schedule A & B), a Statement of Financial Affairs (in which you provide such information as occupation and income, taxes paid or refunded, bank accounts, loans repaid, and your claim of property exemptions), an Information Summary Sheet, and a list of your creditors and their addresses. All of these forms are available from the clerk of the bankruptcy court or from a stationery or office supply store. If you are married, you and your husband can complete a "joint petition."

2) Sign the forms and deliver them to the clerk of the court along with the $60 filing fee (you may be allowed to pay the fee in installments). You or your attorney should retain one copy of each form submitted to the court.

3) Once you have filed the petition, an automatic stay will go into effect, which prohibits your creditors from bringing or continuing legal action or harassing you for nonpayment of your debts.

DEBTS

Bankruptcy protects you against debts incurred up to the time you file the bankruptcy petition, not those that come afterwards. Consequently, the time at which you file the petition is crucial. If you are anticipating a number of substantial bills that could be eliminated by bankruptcy, such as medical bills, it is better to file after they are in hand. The court will not discharge debts that were created with the purpose of intentionally avoiding payment (such as the Mediterranean cruise or the shopping spree six weeks before filing for bankruptcy). In addition, payments made to creditors within the 90 days preceding the filing of the bankruptcy petition may have to be returned to the bankruptcy court for a more equitable distribution.

There are two kinds of debts—secured and unsecured. A secured debt is one which allows your creditor to repossess your property if you fail to make payments. For example, if you took out a loan at a credit union to purchase a new Toyota and later defaulted on the payments, the credit union could repossess the car and sell it to obtain the unpaid balance. However, according to the new bankruptcy law, you may be allowed to retain household property that has been pledged as security or collateral if it is classified as exempt. An unsecured debt is one for which you have not pledged your property as security, such as dining room furniture purchased with a Bank Americard. All credit agreements you sign specify whether or not your property is secured (you can obtain copies of the agreements from your creditors).

Before you file for bankruptcy, you should pay off as many of your secured creditors as possible so that your property cannot be repossessed.

The law defines what debts are dischargeable and which are not dischargeable. Those which are not dischargeable you will continue to be responsible for, in spite of the bankruptcy. Listed below are those debts which are generally considered by the courts to be non-dischargeable:

—*Attorney's fees and court costs incurred during divorce proceedings* are not dischargeable if they relate to child or spousal support.

—*Child and spousal support* are non-dischargeable, but payments made to an ex-spouse as part of a property settlement are dischargeable.

—*Income taxes* are not dischargeable if they were payable within the three years prior to the filing of bankruptcy, or if the tax returns were fraudulent or were not filed.

—*Student loans* are not dischargeable if owed to a governmental body or a nonprofit institution of higher education. Lenders are protected for five years against having loans discharged through bankruptcy. The only argument used by debtors that has been considered valid is that repayment would impose undue hardship. These cases are determined on an individual basis by the courts.

—*Lawsuits and fines imposed for violation of the law.* This includes traffic tickets that are considered by the particular state to be of a criminal nature.

—*Debts incurred by using false financial statements or by fraud.* A rather comical example is the case of Baldwin National Bank v. Stephen P. Brill.[1] Mr. Brill secured a loan from the bank using 15 cows as collateral. Actually, the cows had been sold long before he applied for the loan. Understandably, the court ruled that the debt was not dischargeable.

—*Liabilities for willful and malicious injury to person or property.*

—*All debts that were omitted from the bankruptcy form submitted to the court.* Any debts you forgot to include will not be discharged; nor will any debt you previously waived or that was denied discharge in a bankruptcy action.

PROPERTY

Once you file for bankruptcy, you are allowed to keep in your possession or to own only that property which the law states is exempt. Exempt property is that which state law or federal law has recognized as necessary for the debtor to make a new start. The state and federal statutes each have their own list of exemptions, but the state exemptions vary from state to state. You will need to compare your state's exemptions to the federal exemptions to see which will allow you to keep more of your property. You cannot select exemptions from both lists. However, you are allowed to convert non-exempt assets (such as cash) into exempt assets up until the time you file for bankruptcy. By converting these assets, you may be able to retain much more of your property.

Property considered by the bankruptcy court includes both real property (houses, land, buildings, etc.) and personal property (furniture, clothing, jewelry, etc.). Anything you own is considered your property, even those intangible items not usually thought of as property. Here is a brief list:

Household goods
Automobiles
Home and other real property
Clothing
Jewelry
Works of art
Cameras
Firearms
Pets
Bank accounts/Cash
Pension/retirement plans
Savings bonds
Debts owed to you
Insurance policies with cash value
Social Security benefits
Unemployment compensation
Veterans benefits
Insurance proceeds/benefits

The federal exemption list allows the debtor to keep the following:

1) A residence (a home, mobile home, houseboat, etc.) with a total equity of $7,500 or less. Equity is the market value minus the amount of the mortgage.

For example, suppose you purchased a home in 1975 for $30,000 with a down payment of $5,000. At the time you filed for bankruptcy you owed $20,000 on the mortgage. If the market value of the home is $50,000 it would have to be sold to pay off your creditors since the equity is greater than the $7,500 allowed; you would receive $7,500 from the sale.

$50,000	market value
−20,000	present mortgage
$30,000	equity

Some states provide greater protection to homeowners through the homestead exemption. For example, California allows an exemption of $45,000 if a woman is the head of household. If the preceding situation occurred in California, then, and you were the head of household, your home would not have to be sold to pay off your creditors.

$50,000	market value
−20,000	present mortgage
30,000	equity
−45,000	head of household homestead exemption
0	

2) Motor vehicles with equity not exceeding $1,200.

For example, suppose you bought a car in 1973 for $5,000 and now own it free and clear. If the car is valued at $1,000, you will be allowed to keep it since you owe nothing on it and your total equity is $1,000, which is less than the exemption limit.

3) Equity of up to $200 in each item that falls under any of these categories:

Household furnishings	Books
Household goods	Animals
Wearing apparel	Crops
Appliances	Musical instruments

4) Jewelry with a value up to $500.

5) Up to $4,000 cash value of a life insurance policy

6) Health insurance benefits

7) Tools of your trade (including professional publications) with a value of $750 or less

8) Disability benefits

9) Retirement benefits

10) Unemployment compensation

11) Veterans benefits

12) Social Security benefits

13) Awards made under crime victims reparation laws

14) Up to $7,500 in payments for personal bodily injury

15) Reasonable spousal and child support payments

16) An additional exemption of $400 plus any unused portion of the exemption for your residence, which can be applied to any type of property.

In other words, if you don't own your own home, you can apply the $7,500 as well as an additional $400 toward any other property, even that which is generally not exempt (such as cash, a bank account, or savings bonds).

COURT PROCEEDINGS

The federal court system has exclusive jurisdiction over bankruptcies, so you must file your petition and have your case heard at the bankruptcy court in the district where you reside. In 1979, the Advisory Committee on Bankruptcy Rules issued suggested guidelines on how bankruptcies should be administered; some courts have adopted these guidelines, while others continue to follow local rules. Consequently, there are variations from district to district, but your attorney or the clerk of the bankruptcy court can instruct you on court procedures.

As we mentioned earlier, once you have filed a petition for bankruptcy an automatic stay becomes effective, which means that your creditors cannot harass you or bring or continue a suit against you for default of payment. Any creditor who violates the automatic stay may be found in contempt of court. Criminal actions and those brought for failure to pay child or spousal support are not subject to the stay. The stay remains in effect until the case is closed or dismissed unless the court grants a creditor an exception (that is, allows him to attempt to recover the amount of the debt). You are not required to notify your creditors; it is the court's responsibility to inform them of the bankruptcy.

Within five or six weeks of filing the petition, you will be required to meet with your creditors and with the interim trustee appointed by the court. Creditors who hold at least 20% of the claims may elect a trustee to oversee the administration of the bankruptcy if they wish. The purpose of the meeting is to allow the trustee and your creditors to question you about your assets and debts and the manner in which you have managed your finances. A court reporter, the creditors, the trustee, and the debtor attend the meeting, but a judge is not present.

In a Chapter 7 bankruptcy, all of your property that is not exempt will be relinquished to the trustee, who is responsible for investigating your assets, liabilities, and financial affairs, having the property appraised, overseeing the sale of the property (if such is necessary), paying your creditors, and keeping records and accounts of the payments. You or your attorney should attempt to renegotiate repayment agreements with your secured creditors to avoid having your property repossessed.

The discharge hearing is held once the deadline has passed for creditors to file complaints objecting to the discharge of your debts. At this time, the judge will determine which debts will be discharged, and thereafter you will no longer be indebted to those creditors. Although not required under the bankruptcy code, you may wish to file a reaffirmation declaration, a legally binding agreement in which the debtor consents to pay a debt that has been discharged through the bankruptcy. The agreement must be approved by the court, which will decide whether such an arrangement would impose undue hardship on you. You are allowed to rescind the reaffirmation agreement up to 30 days after it has gone into effect.

If you are unsatisfied with the outcome of the bankruptcy proceedings, you can appeal as long as you meet certain requirements: 1) there must be valid grounds for appeal; 2) you must file a notice of appeal with the clerk of the bankruptcy court within a specified number of days (usually 10 to 30 days); 3) you must file a statement of the issues you will be raising on appeal; and 4) you must obtain and pay for a transcript from the lower court. Generally, you can appeal directly to the court of appeals. In some districts, however, a panel of bankruptcy judges decides appeals from the bankruptcy courts. Foreclosures and the sale of property will be prohibited until the appeal has been heard.

A WORD ABOUT BANKRUPTCY OF YOUR BUSINESS

You can file either a Chapter 7 or a Chapter 11 for bankruptcy of your business. A Chapter 7 involves the liquidation and elimination of debts, and you need to follow the same procedures and complete the same forms required in an individual Chapter 7 bankruptcy. Chapter 11 allows you to reorganize your business and finances and to present to the court a plan of repayment based on the amount of assets and future income. The reorganization plan may involve the sale of some property, a change in interest rates or terms of repayment, or a merger and consolidation. It must be in the best interests of the creditors and be approved by the bankruptcy court. You would be wise to consult an attorney before filing either form of bankruptcy.

Notes and References

Chapter 1—Do You Really Need an Attorney?

Notes

1. U. S. Department of Labor, Bureau of Labor Statistics, *The Female-Male Earnings Gap: A Review of Employment and Earnings Issues* (Washington, DC: U.S. Government Printing Office, 1982), p. 8.

Chapter 2—Selecting an Attorney

Notes

1. Canter v. Lovett and Lender, Ltd. 425 A.2d 1244.
2. Grievance Commission v. Kerpelman BV No7 (Maryland Court of Appeals, 1981).
3. In Re Matter of Adams 428 N.E.2d 786 (Indiana Supreme Court, 1981).
4. In Re Petty 627 P.2d 191.

References

American Bar Association. Disciplinary Law and Procedure Advance Sheets. Chicago: American Bar Association Center for Professional Discipline, 1982.

Aronson, Robert. *Attorney-Client Fee Arrangements: Regulation and Review.* Washington, DC: Federal Justice Center, 1980.

Citizens' Legal Manual: Shopping for a Lawyer. Washington, DC: Halt, Inc., 1979.

Law Journal Seminars. *Attorneys' Liability.* New York: Law Journal Seminars Press, 1980.

Mallen, Ronald E., and Victor B. Levit. *Legal Malpractice.* St. Paul, MN: West Publishing Co., 1981.

Chapter 3—Jury Duty

Notes

1. Constitution of the United States, Amendment VI. "In all criminal prosecutions, the accused shall enjoy the right to a speedy and public trial, by an impartial jury.... "
2. United States v. Wood (1936) 299 U.S. 123, 145.
3. California Civil Procedure Section 198.
4. People v. Jones (1972) 25 CA3rd 776. "Sufficient knowledge of the English language" requires that jurors be fully able to understand written as well as spoken English.

5. 28 USCA 1861. "It is the policy of the United States ... that all citizens shall have the opportunity to be considered ... [and] shall have the obligation to serve as jurors when summoned for that purpose."
6. 28 USCA 1863 (b) (5).
7. Questions supplied by the Honorable Walter L. Gorelick, judge of the Tulare-Pixley Municipal Court, Tulare, California.
8. California Penal Code Section 1070.
9. U.S. v. Wheeler 583 P2d 748.
10. U.S. v. Durham 587 F2d 799.

Chapter 4—Small Claims Court

References

Spurrier, Robert L., Jr. *Inexpensive Justice: Self-Representation in the Small Claims Court*. Port Washington, NY: Associated Faculty Press, 1981.
Warner, Ralph. *Everybody's Guide to Small Claims Court*. 4th ed. Occidental, CA: Nolo Press, 1982.
Willer, S., and J. Ruhunka. *Practical Observations of the Small Claims Court*. Williamsburg, VA: National Center for State Courts, 1979.

Chapter 5—Traffic Court

References

Contemporary Overview of Traffic Law Uniformity in the U.S. Washington, DC: U.S. Department of Transportation, National Highway Traffic Safety Administration, 1978.
Standards for Traffic Justice. Chicago: American Bar Association, 1975.
Traffic Court Procedure and Administration. 2nd ed. Chicago: American Bar Association, 1982.

Chapter 6—Your Rights as an Arrested Person

Notes

1. Miranda v. Arizona 384 U.S. 436.
2. Id. at 492.

Chapter 7—Searches

Notes

1. California Penal Code Section 1523.
2. U.S. v. Ross 456 U.S. 798.
3. People v. Arno 90 Cal App 3rd 505.
4. Blair v. Pitchess 486 P.2d 1242, 1253.
5. Warden, Maryland Penitentiary v. Haden 387 U.S. 294.
6. U.S. v. Robinson 414 U.S. 218.
7. Chimel v. California 395 U.S. 752.
8. Id. at 763.
9. Id. at 763.
10. Id. at 763.

References

Hirschel, Joseph D. *Fourth Amendment Rights*. Lexington, MA: Lexington Books, 1979.

Chapter 8—Divorce

Notes

1. "Family Law in the Fifty States," *Family Law Quarterly* 16 (Winter 1983): 300-312.
2. Orr v. Orr 99 S.Ct. 1102, 1112.

References

CuConto, Joseph N., and Robert S. Taft. *Divorce Math.* New York: Law and Business, Inc., 1982.

Eisler, Riane Tennenhaus. *Dissolution, No-Fault Divorce, Marriage and the Future of Women.* New York: McGraw-Hill, 1977.

Family Advocate 6 (Spring 1984).

Family Law Quarterly 16 (Winter 1983); 17 (Spring 1984).

Friedman, James T. *The Divorce Handbook: Your Basic Guide to Divorce.* New York: Random House, 1982.

Glendon, Mary Ann. *The New Family and the New Property.* Toronto: Butterworths, 1981.

Halem, Lynne C. *Divorce Reform: Changing Legal and Social Perspectives.* New York: Free Press, 1980.

Mitnick, Harold. *How to Handle Your Divorce Step by Step.* Bethesda, MD: Lone Oak Books, 1981.

Wheeler, Michael. *No-Fault Divorce.* Boston: Beacon Press, 1974.

Chapter 9—Child Custody and Support

Notes

1. Dodd v. Dodd 403 NYS2d 401, 404.
2. Borden v. Borden 193 So2d 15.
3. Stuart v. Stuart 209 Cal App2d 478.
4. Ashwell v. Ashwell 286 P.2d 983, 987.
5. Almond v. Almond 257 S.E. 450, 452.
6. California Civil Code 4600(a).
7. Hurst v. Hurst 27 So2d 749, 750.
8. California Civil Code 4600.5(f).

References

Kram, Shirley, and Neil A. Frank. *The Law of Child Custody: Application and Procedural Aspects.* Lexington, MA: Lexington Books, 1983.

Wheeler, Michael. *Divided Children: A Legal Guide for Divorcing Parents.* New York: W. W. Norton, 1980.

Chapter 10—Juvenile Law

Notes

1. Colorado Revised Statute, 1973, 19-1-102(a).
2. Lamb v. Brown (Oklahoma) 456 F.2d 18.
3. California Welfare and Institutions Code Section 602.
4. California Welfare and Institutions Code Section 601.
5. In Re Gault, 387 U.S. 1.
6. McKeiver v. Pennsylvania 403 U.S. 528.
7. In Re Winship 397 U.S. 358.
8. California Welfare and Institutions Code Section 606.
9. Texas Family Code Title 2 Section 51.16.

Chapter 11—Sex Discrimination

Notes

1. Muller v. Oregon 208 U.S. 412.
2. Bradwell v. The State 83 U.S. 130.
3. Futran v. Ring Radio Co. 501 F.Supp. 734.
4. Hill v. Nettleton 455 F.Supp. 514.
5. Griggs v. Duke Power Co. 401 U.S. 424.
6. Hishon v. King and Spalding, heard by Supreme Court May 22, 1984.
7. Marshall v. Kirkland 602 F.2d 1282.
8. U.S. Department of Labor, Bureau of Labor Statistics, *The Female-Male Earnings Gap: A Review of Employment and Earnings Issues* (Washington, DC: U.S. Government Printing Office, 1982).
9. EEOC v. Central Kansas Medical Center 705 F.2d 1270.
10. Usery v. Richman 20 F.E.P. 807.
11. County of Washington v. Gunther 602 F.2d 882.

References

Anderson, Howard. *Primer of Equal Employment Opportunity*. Washington, DC: The Bureau of National Affairs, 1978.

Fair Employment Practices Cumulative Digest and Index and Table of Cases. Washington, DC: The Bureau of National Affairs, 1979-82.

Larson, Richard. *Sue Your Boss: Rights and Remedies for Employment Discrimination*. New York: Farrar, Straus & Giroux, 1981.

Lawrence, Kenneth, and Katharine Klos. *Sexual Discrimination in the Workplace*. Maryland: The Center for Compliance Information, 1978.

1984 Guidebook to Fair Employment Practices. Chicago: Commerce Clearinghouse, 1983.

Pepper, William, and Florence Kennedy. *Sex Discrimination in Employment*. Charlottesville, VA: The Michie Co., 1982.

Reifers, Suzanne. *How to Hire and Supervise Women Legally*. New York: Executive Enterprises Publications Co., 1979.

Smith, Arthur B., Jr. *Employment Discrimination Law*. Charlottesville, VA: The Michie Co., 1982.

Thomas, Claire S. *Sex Discrimination*. St. Paul, MN: West Publishing Co., 1982.

U.S. Department of Labor, Bureau of Labor Statistics. *The Female-Male Earnings Gap: A Review of Employment and Earnings Issues*. Washington, DC: U.S. Government Printing Office, 1982.

U.S. Equal Employment Opportunity Commission. *Job Discrimination Laws and Rules You Should Know*. Washington, DC: U.S. Government Printing Office, 1979.

Chapter 12—Sexual Harassment

Notes

1. Toscano v. Nimmo 570 F.Supp. 1197.
2. Katz v. Dole 709 F.2d 251.
3. Williams v. Civiletti 487 F.Supp. 1387.
4. U.S. Equal Employment Opportunity Commission. *Job Discrimination Laws and Rules You Should Know* (Washington, DC: U.S. Government Printing Office, 1979).
5. Ibid.
6. Tomkins v. Public Service Electric & Gas Co. 568 F.2d 1044.
7. Miller v. Bank of America 418 F.Supp. 233, 600 F.2d 211.

References

Backhouse, Constance, and Leah Cohen. *Sexual Harassment on the Job.* Englewood Cliffs, NJ: Prentice-Hall, 1981.

Farley, Lin. *Sexual Shakedown: The Sexual Harassment of Women on the Job.* New York: McGraw-Hill, 1978.

Chapter 13—Rape

Notes

1. Neal v. State 263 S.E.2d 185.
2. Commonwealth v. Carter 418 A.2d 537.
3. People v. Dorsey 429 NYS2d 828, 104 misc2d 963.
4. Fitzpatrick v. State 558 P.2d 630.
5. Elizabeth Bochnak, *Women's Self-Defense Cases: Theory and Practice* (Charlottesville, VA: The Michie Co., 1981).
6. Provided by the National Clearinghouse on Marital Rape, Women's History Research Center, Berkeley, California.
7. State v. Smith 85 N.J. 193, 426 A.2d 38.

References

Bienen, Leigh. "Rape III: National Development in Rape Reform Legislation." *Women's Rights Law Reporter* 6 (Spring 1980).

Brownmiller, Susan. *Against Our Will: Men, Women and Rape.* New York: Simon and Schuster, 1975.

Drucker, Dennis. "The Common Law Does Not Support a Marital Exemption for Forcible Rape." *Women's Rights Law Reporter* 5 (1979).

Eyman, Joy S. *How to Convict a Rapist.* New York: Stein and Day, 1980.

Field, Herbert S., and Leigh Bienen. *Jurors and Rape: A Study in Psychology and Law.* Lexington, MA: Lexington Books, 1980.

Herschel, Adam. *The Prosecution and Defense of Sex Crimes.* New York: Matthew Bender, 1981.

Hursch, Carolyn. *The Trouble with Rape: A Psychologist's Report on the Legal, Medical, Social and Psychological Problems.* Chicago: Nelson-Hall, 1977.

McDermott, Joan. *Rape Victimization in 26 American Cities.* Washington, DC: U.S. Department of Justice, Law Enforcement Assistance Administration, 1979.

U.S. Department of Justice, Criminal Justice Research Center. *Sourcebook of Criminal Justice Statistics.* Washington, DC: U.S. Government Printing Office, 1978.

Chapter 14—Battered Women

Notes

1. Murray Straus, "Wife Beating: Causes, Treatment, and Research Needs," in *Battered Women: Issues of Public Policy* (Washington, DC: U.S. Commission on Civil Rights, 1978), p. 153.
2. Maria L. La Ganza, "Domestic Violence: For Some Women a Way of Life," Part V, *Los Angeles Times*, Oct. 18, 1982, pp. 1, 3, 7.
3. Natisa Hoodbhoy, "Problems Don't End When the Battering Stops," *Guardian*, v. 35, April 21, 1983, p. 7.
4. Dreas, Ignatov, and Brennan, "The Male Batterer: A Model Treatment for the Courts," *Federal Probation*, v. 46, Dec. 1982, pp. 50-55.

References

Battered Women: Issues of Public Policy. Washington, DC: U.S. Commission on Civil Rights, 1978.

Bochnak, Elizabeth. *Women's Self-Defense Cases: Theory and Practice*. Charlottesville, VA: The Michie Co., 1981.
Dobash, R. E., and Russell Dobash. *Violence Against Wives*. New York: The Free Press, 1979.
The Federal Response to Domestic Violence. Washington, DC: U.S. Commission on Civil Rights, 1982.
Gelles, Richard. *The Violent Home*. Beverly Hills, CA: Sage Publications, 1974.
Martin, Del. *Battered Wives*. rev. ed. San Francisco, CA: Volcano Press, 1981.
Pagelow, Mildred. *Woman Battering: Victims and Their Experiences*. Beverly Hills, CA: Sage Publications, 1981.
Roy, Maria. *Battered Women: A Psychosociological Study of Domestic Violence*. New York: Van Nostrand Reinhold, 1977.
Straus, M., R. Gelles, and S. Steinmetz. *Behind Closed Doors: Violence in the American Family*. Garden City, NY: Anchor Press/Doubleday, 1980.
Walker, Lenore. *The Battered Woman*. New York: Harper & Row, 1979.

Chapter 15—Wills

References

Mennell, Robert L. *Wills and Trusts*. St. Paul, MN: West Publishing Co., 1979.

Chapter 16—Social Security

References

Federal Tax Coordinator, Volume 12. New York: New York Research Institute of America, 1984.
Federal Tax Regulations 1984. St. Paul, MN: West Publishing Co., 1984.
McCormick, Harvey L. *Social Security Claims and Procedures*. 3rd ed. St. Paul, MN: West Publishing Co., 1983.
Social Security and the Changing Roles of Men and Women. Washington, DC: U.S. Department of Health, Education, and Welfare, 1979.
"Social Security Rulings." January 1984. Washington, DC: U.S. Government Printing Office, 1984.
Pamphlets on Social Security are available from the Consumer Information Center, Pueblo, Colorado 81009.

Chapter 17—Consumer Concerns

Notes

1. Truth in Lending Act, Title I or Consumer Credit Protection Act PL 30-321, 82 Stat 146, 15 USC §1601.

References

Analysis and Digest of Consumer Protection Case Law. Washington, DC: Committee on the Office of Attorney General, 1976.
Clark, B., and J. Fonseca. *Handling Consumer Credit Cases*. 2nd ed. Rochester, NY: Lawyers Co-operative Publishing Co., 1980.
Clontz, Ralph C., Jr. *Equal Credit Opportunity Manual*. 3rd ed. Boston, MA: Warren, Gorham & Lamont, 1979.
Clontz, Ralph C., Jr. *Truth-in-Lending Manual*. 5th ed. Boston, MA: Warren, Gorham & Lamont, 1982.
Consumer Credit 1983. Ed. by Harold E. Mortimer, et al. New York: Practicing Law Institute, 1983.

Federal Trade Commission. *Federal Trade Commission—Operation Manual.* New York: Federal Legal Publications, 1976.
Hemphill, Charles. *Consumer Protection: A Legal Guide.* Englewood Cliffs, NJ: Prentice-Hall, 1981.
Horvitz, Simeon. *Legal Protection for Today's Consumer.* Dubuque, IA: Kendall/Hunt, 1980.
Kaplan, Melvin J., and Phillip T. Drotning. *How to Get Creditors Off Your Back without Losing Your Shirt.* Chicago: Contemporary Books, 1979.
White House Office of the Special Assistant for Consumer Affairs. *Consumers Resource Handbook.* Washington, DC: U.S. Government Printing Office, 1979.
Pamphlets on all areas of consumer concerns are available from the Consumer Information Center, Pueblo, Colorado 81009.

Chapter 18—Bankruptcy

Notes

1. Baldwin National Bank v. Stephen P. Brill (Alabama 1982) 20 B.R. 84.

References

Cohen, Arnold. *Bankruptcy, Secured Transactions and Other Debtor-Creditor Matters.* Charlottesville, VA: The Michie Co., 1981.
Cowans, Daniel. *Cowans' Bankruptcy Law and Practice.* St. Paul, MN: West Publishing Co., 1981.
Girth, Marjorie. *Bankruptcy Options for the Consumer Debtor.* New York: Practicing Law Institute, 1981.
Herzog, Asa. *Herzog's Bankruptcy Forms and Practice.* New York: Clark Boardman, 1980.
Kosel, Janice. *Bankruptcy: Do It Yourself.* 2nd ed. Occidental, CA: Nolo Press, 1983.
Norton, William. *Norton Bankruptcy Law and Practice.* Wilmette, IL: Callaghan and Co., 1981.
Samet, Joseph. *Consumer Finance and Lending: Practice under Chapters 7 and 13 of the Bankruptcy Code.* New York: Practicing Law Institute, 1981.
Taylor, Catherine. *Bankruptcy Practice—An Overview.* San Diego, CA: San Diego Trial Lawyers Association, 1982.
West's Bankruptcy Reporter. St. Paul, MN: West Publishing Co., 1982.

Glossary

Administrator—a person appointed by the probate court to settle the estate of one who has died without a will.

Admissible evidence—evidence which has been properly obtained and is allowed to be presented in court to aid the judge or jury in deciding the merits of a case.

Alimony—see **Spousal support**.

Annulment—a declaration by a court of law that a marriage was invalid from its inception and never legally existed.

Appeal—the procedure by which a case is brought to a higher court for review in an attempt to have the decision of a lower court reversed or modified.

Appellate court—a court having the authority to hear appeals from a lower court.

Arraignment—a criminal proceeding in which the defendant is formally charged with an offense and requested to plead guilty or not guilty.

Bail—money or other security given to secure the release of a defendant and to guarantee her appearance in court.

Bankruptcy—a legal process by which a court liquidates the assets of a person who is insolvent to pay off creditors and frees her of most of her debts (Chapter 7 bankruptcy). A Chapter 13 bankruptcy allows the debtor to submit a repayment plan to the court and to retain possession of most of her assets.

Bench warrant—a court order authorizing an arrest (often issued when a person fails to appear in court or when there is a charge of contempt).

Beneficiary—a person named in a will, trust, insurance policy, or other agreement to receive property or a sum of money.

Breach of contract—failure to comply with the provisions of a contract.

Breach of warranty—failure to comply with the provisions of a warranty.

Cause of action—facts sufficient to form the basis of a valid lawsuit.

Civil action—a lawsuit brought in civil court (as opposed to criminal court) to recover damages or to protect a private right.

Class action—a lawsuit brought on behalf of a large group of persons by one or more persons representative of the group.

Codicil—an amendment to a will, written to add to, delete from, or modify the provisions of the will.

Common property—the system of property ownership in which each spouse owns whatever she or he earns.

Community property—the system of property ownership in which property acquired by either spouse during the marriage is owned by both of them, regardless of whose name appears on a title. Property acquired before the marriage or by gift or inheritance is generally considered separate property.

Complaint—a statement of facts that form the basis of a plaintiff's lawsuit.

Contempt of court—an act or omission that interferes with the orderly administration of justice or indicates disrespect for the authority of a court of law.

Contingent fee—an attorney's fee based on a percentage of the amount awarded to a client in a civil lawsuit.

Continuance—a postponement or adjournment of a hearing or other legal proceeding to a later date.

Contract—an agreement in which two or more parties exchange promises to do or refrain from doing an act (often one party agrees to perform a service if the other pays her a specific sum of money).

Conviction—the result of a criminal proceeding in which the accused is found guilty.

Counterclaim—a claim asserting a separate cause of action that is brought by a defendant in response to a lawsuit filed by the plaintiff.

Cross-examination—the questioning of a witness for the opposing party during a trial or hearing.

Damages—monetary compensation awarded to a person who has suffered an injury or loss because of the actions of the opposing party.

Default judgment—a judgment against a defendant due to his failure to respond or to appear in court.

Defendant—the party in a lawsuit who is accused of wrongdoing.

Deposition—a written record of testimony given by a witness under oath that may later be presented at a trial.

Dischargeable debt—a debt for which the debtor is not liable as a result of bankruptcy.

Discovery—the pretrial process by which one party attempts to obtain from the opposing party additional information that will strengthen her case. See **Deposition** and **Interrogatories**.

Divorce—dissolution of a marriage.

Estate—all property owned by a person plus that in which she has an interest.

Executor—the person appointed by the testator to settle her estate in accordance with the provisions of the will.

Felony—a serious crime, generally punishable by imprisonment. See **Misdemeanor.**

Fraud—intentional deception resulting in injury to another.

Garnishment—a legal procedure whereby a person's money or property is taken, while it is in the hands of a third party, to pay off her debts.

Grand jury—a jury of between 12 and 24 persons that determines whether there is probable cause to return an indictment.

Grievance procedure—a process designed to settle disputes between employees and employers.

Guardian—a person given the legal authority to manage the property of another, or to provide for the support and welfare of a person, often a minor.

Heir—a person who inherits property.

Holographic will—a will dated, signed, and written by the testator entirely in her own handwriting.

Implied warranty—an unwritten assurance that a product is of average quality and is fit for the purpose for which it was manufactured.

Indictment—a formal, written accusation of a crime that initiates criminal prosecution.

Infraction—a minor violation of a law.

Injunction—a court order requiring a person to refrain from certain conduct.

Interrogatories—written questions posed to a witness or a party to a civil suit that must be answered in writing under oath.

***Inter vivos* trust**—a trust in which property is transferred to a trustee during the owner's lifetime.

Intestate—not having made a will before death.

Joint tenancy—a form of property ownership whereby two or more persons own equal shares of a property, which automatically pass to the surviving owner(s) upon the death of one of the joint tenants.

Judgment—an official decision by a court.

Jurisdiction—the authority of a court to hear and determine a particular case; the geographical area over which a particular court has power.

Jury—a group of citizens summoned to hear evidence and deliver a verdict at a trial.

Legal age—the age at which a person is legally an adult; the age at which a person can marry and transact business.

Lien—a legal claim upon the property of another as security for a debt.

Minor—a person under legal age.

Misdemeanor—a violation of the law punishable by a fine or a short term of imprisonment; a less serious offense than a felony.

Nolo contendere—a plea of "no contest," generally having the same effect as a guilty plea, although it cannot be used as an admission of guilt in any other legal proceeding.

Personal property—assets other than real estate.

Petition—a document outlining the facts of a situation and requesting the court to take some type of action.

Plaintiff—the party who initiates a civil lawsuit.

Plea bargain—the process whereby a prosecutor and the accused (or her attorney) negotiate the disposition of a case to avoid going to trial.

Probable cause—a knowledge of facts that warrants the belief that a crime has been committed.

Probate—the process by which a court determines that a will is valid; the term is often used to refer to the administration of the estate as well.

Probation—procedure whereby a defendant found guilty of a crime is released without imprisonment, subject to certain conditions and usually under the supervision of a probation officer.

Protection order—an order issued by the court instructing an individual not to harass or harm a certain person or persons.

Punitive damages—compensation awarded to the injured party to punish the opposing party for malicious and willful behavior. Also referred to as "exemplary damages."

Real property—land, buildings erected on the land, and all interests and rights resulting from ownership of the land (as opposed to personal property).

Rescission (rescind)—cancellation of a contract or agreement.

Respondent—the defendant in a lawsuit.

Retainer—a fee paid to an attorney in advance for professional services.

Secured debt—a debt that allows the creditor to repossess certain property if the debtor fails to make payment.

Service of process—the act of notifying the defendant that a lawsuit has been brought against him.

Spousal support—money that the court determines must be paid to a spouse for financial support, either after a divorce or during a separation.

Statute of Limitations—a law that establishes a time period during which a lawsuit can be brought after an injury.

Subpoena—a document ordering a person to appear in court.

Summons—a written notice to a defendant that she is being sued and is required to appear in court by a certain date; also a notice to a person requiring that she appear in court for jury duty.

Tenancy by the entirety—a form of property ownership by husband and wife in which neither spouse can sell her or his share without the consent of the other, and upon the death of one spouse the entire property is owned by the survivor.

Testator—a person who makes a will.

Trust—a legal relationship in which a title to property is transferred to a trustee, who manages the property for the benefit of another (the beneficiary).

Trustee—a person who holds legal title to property for the benefit of the beneficiary of the trust.

Unsecured debt—a debt in which no property has been pledged as security.

Warrant—a written order authorizing an arrest, a search, or the seizure of property.

Warranty—an expressed or implied assurance by a seller that a product is fit for use and is of a certain quality.

Will—a legal document that specifies how one's property is to be distributed after her death.

Index